Person of No Nationality

A Story of Childhood Separation, Loss and Recovery

Person of No Nationality

A Story of Childhood Separation, Loss and Recovery

Ruth Barnett

DAVID
PAUL

First published in 2010
by David Paul
25 Methuen Park,
London N10 2JR

info@davidpaulbooks.com

A catalogue record for this book is available from the British Library.

ISBN 978-0-9548482-7-9

Printed in Great Britain

www.davidpaulbooks.com

This book is dedicated to children everywhere, because upon them depends the future of the human race; and to the memory of more than a million children who perished at the hands of the Nazis.

I also dedicate this book to the memory of my brother, Martin, and my sister-in-law, Maria, who, devoted to each other, both died recently within three weeks. Martin, the mainstay of my childhood, was always close and lives on in my heart. His contributory chapter is now a precious, poignant epitaph.

Contents

Foreword

by Dr Stephen D. Smith

If ever a book showed the complexity of identity, the struggle with confusion and dislocation, the bewildering fear of the unknown, the callousness and insufficient care of adults, the self-awareness little children have about their identity, this book shows it.

At a first glance the story of a four-year-old Kindertransportee with one German and one Jewish parent, placed in foster care in England, seems unchallenging – safe even. As a child Ruth was not aware of the excesses of Nazi ideology. Later, she was not exposed to ghettos, deportation or the concentration camp system. But this story shows just how far-reaching and how damaging National Socialism really was. A child so removed, so safe, and so protected, had her identity ravaged in the maelstrom of Nazi hatred. Even she could not escape its clutches.

Ruth Barnett is in pursuit of personal truth. It takes inner strength to confront difficult realities and the ghosts which have always been there. As she talks about Ruthchen, the little girl who left Germany, and Ruth, the girl who grew up in Britain during the war, the two people struggle in her soul. But out of the two eventually emerges a third – an altogether more rounded and wise person, devastated by the past but strong and clear in the present.

Ruth is aware of the fallibility of memory, and yet paints a vivid and accurate picture of her past. Portraits unfold of people and places, memories of foster homes, schools, games, scenery and pranks. The tension of her embroiled identity soaks the pages, her longing to be in a family, her desperate desire to please, her fear of being rejected again and again.

As a psychotherapist, Ruth understands well the many difficult psychological processes which were at play in her childhood. She recognizes that her self-knowledge comes with the benefit of hindsight. This enables her to give the reader a way into her struggles, which, without that perspective, would be difficult to dig out. She knows why she had to think her mother was dead. She knows why she sought solace with the animals on the farm. She understands why being returned to Germany was an impossible request for a fourteen-year-old to endure after ten years away from 'home'. And she knows why she craved a family and was so bitterly disappointed when every dawn was yet another false one.

Watch for the themes of identity, religion, betrayal, adult failings, language, belonging, hope, fear, trust, mistrust, confusion, family, depression, longing for love and security. 'You cannot fool children', she states with the clarity that only a child that was clearly not fooled could know. She may not have been fooled, but she was not helped either. There were adults all around her, and indeed she was supported physically, but there was no-one to help her to feel truly secure.

As you journey through the bewildering maze of her identity, one is left asking how it was possible for a child to go through so many switchbacks and emerge as a well-adjusted human being, who has made the contribution that she has made to her own family and to the lives of others.

Above all, you will find Ruth Barnett to be honest. It is an honesty which must have been unbearably difficult to confront over many years, and even more difficult to write down. She is honest about her feelings; honest about the actions and reactions of others; honest about those who helped and those who did not. She does not seek to hide her own confusion or anger, but to explain and describe her feelings in clear and intelligible terms. She does not shy away from the things which made the start of her life almost impossible to come to terms with, for no fault of her own.

In so doing, Ruth Barnett helps us to understand her painful journey. She gives us insights into those many children whose stories will never be told, and for the benefit of those children who may look to us today, for whom our support and guidance may make all the difference.

Dr Stephen D. Smith MBE is executive director of the Shoah Foundation Institute at the University of Southern California. He was co-founder and director of the UK's first Holocaust Centre and the Aegis Trust for Genocide Prevention. He is the author of *Creating Britain's First Holocaust Centre* and *The Holocaust in the Christian World*. He was awarded an MBE for his contribution to Holocaust education.

Acknowledgements

First I must thank the British Government of 1938 for rescuing me and my brother, Martin, from the clutches of the Nazis through the Kindertransport, and the Quakers for sponsoring me. Without this amazing rescue operation, my story would probably have ended prematurely.

Next, I would like to thank all the people who have made this book possible: my four sets of parents, who were all vital for my induction as a civilised human being: the parents who gave me birth, my brother who took over when they were left behind in Berlin, and my three sets of foster parents who generously opened their homes to me.

I have my husband, Bernard, to thank for his endless patience that helped me regain my trust in humanity after the shock and betrayal that was my experience of repatriation against my will. Thanks to my dedicated teachers at Petersfield High School, which sadly has been replaced by a block of flats, and thanks to my teachers in my psychotherapy training, who inspired me with, not only with a love of learning but also respect for people's differences. These were the people who made me and without whom I would not have had a story to tell; and of course, I would like to thank my editor and publisher, David Paul.

My thanks also go to the people who encouraged and helped me in the writing of this book; in particular, my huband for his companionship and humour, Bertha Leverton, Iris Guske for her interest in my personal story, the wonderful Smith family of Beth Shalom in Nottinghamshire, and Tessa in Berlin, from whom I have learnt so much about human rights.

Finally, I want to thank my three children, Bruce who did the proofreading, and Barry and Tania, with whom I had valuable discussions; my grandchildren, Adele and Raphael, who were a powerful inspiration; my niece and two nephews, Miriam, Markus and Martin respectively; my nine foster brothers and sisters, the Goodrickes, Ursula, John, Susan, Joan, my life-long 'buddy', and

Guy and the four Haltings, and all the children in my teaching career, especially those distressed adolescents from whom I learnt to understand the real meaning of the psychology of childhood.

Ruth Barnett
December 2009

For the Child in All of Us

When we grow up, the child each of us once was does not vanish completely, but remains alongside the adult in our emotional lives.

For many years, I felt ashamed of the child I once was. I rejected this child by locking her away in some corner of my mind. But the child in me, and in all us, is our source of creativity, curiosity, resilience and zest for life. By denying the existence of this child that was once my whole self, I did not have a complete adult self, and I can now see that I was living at only part of my potential.

I was born in 1935, a German citizen of parents who were German citizens. But eight months later, the Nazis took away my citizenship with their Nuremburg Laws, because my father had been born Jewish. Then in 1939, at the age of four, I had to come to England as a refugee, with my seven-year-old brother, Martin. We were two out of ten thousand children who came to Britain, rescued through the Kindertransport. The words 'Person of No Nationality' were written into my British travel documents until I was eighteen years old and eligible to become a British citizen. This lack of nationality deprived me of a feeling of belonging, and had a profound effect on me.

I disowned my German roots, trying to be more English than the English and desperate to be like everyone else – or, rather, like how I imagined everyone else to be.

Ruthchen was the first name I recognised as 'me'. In Germany, that was what everyone called me. It means 'little Ruth'. But it felt as though everyone in that unfathomable, scary, new world I had come to had rejected Ruthchen, so I did too. Everyone called me Ruth, even Martin. The new Ruth knew Ruthchen had been sent away from her home by her parents, and that must have been because she was unacceptably bad. As Ruth, with a new name, I was desperate to be accepted as good.

Life as Ruth was not easy. I lived with three foster parents and in a hostel. For ten years, I did not know for sure if my parents were alive or dead. Even as Ruth, I was often in trouble. I found it hard to work out what grown-ups wanted of me. They seemed to keep scolding me and sending me away, so I came to regard the child Ruth as just as unacceptably bad as Ruthchen.

I grew up in the countryside, at a time of post-war austerity, surrounded by farm animals, fields, and green hills. I have included many anecdotes about animals. There are stories about the pigs, horses, cows, sheep, rabbits, and other animals, that I remember with affection, for they were important to me as a child who had little to call her own. They were my companions and a comfort to me. They were the only ones who never complained or told me off.

Then my parents, all of a sudden, came back into my life and I had to go back to Germany, where they started calling me Ruthchen again, but my parents had become strangers to me. I was fourteen and no longer a sweet little four-year-old, desperate to please and be loved. I was a very confused and angry teenager and not Ruthchen at all. I refused to allow her back into my life. I ignored her and shut the door on her. I longed to be an adult, so that I would understand everything and wouldn't be found wanting any more.

Of course, adulthood, when I got there, was not like that at all. I still didn't understand why things kept going wrong, and I still battled to keep Ruthchen and the childhood Ruth out of my mind.

These two aspects of me were at loggerheads for a very long time. It was not until the 50th Reunion of the Kindertransport in 1989, when I met many other survivors who all wanted to share their stories and hear mine, that Ruth and Ruthchen were able to make friends and accept each other. So this book is the outcome of their joint project.

I had no idea how essential my childhood was to my character until I got to know and accept my German roots, and recognise that what had happened to me was not my fault. If you cut off your roots, you are like a tree that is not anchored in the ground. Only when I re-connected with Ruthchen and my German past, was I able to feel at peace with myself and to write this story of my life.

I began to appreciate the positive aspects of my childhood and remember the times I had been happy. I was then able to understand where Ruthchen had got stuck and help those parts of her to grow.

I am fortunate that my brother, Martin, has shared some of his own thoughts in this book. Being older, he remembers many things differently to the way I remember them. We both think the other has a faulty memory, but we are each telling our own truth and our recollections have changed with time.

My story also has many gaps, because sometimes we don't know what happened. For example, my mother was never able to talk about what happened to her in the ten years we didn't see her; she simply couldn't bear to talk about it – and we couldn't bear to hear.

The parents of many of the children, who sought refuge in Britain were murdered by the Nazis. There will always be a terrible, painful shadow over their lives. We Kinder, the children who survived, will always remember that more than a million children in continental Europe didn't get the chance to escape and were killed. I have always felt the need to work hard so I can justify having had a place on the Kindertransport. I still can't help thinking that one of those children who didn't get the chance that I got, had he or she lived, might have become a famous musician or discovered a cure for some life-threatening disease.

Through making friends again with Ruthchen and letting her help me to understand the troubled adolescent Ruth inside me, my story has a happy ending. I have a wonderful husband, with whom I celebrated our 50th wedding anniversary in 2008. I have three lovely children and two fine grandchildren and I have some very interesting work, which I will describe later, including talking about the Kindertransport, which all keeps me stimulated and enjoying life.

So I hope my story encourages an enriching dialogue. If it helps readers, young or not so young, to learn to respect and trust one another, and to feel empathy and compassion, then I will feel I have gone some way to fulfilling the task that Ruth and Ruthchen set me.

Ruth Barnett, December 2009

Grandmother, Oma Emma

My mother, Louise

My grandfather, married to Emma

Grandmother, Oma Clara

PART ONE

Pre-War Berlin: My First Home

CHAPTER 1

My First Family

My first home was in Berlin, Germany. I was born by Caesarean section on January 23rd, 1935 in a hospital in Charlottenburg, a district in the west of Berlin. It was a risky operation in those days. A doctor had told my mother three years earlier, when my brother, Martin, was born by the same procedure, that she shouldn't have any more babies because it would be too dangerous for her, and for the baby. My mother always made up her own mind. She was very determined once she had done so. So, here I am. If she had listened to the doctor, I would not be writing this book and the stories in it would not have happened.

When I was born, my two grandmothers, *Oma* Clara and *Oma* Emma were still alive (*Oma* is German for granny). I had an aunt, *Tante* Ella, and an uncle, *Onkel* Erich, who were my mother's brother and sister. I don't recall meeting any other members of the family in Berlin.

Tante Ella never married and never had children. In those days, one child in the family was expected to stay at home and look after the parents when they got older and needed help. *Tante* Ella was the eldest of the three children, so it fell to her to look after Oma Emma following grandfather's death. Most people did not have money for private care homes. They depended on their children to look after them in their old age.

My grandmother lived into her 80s, by which time *Tante* Ella was nearly 50 and too old to have children. I always thought this was sad, as *Tante* Ella was a very patient and loving person and would have been a good mother.

Oma Emma died in 1944. Berlin had been badly bombed and everything was in chaos. During the war, it was difficult to organise a proper funeral and burial, and *Tante* Ella did not have the money to pay an undertaker. So she wrapped her dead mother in sheets and took her in a wheelbarrow to the graveyard in the dark of the night. During the war, just like in England, there were no street-lights allowed and everyone had to have blackout curtains made of thick black cloth. So, no-one saw *Tante* Ella do this. She dug the grave herself and buried her mother. She told me many people did this. They helped each other with the digging. Otherwise, the city council would have put into mass graves the dead not claimed by relatives or by families that could not afford to pay an undertaker. I find it hard to think about this and all the other awful things people had to do in the war. I can't imagine myself burying a dead body. I think it was very brave of *Tante* Ella to do so; she loved her mother and wanted to be able to visit her grave. This would not have been possible if she had left it to the city council.

There were other more distant relatives of my parents that I don't remember ever meeting in Germany. Some fled to San Francisco and some were murdered by the Nazis. I don't even have photos of them as the Nazis destroyed so much. My parents did not like to talk about their relatives after the war.

My father, Robert Bernd Michaelis, was an only child. His father, my grandfather, Martin Ludwig Michaelis, was a bookbinder, but died when my father was very young. I remember visiting his mother, my other grandmother, *Oma* Clara Michaelis, just before we left Berlin. It is one of the snatches of memory I have of the city. My papa took me on the visit and, on the way, we passed a toyshop and he bought me a tiny little, bright golden, furry teddy. *Oma* Clara wanted to hold it and I cried because my papa made me give it to her. I was scared she wouldn't give it back, but she did. I don't remember what happened to that little teddy; I think it got left behind when we came to England, and it represents the part of my earliest childhood that stayed forever lost in Berlin.

Oma Clara had a sister, my great-aunt. I can't remember ever seeing her but I probably did. I don't know her name, or even if she lived in Berlin or somewhere else. I found out, after the war, that the Nazis murdered her and her husband. There were lots of things I didn't know because I was considered too young to be told things when I was in Berlin. But I knew bad things were happening, because I can

My parents' wedding day

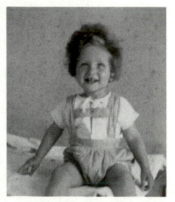

My father, Robert

Far right: Me, in Berlin

With my favourite doll

Martin with sweets on his first day at school

Mother, Martin and me

Below: sitting on Martin's lap

Erich, Ella and Louise

5

remember frightening feelings and not knowing what they were about. After the war, it was too painful and frightening to ask questions and my parents didn't want to talk about anything to do with the Nazi period. They couldn't bear to think about the awful things that had happened.

My great-aunt, *Oma* Clara's sister, had an only child, my father's cousin, George. After the war, he was living in Paris and I visited him there. My mother, Louise Maria, had a brother, Erich, and a sister, Ella. Erich and Ella Ventzke were my uncle and aunt. They lived with my grandmother, Emma Ventzke, in a part of the city that became East Berlin after the war. I often went to stay with *Oma* Emma and *Tante* Ella. *Onkel* Erich lived near by. It was relatively safe there because my mother's family was not Jewish and so the Gestapo would not usually come there looking for Jews.

I have another snatch of memory, this time of my father taking me to *Oma* Emma and *Tante* Ella because he got wind the Gestapo were looking for him. I remember my papa hiding in a broom cupboard. *Tante* Ella tried to make a joke out of it, but I didn't believe her because I saw that my papa was shaking with fear. You don't do that if you are joking. *Tante* Ella tried to convince me it was a joke and he was shaking with laughter, but I had seen the terror in his face. You can't fool children. It's usually best to tell them the truth and not try to hide it. Children sense it when something important is being kept secret, and they have fantasies about the secret. I imagined my Papa had wet his pants and therefore had to hide for fear of being found out. People do wet themselves when they are really scared and I might have seen what looked to me like wet trousers. A little later, when I wet myself in England, I used to hide because I was terrified the Gestapo would get me. (Gestapo is short for Geheim Staats Polizei and means State Secret Police) Of course, I did not know who the Gestapo were; only that they were very bad and terrifying, and you mustn't let them see you. I knew that because my papa was terrified of them. He was a big strong man and not easily frightened.

I liked staying at *Oma* Emma's. *Tante* Ella was very patient and kind. She read lots of stories to me and she always gave me sweets after I ate the things I didn't like, such as spinach. *Oma* Emma always had a sleep after lunch and I was supposed to go to sleep then too, even though I wasn't tired. Once, after I had been tucked up in my cot, I could hear *Oma* Emma snoring away. I was bored and, to have a bit of fun, I pretended I was a lion. I burrowed underneath the mattress of my cot and roared like a lion. That woke *Oma* Emma and she sat up in her bed. When she saw me crouching under the cot mattress, she roared with laughter. Her mouth looked so huge and terrifying that I screamed as loudly as I could. *Tante* Ella came running and picked me up. She understood at once what had frightened me and showed me *Oma* Ella's teeth in a glass of water. *Oma* Ella put her teeth back in her mouth and then we all laughed together.

Martin didn't come to *Oma* Emma's. He was older and went to a Kindergarten outside Berlin for safety. But Martin and I were often together at our parents' flat in Cicero Strasse (number six) and we visited *Oma* Clara together with our parents. We also had a nanny, who was really a general helper, as my mother worked as my father's secretary. This was very important as the Nazis threw all Jews out of professional jobs and gave them to Nazi party members. My father was a lawyer and, after he lost his job, we depended on my mother's salary. She could get another job but my father couldn't. They couldn't take her job away because she was not Jewish; she was what the Nazis called an Aryan. According to the Nazis, Aryans were the only true Germans, and only Aryans could be German citizens. All Jews had their German citizenship taken away by the Nazis, who wanted to create a *Herrenrasse*, a master race of superior Germans, by driving away or killing off everybody they considered not good enough to be an Aryan.

In Cicero Strasse, we had a huge toy dog. It was a lot taller than I was and I wanted to ride on its back, but it always toppled over when I climbed up it. I can't remember if we gave it a name. We also had a rocking horse that was Martin's birthday present. It was a very big one with a rather fierce look on its face. Martin was frightened, and refused to be lifted onto it. I wanted to ride the rocking horse but I was told that I was too young and would surely fall off. That made me determined to ride the rocking horse. I climbed up by myself and, sure enough, I fell off and howled. The grown-ups thought that would be the end of it – but no. I collected all the cushions in the flat and laid them round the rocking horse. Then I rode the horse faster and faster, till I fell off with whoops of joy! So Martin decided to have a go too. I was very proud that I had achieved something before Martin, because he usually did everything first. He could do heaps of things I couldn't do, partly because he was three years older than me but also because he was very clever.

In the first four years of my life, my parents already had huge difficulties because of what the Nazis were doing to Jews. But they looked after my brother and me very carefully and protected us, as much as they could, from what was going on outside our little family. I can remember many happy times, such as romping in my parents' bed on Sunday mornings, sitting on my father's lap and riding on his shoulders. I have often wondered what it was like for them having to make terribly difficult decisions about what to do with two small children, when life was becoming so difficult for Jews. It is almost impossible to think yourself into your parents' shoes, because things change so much between generations. Looking back to 1939, I can't imagine what I would have done if I had been the mother of two small children.

CHAPTER 2

Things Got Worse and Worse

As a baby, I could not know about what was going on in Germany. The Nazis came to power in January 1933, two years before I was born. They immediately started making laws to make life hard for Jewish families. In September 1935, before I was one year old, they decreed that only proven Aryans could be German citizens. Citizenship was taken away from all the Jews in Germany. Martin and I were half-Jewish but that made no difference to the Nazis. If you had one Jewish grandparent, they counted you as a Jew. I had two Jewish grandparents, so there was no way the Nazis would consider me good enough to be a German. Long after the war, I found out that even Aryan Germans with no Jewish ancestry were not safe from the Nazis. If any non-Jew befriended Jews or protested against anything the Nazis were doing, the Nazis arrested them and treated them cruelly. Sometimes they were so cruel, beating and torturing the people they arrested, that the victims died.

Already, before the war, they rounded up children with any sort of serious deformity into vans or buses with windows painted over in grey paint so that no-one could see what was going on inside. To stop them crying and protesting, the children were drugged. They were taken to six secret hospitals, where they were murdered. Later the Nazis murdered disabled adults too and, by the end of the war, they were murdering their own soldiers who had come back from the Eastern front psychologically disturbed by the horrors they had seen there. The Nazis were hell-bent on creating a perfect 'master race' of blond, blue-eyed and able-bodied Aryan Germans that would be superior to all other peoples. All non-Aryans would either have to be killed, to get rid of them, or enslaved to serve the superior master race as labourers.

Of course, I didn't know at that time that I was no longer a German citizen. I was a normal lively baby and toddler. My parents sheltered me from what was going on in the world outside our flat, and I spent a lot of time with *Oma* Emma and *Tante* Ella when the Gestapo were out searching for Jews. But I must have sensed there were bad things happening when the grown-ups whispered together. Because my father had his job taken away, my mother had to work longer hours to support the family. Then our nanny had to leave because the Nazis decreed that Jews were not allowed to employ Aryans. That meant *Tante* Ella had to look after me and I spent even more time at *Oma* Emma's. Martin was sent to a Kindergarten outside Berlin. Out shopping with Tante Ella, there would be crowds and she would pull me away quickly to go another way. I didn't know what was going on in the crowd but I knew it was something bad because Tante Ella was anxious. Very young children always tune in to the adult's mood. If the adult is calm, the children do not get upset but, if he or she becomes anxious, the children sense it.

Then on November 9th, 1938, there was *Kristallnacht*, which means 'Night of Broken Glass' and it was called that because so much glass was broken. All over Germany at the same time, groups of Nazis set the crowds rioting. They smashed Jewish shops and set synagogues on fire while the Gestapo raided Jewish homes. The Gestapo arrested all the men and took them to labour camps, where they were brutally treated. Many died there or came home broken in body and spirit. Some committed suicide. My father would certainly have been arrested, if he had been at home, and maybe Martin too. But my father didn't stay at home. He took Martin and they walked the streets on the edge of the crowd until the rioting was over and they could go home. I was safely at *Oma* Emma's.

It was a shocking experience for a young boy, just one month short of his seventh birthday. He told me, much later, that it had forced him to 'grow up suddenly' and realise that you couldn't trust adults to behave any better than children. He had been taught to respect adults because they were reliably good; then suddenly crowds of adults, shouting and hurling bricks at windows, confronted him. He knew that this was behaviour that would not be tolerated, if done by children. It made a lasting impression on him. In a way it shocked him into a sort of premature adulthood. He realised he could not count on adults and had to think and make decisions for himself. (See Martin's Story at the end of the book). Children should not have to do this so early in their lives as seven years old. Sadly, many children today, even some in our own country, don't have reliable adults to look after them, and have to find ways of surviving by themselves.

The Nazis hid a great deal of the bad things they did but they couldn't hide *Kristallnacht* from the eyes of the world. It was in all the newspapers. The Nazis claimed that the Jews had started it and that the crowds were defending themselves against the Jews. They even made the Jews clear up all the broken glass the next day and pay for the damage! Nobody believed the Nazis; everyone knew it was not the Jews, but the Nazis themselves who planned it all and incited the crowds to riot. After *Kristallnacht*, the British Government allowed an unlimited number of children to be brought to safety in England, but not their parents. Each child had to be sponsored; someone had to take responsibility, so that the government did not have to pay anything.

I don't blame the government for not wanting to pay. It needed all its resources to prepare for the war that everybody knew would come, but it was tragic that they refused to allow the parents to come with their children. The parents had to make heart-rending decisions in sending their children to safety. Many rightly feared that they might never see their children again. They did not know what their children would experience in England, whether they would be treated well or harshly, or whether they would be able to cope with the separation.

My father decided to convert to Christianity to try to protect the family. I did not understand anything about this till much later in my life. I thought, for many years, that he had converted six years earlier, in 1932, when he married my mother. At that time, *Oma* Emma hadn't wanted her daughter, my mother, to marry a Jew, because anti-Semitism was rife in Berlin and it was dangerous to be involved with Jews. *Oma* Clara would have preferred her son, my father, to marry a Jewess. But in 1938, my father's conversion after *Kristallnacht* enabled our parents to ask for Martin and me to be raised as Christians in England, which they felt would make us safer.

Between *Kristallnacht*, in November 1938, and when war broke out in September 1939, nine months later, almost 10,000 children were brought to England, mainly from Germany and Austria. As they came on special trains arranged by the organisers, it was called the Kindertransport. ('Kinder' is German for 'children'). There were individuals who were philanthropic and rich enough to sponsor some children; but most children were sponsored by organisations like World Jewish Relief and Christian charities. The Quakers sponsored Martin and me. It was a pity that the British government didn't allow the parents to come with the Kindertransport children. The parents would have been only too happy to work for the British government against Hitler. They could have worked in the factories making necessities for the war and the British government would have gained by that.

Thousands of Jewish families left Germany in the early 1930s, as soon as Hitler came to power. But most Jews, including my parents, believed that it would all blow over, as so many attacks on the Jews had done before. At that time, very few people could imagine the awful extent to which the Nazis would take their hatred of Jews. By *Kristallnacht*, Jewish families had been dispossessed by the Nazis of nearly everything they owned, and no country was willing to take in families with no money at all. German Jews realised how much danger they were now in, but the parents were trapped and couldn't get out. Many of the parents of Kindertransportees were murdered by the Nazis and never saw their children again. Those children, such as Martin and me, who were reunited with their parents after the war, did not find that easy. You might think that it would be wonderful to be reunited after such tragic separation. When it comes down to it, you simply can't pick up a relationship where you left off ten years ago! Life does not stay still. Both parents and children had moved on during the separation. They were not exactly the same people as they were before. They had been through harrowing experiences that would be difficult, if not impossible, to talk about.

CHAPTER 3

The Journey to England

I don't know what arrangements my parents made or how my brother and I came to be selected for the Kindertransport. Martin remembers being told some time ahead that we were going to England, and he was given some special English lessons to prepare him. I don't know if anyone tried to prepare me, but I don't remember anything about it. Martin can remember everything that happened on the day we left Berlin, February 21st,1939. He can remember all the preparations before we left, such as clothes being selected, toys being sorted and packing his own suitcase, because he was three years older than I was. He was seven and I was only four. Those three years make a big difference.

I do remember we all set off in a car to the Zoo Station in Berlin. As I often went to stay with my granny, *Oma* Emma, and aunt, *Tante* Ella, I was used to bags being packed and going on journeys, usually by car. I don't remember this one as any different to begin with. I must have just thought this was another visit to *Tante* Ella or one of my grandmothers. But going on a train was something different and special.

I remember the journey to England in great detail, but I don't remember much before that big journey. It is a strange thing that later on in your life, if you work hard at trying to make connections, you can get back some early memories that you didn't even know were there. Later, when I visited Berlin as an adult, some of the places where I went triggered such memories. One of those triggers happened when I visited the Zoo station. I suddenly remembered that when we got out of the car at the station I threw a tantrum because I wanted to go to the zoo and not to England. I would not have known what 'England' was, but I knew and loved the zoo. *Tante* Ella used to take me there, and I remembered how she would lift me up to see the monkeys. I loved the monkeys. They would clap their hands to get us to throw nuts down into their pen. *Tante* Ella would give me bags of monkey nuts, but I would clap my hands when the monkeys clapped, so I would usually end up dropping as many nuts as I threw!

I remember the seemingly endless train journey to England. There was my mother, another lady who was helping her, and Martin. I asked again and again, 'Is this England yet?' until I got tired and fell asleep. I recall waking up and asking again if we were in England, but we were still in Germany. I was amazed that Germany was so big; it seemed to go on forever.

Next thing I remember was being woken up, as we had to get out of the train. It was dark, and I was frightened and bewildered. I had been in a deep sleep and could hardly stand on my feet. Martin dragged me along. Then we were walking along a quay beside a gigantic boat. I was amazed when we walked up a ramp, up and up, and right onto the deck of this big boat. I saw a huge pile of suitcases and porters stacking them into racks on the deck.

Lots of people were all around and disappearing down some steps into the inside of the boat. More and more people were coming up the gangplank. I suddenly felt very frightened. How could there be so many people and cases? How could such an enormous boat, with so much in it, possibly float? I was sure it would sink like the toy boats at bath time if you put too much in them.

I asked Martin and he just told me not to ask silly questions. He didn't seem to be afraid. He seemed to be excited and enjoying it, so I wasn't frightened any more. He was my big brother, and if he was there and not scared, then everything must be all right. I remember all this very clearly, but the strange thing is that I remember what was said in English although it must have all been said in German. Memory is more strange and complex than you might think! Much later, when I studied psychology, I learnt that it is impossible to remember what actually happened because, every time you recall a memory, you automatically update it. That means you change its meaning in line with all that has happened to you since you last thought about that memory.

On the big boat with all the people and suitcases, we were suddenly going down the steps too, down into the inside of the boat. There were long, strange-smelling corridors, and it was dark, gloomy and very crowded. I was afraid of getting lost and I clutched my mother's coat very tight. The four of us squeezed into a tiny room, with four bunk beds in it. My mother undressed me and told me to climb a little ladder on to the top bunk on one side. Martin climbed up into the top bunk on the other side. My mother and the helper had the bottom two bunks.

By this time, I was not sleepy any more. Martin and I reached out and poked each other, and giggled, and talked together, until the helper got very cross. I must have gone to sleep eventually, because I woke up feeling awful. I didn't know where I was or what was happening. There was a strange sort of buzzing noise and I felt as though I was on a see-saw. It was dark but I could see the dim outline of Martin's bunk. I clutched the side of my bunk and looked over the edge. It looked a long way down. I called my mother. As she looked out of her bunk, I was sick all over her. I had already been sick all over my bedding. My mother lifted me down and took me out to a washroom to clean me up. By the time we were both cleaned up, the see-sawing had stopped. Martin said the boat had reached England, but I was feeling too weak and groggy to be interested. It was a strug-gle to get dressed and back along the corridors to the stairs up to the deck.

I don't remember going through the customs. I think I fainted once or twice. After the war, my mother told the story of how she smuggled jewellery into England. I was allowed to bring my favourite doll, Christine. My mother dressed the doll in lots of little outfits and gave her to me to carry. Of course, the doll looked suspicious, so the customs officer wanted all her clothes off. My mother obligingly un-dressed Christine to the accompaniment of my screams of protest, which my mother had counted on. When there was nothing but a naked doll, the customs officer wanted to shoo us on. Just as my mother had hoped, I made a huge fuss until Christine had all her clothes back on, by which time the customs officer was fed up with us and only opened one suitcase. Luckily, it was not the one in which my mother had hidden the jewellery. No-one was allowed to take valu-able jewellery out of Germany. If the customs officer had found my mother's jewellery, it would have been confiscated and she would have had to collect it on her way back to Germany. But she wanted to get it out of Germany. I think that is how she paid for my father's boat passage to China from Southampton.

After the boat docked in Harwich, we had another long train journey to London. I was terribly disappointed. Firstly, that we were again cooped up in a train. I had had enough of trains. Secondly, this was England and it didn't look any different to Germany, with fields and trees flashing past. I don't know what I had expected England to be like, but I certainly did not expect it to be like Germany. In London, we arrived at Liverpool Street Station and had to cross part of the city to Victoria Station to get yet another train to Maidstone in Kent.

I found London was very different to Berlin, though I can't really explain the difference except for the double-decker buses. I found it shocking that they were bright red, the colour of blood, when double-decker buses should be a nice gentle yellow as they were in Berlin. I asked Martin why the Londoners painted their buses red. He told me that Englanders needed their buses to be a bright colour because they had much weaker eyesight than Germans and might get run over if they were yellow. He added, 'you will have to get used to it as in England they are all mad.' Of course, because my big brother said it, this explanation satisfied me at the time.

The helper left us in London, as she had to go somewhere else. We took the train to Maidstone and then Sittingbourne, and, finally, to Merston Rectory, our first home in England. I can't remember whether we were collected from the station or took a taxi, and I don't remember our first meeting with the Reverend Stead and his wife. What I do remember is that we all sat round a big, shiny, dark wooden table with the Reverend Stead and his wife, and were served tea and cakes. I think it was rather like the visits we must have made to family and friends in Berlin. I was used to that, so it was like just another outing for me. After tea, my mother put us to bed and tucked us up with a story. It all seemed like an adventure. That is until I discovered in the morning that my mother was no longer there.

Neither Martin nor I can remember saying goodbye to her, nor do we recall seeing her leaving. Martin thinks she stayed a few days at Merston Rectory, but I doubt this. I don't think the Steads spoke any German and my mother couldn't speak any English. It would have been very difficult for her to stay. I also find it hard to believe that she sneaked away after putting us to bed and didn't say 'goodbye'.

As an adult, I worked with many former Kindertransportees, and they either have a memory gap over the parting or it is painfully etched in their minds in horrific detail. The human mind has many built-in protection devices. One of them is to shut off an experience that is too traumatic to deal with at the time and lock it away in some corner of the mind. Sometimes it can be unlocked and dealt with later, and sometimes the key has been thrown away and it can't be remembered at all, however hard you try. If an experience can neither be dealt with nor understood at the time, nor locked away, it is burnt into the mind. Then it is very difficult to keep it out of the mind and it even comes as nightmares at night. So this memory gap around our mother leaving probably helped Martin and me adjust to being in England without our parents.

I remember missing my mother terribly. Mrs Stead was furiously angry when I cried, so I fought it to try to please her and her companion, Miss Wright, who looked after us most of the time. When I asked Martin where our mother was, he said she had work to do and would come soon. This made sense, as I was used to spending time with Tante Ella and Oma Emma. But they were never angry with me and always brought me home to my parents after a while. Soon Martin, too, got angry when I kept asking about our mother and I gave it up.

Everybody seemed to be angry with me most of the time. I couldn't understand what they wanted. It wasn't like that in Berlin. I got to believe I was very bad, because I was always being told off. I thought I must have been so bad that my parents sent me away. Although I understood a bit later that we had to leave Germany because of the Nazis, I still thought I had been too bad for my parents to want me. Martin didn't get into trouble as much as I did and, anyway, he was there to look after me. Finally, because she didn't come to take me back, I decided that my mother must be dead. It was just too unbearable to think that she chose to be somewhere else and not with me. If she was dead, she couldn't be with me and nor could she be with anyone else, and that was bearable. I started telling people my mother was dead and no-one contradicted me. With no mother, I realised I had to look after myself, even though Martin was there.

Reverend Stead with Martin and me in the Merston Rectory garden

Foster Families:
Seeking a Place to
Call Home

CHAPTER 4

Merston Rectory

Merston Rectory was our first home in England. A large, old manor house, it stood at the top of a long drive between fields and a little copse. It had a large and very beautiful rose garden in front, scenting the way to steps leading up to a porch with Greek pillars either side. To the right was a lawn with a big cedar tree and flower borders, and to the left was the copse. Behind the house, there were more flowerbeds, a large vegetable garden and stables. There were no horses in the stables; instead, they were filled with gardening tools and other things for the garden, and a big coalbunker. Just inside the front door, after a small hall, there was a corridor. To the right were all the posh rooms: the dining room, the Reverend's study and other rooms we seldom entered. To the left were the ordinary rooms and the kitchen. And, at the end of this corridor, there were two staircases, a posh carpeted one on the right and an ordinary uncarpeted one on the left. Upstairs, there was a similar corridor with smart-looking bedrooms at one end, and ordinary bedrooms and the schoolroom at the other end.

The Reverend Stead was a tall, slim, slightly stooping, elderly man. He had white wispy hair and spectacles. He always wore a smart, dark suit but the knees were baggy from long hours sitting in his study. He was gentle and kind, and I always felt safe in his presence. He used to take Martin and me for long walks in the countryside. He would hobble along with a walking stick, while Martin and I scampered on ahead, until he called us back when we got too far away. One particularly enjoyable walk was round the Green Lake. This was a huge chalk pit with the centre, where the chalk had been dug out, filled with water that looked very green against the white chalky cliffs all round it. It was a lovely shade of dark pastel green; a colour that I have always been fond of, as it reminds me of these lovely walks. There was a path all round the green lake. At first, I was a bit frightened because the path was narrow and I feared tripping and falling in the water. Martin told me not to be a scaredy-cat and, even if I did fall in, he would fish me out because he could swim. I believed him and so I wasn't scared any more.

Mrs Stead was exactly the opposite to her husband in almost every way. She was much shorter and rounder than he was. Her hair was not even grey, because she was much younger than her husband, and she wore it in a tidy bun. She usually wore a smart woollen twin set and tweed skirt. She was nearly always cross with me, whenever I saw her. I wanted so much to please her, so that she would report back to my parents that I was being a good girl and then they would take me home; but I could not understand what she wanted from me. It wasn't just the language, because Martin and I learnt English very quickly.

Mostly, we were looked after by Miss Wright. She was Mrs Stead's companion, and our nanny and teacher. Miss Wright was even younger than Mrs Stead with short, curly, golden-brown hair. She was jolly sometimes and very cruel at other times, and I never understood what she wanted from me either. My life in Merston Rectory was a nightmare of confusion, fear and pain that I can't really remember in any sort of order.

The Reverend and Mrs Stead had no children of their own. I think the Reverend took in Martin and me as his humanitarian contribution to the war situation, without considering that his wife might find it hard to look after someone else's children. I prefer to think that she and Miss Wright were rather clueless about how to look after children than that they were deliberately cruel. Martin describes visiting Mrs Stead after the war. But I was too scared to go with him, even though I was in my 20s by then.

For many years, I was haunted by a memory of not being given any food at the meal table until I asked for it in perfect English. I thought that was to make me learn English, as Martin already knew enough to talk in English at meal times. That meant I was very hungry and couldn't sleep. We slept in separate bedrooms but next door to each other.

I was frightened of the dark. We were city children and, in a city, there are street-lights so that it is never completely dark. Merston Rectory was deep in the countryside and, when it was dark, it was pitch black. If I woke in the night, I would be terrified and pinch myself to see if I was still alive. I would tap on the wall to call Martin. He used to go down, when the house was quiet, and everyone else asleep, and raid the larder to feed me. Memories are unreliable, especially when you are only just four years old. Years later, when I studied psychology, I realised that it is normal behaviour for small children to refuse food from strangers and that is probably what I did. After all, most parents tell their children not to take sweets from strangers, and that is most likely what my parents had said to us. It was great fun having our midnight feasts. Martin was surprised that the grown-ups didn't discover how much food was missing from the larder. Then one day he told me he had heard them talking about rats in the larder and how poisoned food had been put down to kill them. Martin said he was not sure whether they believed there were really rats or were talking about us as rats. As we didn't want to be killed by poison, Martin didn't raid the larder any more. In any case, by then, I was happy to eat at mealtimes. Soon after that, we had to sleep in the cellar, which was the air raid shelter for the family, and Martin couldn't go any more to the larder. We got fairly good food at the rectory but we were not allowed to ask for second helpings. So we were usually left still feeling hungry and we both grew taller and thinner.

From the beginning, we had lessons in the schoolroom with Miss Wright. There were a few other children with us for the lessons. I think they must have been other Kindertransportees billeted with other families. When they didn't come any more, we lost touch with them. The first lesson every day was elocution. That meant you had to look in a little hand mirror and make your mouth into the proper shape to pronounce English words correctly. I hated elocution because I always got the sounds wrong. In the end, I succeeded, and I soon learned to speak English without any foreign accent. We were forbidden to speak German, probably to help us improve our English. But I thought it was silly not to talk German on our own. Martin said it was dangerous to speak German because there were English soldiers around on manoeuvres and, if they heard German, they would shoot at us. Of course, I believed Martin and I don't think I spoke another word of German.

Martin had already learnt a little bit of English, before we came over to England. I wished I had been allowed to learn some English in Germany, too; it might have helped me to understand what English people wanted. Martin could read German before we came over, and he very quickly learned to read English. I wanted to do everything that my big brother did, but I found learning to read an awful struggle. I was really too young. But I could learn poems by heart. Martin was given poems to learn and he wanted me to hear him practise them to get them right, so I simply learned the poems with him. I couldn't understand why Miss Wright was cross with me for that! Sums were a different matter. I learnt to count up to a thousand and more very easily but, when you had to put numbers underneath each other and get other numbers out of them, I simply couldn't get it. Martin said I was stupid like all girls, and Miss Wright was cross and said I didn't listen or pay attention. We also had art and geography lessons. I enjoyed painting and sketching; Martin said my pictures were pretty good, but Miss Wright was unimpressed.

Miss Wright was cross about all sorts of crazy things. You had to go to the toilet straight after breakfast and do 'number two'. She would come and inspect to make sure you weren't making it up. So, when I just couldn't squeeze anything out, I dropped a sausage made of hard-squeezed mud into the toilet. I kept a mud-sausage in the pocket of my pinny for that purpose. The trouble was that I would then need to go to the toilet later in the day, and that made Miss Wright very angry. You were only supposed to go to the toilet after meals, even just for a pee. If you wanted to go for a pee any other time of day, she would be very cross. It was very hard to hold it in, but I could manage it in the daytime. At night, it was impossible. So, most of all, Miss Wright was cross with me for wetting my bed. I knew it was a bad thing to do to wet the bed. I tried ever so hard not to, because I really wanted to be good.

We were sleeping in the cellar under the rectory, because the German bombers came over at night and dropped a few bombs in Kent on their way to London. The cellar was dark and damp-smelling. The toilet was right at the end of a long, frightening corridor. One night, I walked along in my bare feet on the icy cold, damp floor, and felt my way to the toilet. I could feel the cold ring of the toilet seat on my bottom and then – wet warmth! I woke up in horror to find myself still in bed – it had all been a dream.

Miss Wright scolded me furiously and called Mrs Stead. Mrs Stead came with a leather strap, threw me face down on the wet bed, rubbed my nose in it and then belted me on my back with the strap. And I wasn't supposed to howl! I got more strokes if I cried. Mrs Stead would say as she hit me, 'This will cure you!', and I believed her. Sadly, it didn't work, even though I tried very hard not to wet my bed. I got so many beatings that my back became a mass of sore welts and I couldn't lie down in my bed except on my tummy. I sat up and chewed my fingers, which is what children do when they are anxious to comfort themselves. Miss Wright painted my fingers with something nasty, mustard or something, but I couldn't keep my fingers out of my mouth because I needed comfort so badly. Then they put mittens on my hands and tied them to the railing on either side of my bed, so that I couldn't reach my mouth. Of course, I slept badly and, when I eventually dropped off into a deep sleep, I woke up with a nightmare in a wet bed.

Martin was worried about the sores on my back and so, when the doctor came to vaccinate us, he asked him to look at my back. The beating stopped after that but not the punishments. Every time my bed was wet I had no nice food like chicken or sausages, just a heap of potato and greens and bread without butter. I liked vegetables, so I didn't mind too much.

But my body knew it needed protein. Whilst we were playing in the garden, I discovered a big, thick cheese rind thrown out with a whole lot of rotten apples on the compost heap. There was lots of cheese left on it, so I brushed it on my pinny and nibbled the cheese off it till there was really only the rind left. Miss Wright came out at that point and snatched it out of my hand, demanding to know what I was doing. I simply said I liked cheese and had felt hungry. She was livid with fury and called me a 'nasty little thief'. Martin stood up for me and said it was not stealing because the cheese rind had been thrown away as rubbish. Miss Wright was so angry she probably did-n't even hear him. She called Mrs Stead, who scolded me again and called me a 'dirty German thief'. Martin tried again to protect me by saying eating rubbish was not thieving and that I needed more food. He also said we were Jews, not Germans, and had to come to England because we were not Germans. Mrs Stead listened and then said I had to be cured of my dirty thieving tricks. At the next meal, I got nothing but the remains of the cheese rind on a plate and I was or-dered to eat it. I was hungry and would have eaten it, but Martin told me it had mould on it, and that could make me ill and I might die. So, I refused to eat the cheese rind, even though it came back at every meal and I was allowed nothing else. Martin cleverly stashed some of his food away in his pocket, when Miss Wright was looking the other way, and gave it to me later when we were alone. I don't know how long this went on for but it stopped when Reverend Stead came to take us for a walk. Martin told him we were both too hungry to walk and then, of course, it all came out. Reverend Stead insisted we sat down with him in the kitchen and had a good feast.

Then there was bath time. Martin and I were in the bathroom to-gether and supervised by Miss Wright. I hated bath time for many reasons. Often the water was scalding hot and that hurt badly, and I would come out bright red up to the water line. We had to soap our-selves all over with a coarse wartime soap that felt unpleasant and smelled foul. Then Miss Wright would wash it all off with a big sponge. She hit me in the face with this sponge and, when I choked and spluttered, told me I wasn't breathing properly.

Martin said he knew she did it deliberately, because he watched her. I don't remember it, but Martin told me that she hit me so hard with the sponge one time that I fell backwards into the water and al-most drowned. Martin pushed Miss Wright out of the way and fished me out. He said I lay on the bath mat, still and white, for a few mo-ments and then vomited. Martin had saved my life and then he got into trouble for it because Miss Wright told Mrs Stead that he had at-tacked her. When Martin told them what really happened, they both called him a liar. Martin was not in the least put off, even though he was only eight or nine. He said, if Miss Wright did that again, he would go and fetch a policeman! Martin tells this story somewhat differently, as he was not as frightened of Miss Wright as I was. What would I have done without my big brother to look after me? Later, when I had children of my own, I used to let them have lots of toys in their bath and we splashed and had fun. For them bath time was great fun, and it makes me sad to think of the nightmare bath times with Miss Wright.

We came to Merston Rectory in February, 1939, and it was hot summer, July or August, when we had a visit from our father. He was on his way to Shanghai in China and his boat was due to sail from Southampton. I was very surprised and delighted to see him. He brought me a dapple-grey rubber horse on wheels. You had to blow it up with air. I don't think it lasted very long, because it kept going down and had to be blown up again. He took Martin with him to London for a few days. That was terrible for me. Of course, I would have liked to have gone too. But my father probably would have found it too much to look after me, as well as Martin. What was terrible was that they didn't tell me. I can't remember what I was doing, but I suddenly realised Martin wasn't there. I looked for him everywhere, getting more and more anxious and distraught. Miss Wright, of course, was very cross and told me not to be a cry-baby. She said that they would soon come back, but I didn't believe her. I thought I was now completely on my own. I didn't miss my father because I was used to him being away a lot. I didn't miss my mother because I already believed she was dead. Martin had taken the place of my mother. He made everything all right, however scary and hurtful things got. Like most four-year-olds can't do without their mothers, I couldn't do without Martin. I was terrified and just sat and chewed my fingers. That made Miss Wright even crosser. I couldn't concentrate on schoolwork or eat. That too made Miss Wright cross. I couldn't even cry, because that wasn't allowed. But Martin did come back and told me that he would never leave me again. I believed him and that helped me to get over the upset.

Whenever the weather was fine, we would be out in the garden. There was a big yard outside the stables, covered with cobblestones, which never got muddy. We could play there, even just after rain. We found some bits of wood and an old rubber ball in the copse and played our own version of cricket, which we called 'rubber moon'. I can't remember why we gave it that name. We used to make little cups and saucers, plates and teapots out of mud, moulding it like play-dough or Plasticine, and have pretend tea parties.

Most of the time, we had to weed the garden – and it was a very big garden. By the time we got to the end, the weeds would be grow-ing again where we started. But it was usually peaceful and nice. Miss Wright seldom came out, and only watched us now and then from one or other window. We spent so much time chattering that we did-n't get enough weeding done to please Mrs Stead and so we were made to work separately. We had a little wheelbarrow each and, when it was full, we took it to the compost heap in the copse. You couldn't see the compost heap from the house because of the trees. Martin would whistle to let me know that his wheelbarrow was full, and I would then hurry to fill mine and join him in the copse. There we could chat and play games for a while. Martin was careful and well-organised. To avoid suspicion, we never both went in or out at the same time.

On Sundays, everybody went to church. After breakfast, we had to wash and put on Sunday best clothes: a pretty, little dress for me, and a little suit for Martin. I quite liked this special routine; it was better than the usual lessons in the schoolroom on all other morn-ings. We all piled into the shiny black car that was very big rather like a taxi, only it wasn't a taxi. It was a short drive to the church, but too far to walk. The church looked huge to me. I was very surprised when Martin and I visited it about 30 years later, to see how very small it re-ally was. Reverend Stead would always take the service, so we had to go there earlier than other people. There was a special children's cor-ner with interesting pictures on the wall, lots of picture books and coloured pencils with books to draw pictures in. Martin and I always went straight to the children's corner. We forgot about everything until someone collected us and took us to our pew.

It was all new and dazzling to me. I don't think we went to any sort of church or synagogue in Berlin. I loved the music and singing, although I didn't understand a word. I was very well-behaved. The choir looked angelic in white gowns over long red skirts and I would stand rapt with awe. When it was time for the sermon, Martin took my hand and we went back to the children's corner and had a very nice time there. After the service, everyone wanted to shake the Reverend's hand, and they all smiled at Martin and me. Everyone was cheerful and nice, even Mrs Stead and Miss Wright. That is, until the car drew up in front of the rectory. Then it was back to the everyday nightmare of crossness and cruelty. So I learnt the meaning of hypocrisy, although I didn't know the word at that time. Once I had learnt enough English, I realised that all the nice things they said in church meant very little in the outside world of everyday things.

But it wasn't all bad, by any means. Apart from the regular country walks, which were always peaceful and enjoyable, there was Christmas. We played in the snow and made snowmen, and there were plenty of parties. The house got decorated with holly and ivy, with a huge Christmas tree in the hall. The tree was festooned with coloured baubles and wax candles that were lit every evening of the twelve days of Christmas. The parties were for grown-ups, but we were sometimes brought in for a little while. Martin would be asked to recite the poems he had learnt. I wasn't supposed to, but I also recited a poem or two. I knew that Miss Wright would never be cross with me in front of guests and I hoped she would forget to be cross afterwards. I always wanted to keep up with my big brother and do all the things he did. We weren't allowed to have the party meal, but we always got some of the leftovers next day. The church was also swathed in greenery and beautiful white flowers.

The party I liked best took place when the whole of the church choir came to the rectory and crowded round the Christmas tree. They sang carols and it was all just wonderful with the flickering candles on the tree. Big plates of delicious savouries, sweetmeats and mince pies would be handed round to everyone. Then the choir would sing some more. After that, they each got a bottle of beer or some refreshment to take away.

In the summer, there was a church fête on the big rectory lawn. A huge marquee would go up a day or too before, in case it rained. It never did rain, but tea was served in the marquee, where there were little folding tables and chairs. It was all very elegant, and people looked lovely in pretty summer dresses and smart blazers. There were lots of stalls and games with prizes. Neither Martin, nor I, ever did win a prize, because the games were too difficult for us. But there was a bran tub. We paid our money, and dug our arms deep into the sawdust and chose little parcels. We were certain of getting prizes, though sometimes all we got was an apple or an orange; it was worth it, however, if we pulled out a little doll or a car. People came and had a good time, and spent lots of money, because it was all going to the war effort.

CHAPTER 5

The Friends' School

Many young children are very unhappy when they are sent to boarding school. Those who are very attached to their parents, and their parents' home, get very homesick and miserable at boarding school. The older children, who have got used to the school, often tease the newcomers and add to their misery. Most children, at any school, long for the next holiday and can't wait for the end of term. For Martin and me, it was quite different. We could hardly wait for the holidays to be over, so that we could return to the Friends' School. It was a huge relief to get away from the oppressive and cruel treatment we experienced at the Steads. Any school would have been preferable to being in Merston Rectory with Miss Wright and Mrs Stead.

The Friends' School, run by the Quakers, was paradise for us. That was largely because the Quakers are such special people who focus on talking and understanding, and avoid all kinds of violence. They keep a quiet pace of life, avoid shouting or getting angry but, although they are very much against any kind of fighting or wars, they will defend themselves if attacked. Defending yourself when attacked does not necessarily mean hitting back. If someone comes up to you at school and thumps you for no apparent reason, he or she probably expects you to hit back and then they can say that you started the fight. I am sure you can think of better ways to defend yourself in such a situation without hitting back. Usually Quakers are liked and respected, so that they are not often attacked.

One September, nearly two years after we arrived in England, we were put on the train at London's Liverpool Street, by Miss Wright. Martin was almost nine and I was still five. There were several other Friends' School pupils on that train, who were older and looked after us. We had to change at a small station in Essex onto a train that was run especially for the school. Teachers met the train at Saffron Walden station to greet all the new children and walk with them up a hill to the school. Our luggage was taken separately and the only thing I carried with me was my doll, Christine. Martin went with some older children to School House and I had to go to Junior House with the little ones. A very nice teacher told us both that the two buildings were very close, and that Martin and I would be able to meet and go for walks together as much as we liked.

The school was a lovely, amazing, old building with arches, towers and creepers growing up it, and a lawn in front. It was much bigger than Merston Rectory, and I used to think that was huge. Martin disappeared through the archway and I was taken a little way to the side to Junior House, which was about the size of Merston Rectory but more like an ordinary house. The teacher took me with the other new girls to the dormitory to sort out beds. As soon as I saw the rows of beds, I couldn't stop myself bursting into tears. Mrs Stubbs, the matron of Junior House, came in and sat me on her lap, and rocked me. No-one had done that with me to comfort me since I left my home in Berlin. I trusted the Matron at once and told her how scared I was of wetting my bed. She said that would be no problem; then she walked me round the dormitory and showed me that every single bed had a rubber sheet under the ordinary sheet. She told me that most children wet their beds when they first came to the school and there was a big laundry, which could deal with all the wet sheets. I don't think I wet my bed at all, because I was no longer anxious.

We were only just over two years at the Friends' School, and I enjoyed every minute of it. I sometimes got into trouble because I was a lively, excitable child, but 'trouble' meant talking about whatever happened that should not have happened, and learning how to do better in future. I could understand that, whereas I never understood what Mrs Stead and Miss Wright wanted me to do, or what they got so angry about. The teachers at Junior House practised what they believed in. They seldom got really angry, preferring to be helpful and to explain things quietly. I thought they were wonderful.

Most of the children got very excited at the end of term, when the time came to go home. Martin and I didn't, because we dreaded going back to Merston Rectory. But it was never so bad again, because we knew the holidays would come to an end, and then we would go back to school. Most children get sad at the end of the holidays and don't want to leave their home; Martin and I counted the days and eagerly looked forward to school again.

Junior House had about 50 boys and girls under nine. There were just two classes. I was the smallest and the youngest, which meant that when we lined up to go in, or out, or to the swimming baths, I was always at the end of the line, at least for that first year. Although I was the youngest, I was astonished to find that I was the only one in my class who could really read and write. That was because I had been trying to please Miss Wright and wanted to catch up my big brother. Miss Wright's harshness and pressurising had at least led to some benefits. She taught me to write with special paper with lines that you had to get the letters exactly between and only the tails could go above or below. She got very angry when there were gaps or wiggles in the letters. Because of her elocution lessons, which I hated, I had no accent at all and none of the children could tell that I had come from Germany.

The teachers were very understanding and didn't let me get bored. Miss Barry asked me what kind of stories did I like. I liked animal stories and so she got some nice books for me from School House. My favourite was *Bambi* but I had stacks of other stories too. I simply sat at the back of the class and read my books when the class had reading lessons. Because the books were so interesting and absorbing I learnt to cut off everything that was going on around me. That is a very useful skill to develop. The teachers at the Friends' School were very advanced in their teaching methods compared with most schools, and did a lot for Martin and me, which helped to counteract the damaging experiences in our first foster home. The science teacher stimulated in Martin a life-long interest in science.

Like most children, I simply wanted to be like everyone else and I joined in everything. Swimming was my favourite activity, although I was not very good at it. It was a long time before I could swim, because I couldn't resist playing about in the water. The teacher was very patient with me, not at all like Miss Wright.

Quakers have special prayer meetings that are very different to the kind of Christian services I was used to in the Merston Church. They are very quiet and peaceful. At first, the Junior House children went into prayer meetings for a short while, just at the end. In my second year, we went for the whole time, over an hour. We all sat comfortably and silently. The atmosphere was friendly and peaceful, and we didn't have to do anything. Sometimes it was silent the whole time, and sometimes one or other adult stood up and spoke. It always felt calm and friendly and the atmosphere didn't change after the service, like it did at Merston Rectory. People were nice all the time. Of course, children sometimes got angry with each other, but never at prayer meetings, and the teachers used to sort it out very quickly. Besides, there was so much to keep us happily busy. Lessons were interesting and there were games to play in playtime, trees to climb in the garden and room to run about. We even had little individual garden plots in which to grow flowers and vegetables.

I grew potatoes and Michaelmas daisies in my garden plot. They were supposed to be for the harvest festival, but each of the two years we were at the Friends' School, I missed the festival. I got a fever and had to go to the sanatorium, which was a kind of little private hospital. There were only two wards, one for girls and one for boys, and a little quarantine room. Children were put in isolation, if they had something that was contagious. I was only ill for a day or two but I was kept a few days longer to make sure I was better. Then we had fun with pillow fights at bedtime and sometimes we climbed out of the window, which was very low down anyway, and ran round the garden. One time, a pillow split and we created a snowstorm of feathers.

On Saturdays and Sundays, we had a lot of playtime in the Junior House garden and the teacher in charge would show us new games to play. I was allowed to go out with Martin. He would come over to Junior House to fetch me, and we would go for long rambles in the countryside by ourselves and chatter together. Often we played tag and chased each other all around. I would also walk with the teacher because she would tell us the names of trees and flowers. I learnt to love the countryside.

There were also Junior House walks on Sundays after the prayer meetings. In winter, it was huge fun making snowballs. Once, we made a big snowball and rolled it down a hill. As it rolled down, it collected more and more snow, and we could hardly keep up running after it. At the bottom of the hill, the snowball was taller than I was.

I don't remember ever being very hungry after mealtimes, although I often could and would have eaten more if it had been there. Food was rationed, and there was very little of what were called luxury foods. You were allowed only one half-slice of white bread, but two slices of brown. I always traded my half slice of white for a whole slice of brown bread. I never liked white bread very much, because I thought brown had more taste to it. Even today, I much prefer most brown and black bread to most white kinds. When there were baked potatoes, I used to trade my potato middle for two whole skins. I liked the skin much more than the middle. Sweets were on ration coupons. Once a week, we marched in a crocodile to the shops, where we could choose what to spend our coupon rations on. It seemed to me that we could get more chocolate than other kinds of sweets, so I nearly always chose chocolate. I have been a chocoholic all my life since! I had a sweetheart called Glen and I used to share my chocolate with him, but nobody else.

When there was a birthday, we could choose the meals for the day, except breakfast, which was always porridge and toast. I chose bubble and squeak and toad-in-the-hole for lunch. For tea, there would be a special cake with candles. And we could choose all the children we wanted on our little table. Of course, I chose Glen. For supper, I chose bread and butter pudding, with lots of sultanas and almond flavouring.

After supper, we could choose the story. I chose *Dr Dolittle* and I really believed he could talk to the animals in their language. Because of *Dr Dolittle*, I always tried to speak to animals in their own language of grunts and squeaks. Sometimes it worked too. Later on, long after the war, when we were coming home from the theatre in Germany one time, I gave a mournful howl or two and got all the dogs in the neighbourhood howling in sympathy.

Every year there would be a school play. Everyone had to be in it somehow. I can't remember what the play was, but I was a soldier in a big, black Busby made out of papier-mâché and a red coat, with a broom handle as a lance. It was a lot of fun dressing up and making all the things we needed in art lessons. The only sad thing for me was that most of the children had their parents, or some relative, who came to watch the play. That was a time when I felt that I had no parents. The Steads, of course, didn't come and I would not have wanted them to, as that would have made me scared. At least, I had Martin, who came with other brothers and sisters from School House to watch the play.

Then, at the end of one summer term, when all the other children went home, we were told that we could not go back to Merston Rectory. The Reverend Stead was very ill and Mrs Stead did not want 'noisy children' around. At first, Martin and I were overjoyed at the thought of not going back to Merston Rectory. But then we began to wonder what would become of us. Did nobody want us? Were we going to have to stay at the school, all through the summer holiday?

Without other children around, it was not much fun. We had meals with the headmaster's family for a time and went for lots of walks. Then, suddenly, we were taken by a teacher and put on the London train. A total stranger met us in London and took us to a hostel in Richmond. At that time, we had no idea that we would never come back to the Friends' School, where we had been so relaxed and happy. We had no chance to say goodbye to our school friends, who had all gone home, and most of the teachers had gone too. Life seemed to be full of abrupt endings, with no time to say goodbye and no explanation of what was going on.

Fifty years later, in 1996, the Friends' School organised a reunion of all the former pupils who had been there during the war years. They had kept lists and contacted everyone they could. Martin and I went to that reunion and met quite a lot of people we had known at the school. We were interested to learn that the Friends' School took in a lot of refugee children during the war years. Some of the other refugee children were there at the reunion. I even remembered one or two, but had no idea at the time that they were refugees too. I was sad to learn from her brother, who had been Martin's friend, that my best friend, Benita, had died very young of cancer. I met Glen too, but the magic of that time long ago had vanished. Nevertheless, it was a very moving weekend talking together, meeting old and new friends, and learning about the past and its influence on the present.

CHAPTER 6

The Hostel in Richmond

Martin and I had spent two and a half years, from September 1941 to July 1943, at the Friends' School. We would have liked to stay there for all our schooldays, because we were so happy there. We were not given that choice. As I now know, the Jewish Refugee Committee had taken over our sponsorship.

You can imagine how confused, apprehensive and insecure, Martin and I felt in July 1943. All the other children went home for the summer holidays and we were told we had to stay at the school for a few more days. Reverend Stead was very ill and we could not go back there. The Jewish Refugee Committee was trying to find us another foster family. We were overjoyed at not going back to Merston Rectory, but what would become of us? Suppose the new foster family was just as unreasonable and cruel, and, could it be possible, even worse? The few staff still at the school tried to reassure us and keep us occupied, so that we would not become too anxious and depressed. The school was silent and empty, and a bit eerie. After a few days, the last of the staff left and we had to go too. Mrs Stubbs, the kindly matron, accompanied us, with our luggage, to the London train. It was a bit scary, but we felt rather grown up too at being all alone, at age eleven and eight, with only strangers on the train. That was a bit spoilt by not knowing where we were going when we reached London, or whether we would get lost.

A stranger met us in London. I didn't know how she recognised us, however we must have been the only two small children getting off that train on their own. She was nice and friendly, so we were relieved at being 'found' by her. She took us on a journey across London and told us about all sorts of things. Then we had to walk the last, quite long bit, until we finally reached a huge house, hidden in trees and bushes, in Richmond. It was a hostel for displaced children. It looked like a normal house but I was surprised at how crowded it was inside, and very shabby and dirty. The noise and smell were overpowering. It felt as though there were hundreds of tiny children, little more than toddlers, swarming up and down the stairs, and making a lot of noise and fuss. It was a hot summer, and most of them were naked or just had a vest on. I was used to grown-ups keeping everything clean, tidy and strictly in order. The Richmond hostel was a bewildering, buzzing confusion that terrified me at first, until Martin told me that we were perfectly able to look after ourselves. That was all right for me; while I had Martin to look after me, I didn't need anyone else.

Most of the time, there was not an adult to be seen. Some older children in their teens looked after the babies for much of the time. It was a non-stop job feeding them all. There were a few tiny babies, who had to be bottle-fed. That was something I had never seen before and I was amazed that the bottles were crescent-shaped with teats each end. I was told that was to let air in, as the babies sucked the milk out, but I never understood why that was necessary. I have never seen a baby-bottle with two teats since. The teenagers let me hold one of the babies and feed her the bottle. I was delighted when the baby smiled up at me. Then a moment later, she was sick all over me. After that, I preferred helping with feeding the toddlers, who had to be spoon-fed.

There were no proper mealtimes. You could never know when the next meal was going to be. My tummy was used to regular meals and didn't like it at all. Often, when we were hungry and asked when the next meal would be, we were told to go to the kitchen and make something ourselves. Usually there was something left over from making the toddlers' meals. One day I was hungry and went to the kitchen. Two teenage girls were making fried bread and offered me some. It looked and smelled rather nice, crisp and brown with a lot of salt sprinkled on it. I had never eaten fried bread before. It was yummy. I wanted more. The girls showed me how to make it and left me to it. It was so delicious that I ate more and more. Of course, it was not long after I had eaten myself full that I got a tummy ache. That night I was dreadfully sick. I had diarrhoea for several days and couldn't eat anything. I recovered but it was many years before I dared to eat fried bread again.

Summer 1943 coincided with the peak of the war. Looking back it was not surprising the hostel was disorganised with so little supervision. Most of the grown-ups who were not in the armed forces were in the munitions factories. There simply would not have been people to spare for running hostels for displaced children. No wonder we were allowed to run wild and get into all sorts of trouble. I am not sure whether Martin and I were allowed out of the hostel grounds; anyway, we went for walks to explore the district. Mostly, we found our way to the Thames and, as it was very hot, we had fun splashing in the water. Martin could swim, but I stayed on the muddy edges. As we had no towels, we would walk back to the hostel in our wet pants, and, by the time we got there, we were dry.

We were aware that the Thames water was murky but, as other kids were swimming and splashing in it, it never occurred to us that it might be dangerous. But it must have been from the polluted Thames water that Martin caught hepatitis. We didn't know at the time that it was hepatitis. Martin developed a high fever and was unable to get out of bed. I couldn't find any grown-ups to tell; the teenagers were too busy to be interested in anything I had to say. So nobody thought of calling a doctor. Martin became delirious and all his skin turned yellow.

I was very frightened. I could not bear the thought of losing him, but that didn't protect me against thinking it. I read stories to him and mopped his hot, flushed face every now and then with a wet flannel to soothe him. He said that 'an apple a day keeps the doctor away.' He was convinced that he needed an apple a day to get better. So I took Christine, the only doll I had left, and went out in the road. By and by, I found a lady with a baby pushing a pram. I was able to buy a big bag of sweet-smelling red apples with the few pennies she gave me for the doll. Martin was so ill that I don't know how he managed to eat an apple a day, but he did. I think my willing him to get better helped more than the apples. He gradually recovered, but I don't think it was really much to do with the apples. I think it was because he had faith in them. And I had faith in whatever my big brother said. As far as I was concerned, he couldn't possibly be wrong.

It was a huge relief when Martin was well again. It took a long time. He was still quite weak, and sleeping a lot, when there was an outbreak of head lice in the hostel. I am not sure if Martin and I had caught them too. We were not aware of itching or scratching, like a lot of the little children were doing. The teenagers decided that the solution to the problem was paraffin. Everybody had to have their head plunged into paraffin and held there for a minute or so. The smell of the paraffin made me feel sick and there was so much splashed about that the whole hostel stank of it for days afterwards. After a few hours, my neck and forehead came up in blisters – big, yellowish bubbles that burst and oozed yellow liquid. It was very painful. I could hardly move at all without it hurting, excruciatingly. Someone put some cream and a bandage round my neck and head, but that stung horribly. I was swathed in bandages when Mrs Goodricke came to fetch Martin and me to take us to our new home.

CHAPTER 7

A Real Family at Last

I remember thinking how nice Mrs Goodricke was to come herself, instead of having us put on a train. She looked very old and very wise, because she had grey hair, although she could not have been more than 50. She didn't rush us out of the hostel. Instead, she took a lot of trouble to talk with us. She wanted to know what we had been doing, and encouraged us to tell her about ourselves. She was very concerned about the scruffy bandage round my neck covering the blisters that had come up when my hair was washed in paraffin to kill the nits. She told me she had been a nurse before she married and she would put some healing cream on it. I think someone must have told her about my sores, because she had brought the cream and a clean bandage with her. I protested, because it had hurt a lot when the hostel staff had ripped the previous bandage off. But Mrs Goodricke was very gentle and did it all slowly, so that it didn't hurt much. She had also brought a jersey for each of us. Mine was a speckled blue, and I got very fond of it and wore it until it was in holes. I trusted Mrs Goodricke immediately and wished she were my mummy.

Then she told us about her family, and asked us if we would like to come home with her. She said that her five children, Ursula, Susan, John, Joan and Guy were looking forward to meeting us. There would be places to explore, animals to meet and things to do. They had an orchard with fruit trees, chickens and rabbits, and a field with ponies. It all sounded interesting and inviting, so that, naturally, I wanted to go with her. She was friendly and warm like the Quaker teachers, and not at all frightening like Mrs Stead and Miss Wright. That made it easier to go off once again into the unknown, and leave behind all we had got used to in the hostel and its surroundings.

The journey didn't seem too long. It was a bit shocking at first, because we had to get a bus through some parts of London that were badly damaged from bombs. But Mrs Goodricke reassured us that, out in the country where she lived, there was no bomb damage and we would be safe. The train was already puffing and blowing its steam whistle, when we got to the station and jumped on. At that time, there were only steam trains. They puffed clouds of smoke as they chugged along with a clickety-clack, clickety-clack rhythm and a choo-choo, chug-chug, choo-choo sound. In spite of the smoke, these trains were always clean and shining because the engine drivers and their crew took great pride in them.

Mrs Goodricke chatted with us and brought us a couple of books; one for me with interesting pictures of farm animals, and one for Martin with more words than pictures. This made the time go by very quickly, and soon we were in Maidstone station. A bus took us to Horsmonden and dropped us a short walk away from the Goodrickes' home. The house was enchanting; it was a real Tudor cottage with higgledy-piggledy, black beams and white plaster in between. It was the first house I got to know that had a name of its own – Westen-hanger. It was much smaller than both the rectory where the Steads lived and the Friends' School. It was even smaller than the big, rambling, three-storey hostel. It was a country cottage with climbing wisteria and rambling roses in the front garden, and a rather dilapidated oast house alongside, where hops had once been stored and treated to make beer.

Some farmer had filled it with hay. It was dark and dusty inside, but it was to be an ideal hide-out, and perfect for romping around. We loved to slide down the hay on the upper floor and fall down into the hay on the lower floor.

When we arrived, Mrs Goodricke told Martin to open the front door. At that time, at least in the country, people didn't lock their doors. It was quite safe, because local people could be trusted and, in any case, nearly every family had a working dog to bark and let them know if someone came. Sure enough, as soon as Martin turned the doorknob, you could hear Rover barking. Mr Goodricke and the five children heard Rover's bark and were all at the door by the time it was open. Mrs Goodricke introduced us and told us to wash our hands, as tea was ready. In the country, it was usual to have high tea at about 5pm or 6pm and that was the last meal of the day. There would be only a drink of milk at bedtime after that. It was called high tea, because there was usually something more than bread and jam and tea. Sometimes there would be an egg, or fried or baked potatoes, and, on Sundays, there would be cake.

At this first meal, all of us children were rather quiet and a bit shy as we looked at one another. I was excited because this was a real family, like the pictures of families in the storybooks I had read at the Friends' School. Back at the Steads, our meals were brought to us in the schoolroom upstairs. Miss Wright used to sit with us, but Reverend and Mrs Stead ate their meals in the dining room downstairs on a shiny polished table and carved chairs.

Now, at last, I was in a real family that all had meals together. Mr and Mrs Goodricke would eat with us and encourage us to have proper conversations. They were quite strict too. No-one was allowed to talk with their mouth full, and only one person could speak at a time. Everyone had to wait for their turn. We had to use our knives and forks properly, keep our mouths shut when we were chewing, and ask politely for dishes to be passed to us. I never took the last piece of anything on a plate without first asking if everyone had had something from that plate. Mr and Mrs Goodricke would explain, if I asked why things had to be done the way they said. It made sense when they explained, so I didn't mind doing it their way.

The Goodrickes were not Quakers, but they seemed to me very similar. They did not believe in war or any sort of violence. But they believed in defence. England had to be defended against Nazi attacks. Everyone feared that Hitler would cross the channel and invade England. So far, Hitler's forces had invaded and occupied the Channel Islands, but only attacked England by air. The Battle of Britain was fought in the air between British Spitfires and German Messerschmidts. We had grown used to hearing planes going over and trying to see if they were 'ours' or 'theirs'.

Although Mr Goodricke was opposed to aggression, and was a compassionate and gentle person, he joined the Territorial Army where he was promoted to lance bombardier. He worked on experimental radar on the cliffs of Dover during the bombing of London in the Blitz. Radar was developed to interfere with the pilots' electrical equipment, so that they could not find their way. When his health deteriorated from stress, he was made a chaplain and then invalided out of the forces. While Martin and I were living with the family, Mr Goodricke was doing his bit for the war effort as a farm labourer. This was very important, as so many men were away in the forces. Older men had to grow and harvest food crops, and a Women's Land Army was recruited to help them.

We sometimes visited him at work. It was a huge farm where hops and fruit were grown. I was always a bit scared and in awe of Mr Goodricke. He was very strong and could lift huge sacks and enormous baskets of fruit. In the autumn, there was fruit to be picked from the trees, hops to be picked off the vines and potatoes to be lifted out of the earth. The produce all had to be put into special baskets by hand. The baskets were then weighed, because the 'pickers' were paid by the weight they picked.

Lots of Gypsies and East Enders from the poorest part of London used to come to do this work. These seasonal workers were welcomed, because the local people could not do it all. The local men were mostly away at war and the women were working in factories, making supplies for the war. The Gypsies came in their caravans and there were temporary huts for the Londoners. They were friendly, fun-loving people who sang while they worked and around their campfires at the end of the day.

Mrs Goodricke didn't engage in farm work, but she must have worked very hard to cook for a family of nine people and to keep the house clean and tidy. And then there was the garden, the orchard, and the chickens and rabbits to look after.

The older children helped a lot and even we younger ones did our bit. Keeping house was very different then and much harder work than now. There was no electric kettle; only a big, black kettle on the hob that was too heavy for me to lift. There was no washing machine; so all the washing for nine people was done by hand. We children used to help hanging it out in the garden on the line. And there was no dishwasher; everything had to be washed and dried by hand, and we all took turns with this.

Food was scarce and therefore rationed during the war. Everybody was entitled to a certain number of coupons for different kinds of food – meats, fat, flour and sweets, and even for clothes. The Goodrickes' big garden and orchard supplied us all with fruit and vegetables, eggs from the chickens and honey from the beehives. So we didn't get as many coupons as town people did. Even then, Mr and Mrs Goodricke sometimes gave their coupons to families who were very poor and struggling. Mrs Goodricke also made lots of jam and pickles for the poorer neighbours. During the war, with its misery and privations, people did what they could to help each other. That special wartime spirit of co-operation and friendliness is still talked about today.

During the war, and for a long time afterwards, ordinary folk couldn't afford to feed pets. Many people ate rabbit at that time, because other meat was scarce and they might have gone hungry otherwise. So, though the Goodrickes kept rabbits and we could feed them, we weren't allowed to get fond of them, because their purpose was to be killed and eaten. Mr Goodricke would inspect them like a doctor looking for illness. They would struggle in his arms, as he didn't tame them, and we were not allowed to play with them. That way we could all enjoy eating rabbit pie and rabbit stew.

Mrs Goodricke was very strict about not wasting anything. We simply did not throw away anything that could possibly be used for something. Fruit and vegetable peelings were saved in a bucket for the rabbits and chickens. Packaging was never discarded until it fell apart. Envelopes, paper bags and boxes were very valuable. Disposable plastic bags had not been invented and there were only a few plastic products, though lots of toys and other things were made of celluloid. When we went shopping, we took empty paper bags and cardboard boxes for refilling. There were no packaged foods to buy. Everything was scooped out of a sack or jar and weighed into the bags we had brought. We could hand in spare bags for a penny or two, and then careless people who came without a bag could buy one.

Ursula was the eldest of the Goodricke children. Aged 15, she seemed like a grown-up to me. She was very fond of reading and didn't join in our games very much. Susan was next, aged 13, a very jolly girl who encouraged our games, but also stopped us if anything got dangerous. John was next. He was away at boarding school a lot of the time and teased us younger ones mercilessly when he was home. He was the leader in our games, when he was there. He was 11, the same age as Martin, but they did not get on very well, as they were so different from each other. Joan was the second youngest and she was eight, the same age as me. We became best friends and were nearly always together. Guy was only six and the youngest. He was a delicate child with serious asthma, but he was always amusing us with his funny antics.

Life at the Goodrickes was interesting and enjoyable a lot of the time for me, but it did not seem so good for Martin, who did not fit in well with the children. He was only enthusiastic about science and, unfortunately for him, no-one else in the family shared his interest. Mr and Mrs Goodricke were very tolerant of Martin's science experiments, which sometimes caused a lot of mess, as he describes later on. I enjoyed the company of the other children, even though there was a lot of teasing, rough and tumble, and scolding, when you didn't get things right. But that is family life.

CHAPTER 8

Life at Westenhanger

The five Goodricke children, Ursula, Susan, John, Joan and Guy, called their parents 'Mummy' and 'Daddy'. I very much wanted to be part of the Goodricke family in every way, so I started calling Mrs Goodricke 'Mummy' too. She didn't scold me, but took me to a quiet corner and explained to me that I had a mummy and daddy who wouldn't want me to call her Mummy. I burst into tears, and told her my mummy was dead and I wanted her to be my mummy. Mrs Goodricke didn't contradict me, probably because she didn't know whether my mother was alive or not. In my mind, my mother was dead, otherwise she would be there with me. It was unbearable for me to consider that she could choose to be somewhere else and not with me, therefore she had to be dead.

Mrs Goodricke knew my father was in Shanghai. We had received a letter from him, via the Red Cross in Switzerland, while we were at the Friends' School, and I had shown it to Mrs Goodricke, together with a photo and a Chinese money note he had also sent. So she told me that my daddy would be very upset if I called her Mummy. She explained to me that, after the war, my daddy would come and fetch me, or he would send a ticket for Martin and me to go on a boat to Shanghai. She said it would be exciting to go on a big steamship to China, and my daddy would be pleased to see me, but he wouldn't want me to call anyone else Daddy or Mummy. She said I could call her 'Auntie', but I didn't like that. We had to call our first foster mother, Mrs Stead, 'Auntie' and I didn't want to be reminded of her, as she had been so cruel. So it was always Mr and Mrs Goodricke.

Martin and I arrived at Westenhanger in October. The children were back at school, and Martin and I joined them. Every day, we set off at 7.55 am. Mrs Goodricke packed a sandwich, or a couple of oatmeal biscuits she had baked, in each of six little cloth bags, as it would be a long time till lunch and we could eat them at mid-morning break.

The radio, an old-fashioned one with tuning knobs to twiddle, was always on over breakfast. When the announcer said, 'Lift up your hearts', to herald a few moments of reflection on the news of the day, we had to 'lift up our feet' and set off. It was over a mile to the stop for the Tunbridge Wells bus. Ursula and Susan would chivvy us little ones along, because they were responsible for us getting on the bus. We girls got off at Pembury for our school, but Martin and Guy had to go right into Tunbridge Wells for their boys' school. There were other St. George's boys on the bus, who made sure they were all right.

I was only one term at Pembury Girls School, because the school closed at the end of that term. I remember there was a dinner dance for the ending. We all wore long, pretty, coloured taffeta dresses. I think they must have been hired, as we only wore them once. Christmas dinner came with jelly and ice cream, which was a great treat. There was a little present on the Christmas tree for each person, including the teachers. We had special dancing lessons well before the party, so that we could enjoy the dancing. I was too excited and rather clumsy, and I envied Joan, who danced so elegantly.

Then Christmas came at Westenhanger. That was magical, compared to previous Christmases at the Steads. There was no money to buy shop decorations, so we made our own. We all went over the fields to the woods, and came back laden with huge bundles of yew and holly branches. The house was decorated with green branches and clusters of red berries. I remember twining branches in the banisters, all the way up the stairs. The Christmas tree had only a few shining balls and some tinsel that had been kept in a box in the cupboard from year to year. But it had real candles that had to be very carefully fixed, and looked wonderful when they were lit.

On Christmas morning, there were presents at the foot of each child's bed. I was not allowed to bring many toys from Berlin, except for one big doll and one little one. The big one, Pupchen, had a porcelain head and got broken. All the toys we had at our first foster family got left behind there, when we went straight from boarding school to the hostel in Richmond. The other doll, Christine, I sold to the lady who had given me a few pennies, so that I could buy apples for Martin when he was ill in the hostel. I missed my teddy bears and the other toys left in Berlin. You can imagine how thrilled I was to discover that Father Christmas had brought me a teddy bear. I don't know how Mr and Mrs Goodricke managed to buy toys for seven children during the war, when everything, especially money, was so scarce.

Clutching newly unwrapped presents, the children crowded into Mr and Mrs Goodricke's bedroom on Christmas morning and sang carols by candlelight, because it was still dark. Every meal was extra special, and the service in the church was special too, with more candlelight than usual and singing. I often wonder about the experience of children today who get dozens of presents at Christmas, and have chocolates and cakes all the year round. Do they enjoy them as much as we enjoyed our one Christmas present each and all the special delicacies that we only had at Christmas?

We had very few actual toys, but we had loads of fun. On winter evenings, we all made our own toys from garments that couldn't be patched and darned any more. Joan and I each made a fabulous hobby-horse. They were really only old socks stuffed with wool for horses' heads at the end of a stick. But to us, they were real horses. We rode our horses everywhere for weeks and weeks in make-believe rodeos and show jumping.

John had a proper lathe in the garden shed, and he made all sorts of toys from bits of wood: skittles, jacks, dice and little boats to float on the water in the stream, so that we could play at torpedoing them. We even made our own board games and jigsaws.

After Christmas, the girls went to Tunbridge Wells High School, which meant we all went on the bus right into town. Whereas Joan and I were in the same class at Pembury School, we were put in different classes at Tunbridge Wells High. We didn't like that, but we found each other at break and dinner times. We were fond of tying our legs together and going everywhere three-legged. Because we got so used to it, we easily won the three-legged race, when it came to sports day in the summer. While at school, I won a prize for one of my drawings. It was a snow scene of children snowballing and sliding in the school playground.

It was not long after Christmas that a visit to the doctor for a heavy cold and headache resulted in my going into hospital to have my tonsils out. I had not been in hospital since my birth in Berlin. I didn't like it at all. It was still morning, and I had to undress and get into bed. It was a frighteningly big ward with two rows of more beds than I could count. Even worse was that elderly women occupied them all. There were no other children. I wasn't allowed to eat anything and I could only drink water. In the evening, a nurse came round with a trolley. She gave some little things to each patient, which I thought were sweets. Mrs Goodricke explained to me later that they were tablets of medicine. The nurse gave me a tiny glass with a dark liquid in it. It smelled good, and I was hungry and drank it up. I asked the nurse for more, and the women in the beds around me burst out laughing. Some of them had no teeth and looked like cackling witches. I was terrified. The nurse told me I couldn't have any more because it was syrup of figs to make me go to the toilet!

The next day, I had my operation. A nurse pushed a wad of cotton wool in my face. It was chloroform and smelled horrible. Instinctively, I snatched it and flung it across the ward. The Sister scolded me, 'Bad girl!', and that was the last I remembered, as two nurses pinned my arms down and I was chloroformed. I still remembered 'bad girl' when I came round. My throat was horribly sore, and I thought that must have been my punishment for being a bad girl. I was absolutely starving hungry but my throat was too sore for me to speak. I rang the bell because I was so frightened, but I couldn't say anything when the nurse came. She picked me up and dumped me on the toilet, and left me there for ages. In fact, it was Mrs Goodricke, who had come to visit me in the evening, who rescued me. I hadn't dared to get off the toilet, in case that would make me into even more of a bad girl.

Sundays were special in the Goodricke family. We started by making breakfast in bed for Mr and Mrs Goodricke. As they worked so hard all week, it felt good to give something back to them. We loved making breakfast, even though it was always the same: sausages, toast with jam, and tea. There was a strict rota, so that everyone had a turn at frying the sausages, which was considered the best job, and the others had to do the rest. Ursula, as the oldest, always carried the tray of breakfast upstairs to her parents, but we all had turns in bringing the tray down when they had finished. Susan, who was good at organising – we called it bossiness – made sure everything was done properly. Ursula sat in her mother's place at the head of the dining room table, while we had our breakfast. Then we did the washing-up and made sure the kitchen was clean and tidy by the time Mrs Goodricke came down.

On Sunday mornings, after breakfast, we all went to church. Most of the clergy had been called up as chaplains for the armed forces, and there were only peripatetic clergy left. They went from church to church, sometimes leading three or four services at different churches in one day. When there wasn't one available, Mr Goodricke would take the service. I liked it when he gave the sermon, because he put a lot of expression into it that made it exciting even if I didn't understand much of it. The peripatetic clergy usually droned on and on, and then it was boring. I was often in trouble for fidgeting or whispering to Joan.

I don't know how she did it, but Mrs Goodricke always had dinner ready soon after we got back from church, although she had been there with us. I remember, one Sunday, she didn't come with us, because her parents were expected. They had dinner with us. All of us children found it very funny that Mr and Mrs Goodricke called her parents 'Mater' and 'Pater'. We giggled like mad until we were sent out into the garden to play.

Sunday afternoon was always a treat, as Mr Goodricke played games with us. If it was rainy, we would be indoors playing board games and hide-and-seek round the house. Sometimes Mr Goodricke played the piano and we had a singsong. I had a poor ear for music, although I enjoyed singing. They all teased me about it and I sometimes got upset. When it was fine, we would play all sorts of games in the garden. The one I liked best, involved performing acrobatics on a big, horizontal, iron bar across two wooden pillars put up by Mr Goodricke and John. I was not very good at it, but it was fun watching the others. John was particularly agile and daring; it was quite scary, but exciting to watch him.

On weekends, summer evenings and in the school holidays, we were allowed to cross the road in front of the house and go across the cherry orchard, to play in the stream. We made make-believe houses, castles, boats, and tanks out of bits of rubbish and branches of trees. John was the leader and sometimes we were soldiers, or bandits, or

Robin Hood and his merry men. We spent hours building bridges over the stream and dams, and we paddled in the ponds we had created. Joan, Guy, and I usually got pushed in, and we all would arrive back home soaking wet.

There was a railway line, a bit further on past the stream. We were not supposed to go there, but John led us there to play 'chicken' on the railway line. The game was to see who would be the last one left on the line when a train came. I was usually the first to jump off, and, mostly, John won the game. The one occasion I saw Mr Goodricke red in the face with anger, was when the railway inspector paid us a visit to report our dangerous games. After that it stopped.

We went for lots of walks through the fields and woods with Rover, a big, energetic, ginger dog. We would pick mushrooms or blackberries, or collect wool.

There were many sheep in the fields around Westenhanger. Sheep have a habit of wriggling through fences, because the grass always looks greener on the other side of a fence. They would leave a lot of wool behind, especially on the thorn hedges and barbed wire fences. Joan and I took a bag each when we went for walks, and we would compete to be the one who could collect the most sheep's wool. It was fun finding and pulling the tags of wool off the brambles and barbed wire. We usually both came home with full bags.

Mrs Goodricke taught us how to card it with a wire comb, to make it smooth. Then it had to be soaked in 'neap' to get the oil out, and then soaked in dye to colour it. Onion skin would make it a lovely yellow. Cochineal made it red. Then we would spin it into thread, using a spindle made out of a dried lump of clay soil, with a pencil through the middle. We got very skilful at spinning the clay spindle and pulling the wool into evenly thin yarn while it was spinning. We would then wind the yarn into balls or skeins. You could then knit with it or weave it. At school, we learnt weaving in craft lessons and I could use the homemade yarn. At home, we knitted squares. Every village collected squares for the women's guild to sew into blankets for the troops abroad. Some people knitted socks and pullovers for them. I sometimes thought about the soldiers and hoped that our homespun woollen squares kept them warm.

School ended and it was the summer holiday. The Goodricke family always went to stay for two weeks in the summer with either Mrs Goodricke's parents in Cornwall or Mr Goodricke's parents, who lived somewhere further north. Mrs Goodricke told me that her in-laws' house was not big enough to have more than five children. They arranged for Martin and me to go somewhere else for a fortnight; Martin went to a boys' hostel in Eastbourne and I went to a hostel for younger children in Hastings.

Though I was sad to be separated from Martin and upset to feel that I was not part of the Goodricke family, I had a good time. It was my first experience of swimming in the sea. I had only just learnt to swim and I was very proud of this. I was mesmerised by the waves. There was only a little bit of safe beach for children, as it was wartime. Most of the beach had huge, concrete tank traps as a wall between the sea and the promenade. We were told there were mines too. I stayed in the water until I was blue with cold. It was such fun, and there were other children to play with. But I also felt that the war had been going on a long time, and I wondered if it would ever end and whether I would ever see my daddy again.

When I was back at Westenhanger, I developed very bad constipation, lost my appetite, and felt nauseous and lethargic for many days. The way that depression was treated at that time was to tell the sufferer to 'snap out of it'. When you are depressed, that is just what you can't do – even if you want to. Every movement was too big an effort, and felt like walking across a ploughed field in the rain in boots that got more and more clogged with mud. I didn't know at the time, but I was quite seriously depressed, probably due to the loss of my fantasy that I was a Goodricke and not wanting to have to be myself. I really didn't know who I was. I had been sent away from my original home because I was not a 'good enough German'. I had tried hard to be a good Goodricke, but I wasn't good enough for that either. Joan was a true friend. She stuck by me and kept me company, while the other children were down at the stream having fun. By the time the autumn term started at school, I had pulled out of my depression and got back to normal.

CHAPTER 9

Doodlebugs over Kent

A little over a year after Martin and I went to live with the Goodricke family, the Nazis started sending doodlebugs to London. The Goodrickes' cottage, Westenhanger, was in Kent, and that was in the path of the doodlebugs on their way to London. Doodlebugs were pilotless planes that were really bombs on wings.

Doodlebugs were catapulted from Peenemünde on the Baltic coast of Germany with just enough fuel to reach London. When they ran out of fuel, they dropped on London as bombs that burst into flame, and caused enormous damage. My father-in-law was in the London fire service

Doodlebug

during the war. His crew had to put the fires out and rescue any people still alive in the damaged areas. It was very skilled, hard and dangerous work. Many of his mates were killed on the job. So, the Royal Air Force did what they could to stop the doodlebugs getting to London. They stationed a lot of anti-aircraft guns in Kent to shoot the doodlebugs down in the country where they would do much less damage. That meant the anti-aircraft guns were all around Westenhanger.

In the autumn of 1944, the doodlebugs started coming over, mostly, at night. The warning siren would wake us up. Joan, Guy and I would sit on the bedroom windowsill with our feet dangling down, and wait for the fun to begin. It was like Bonfire Night. First, the red flares would go up, to warn the gunners that the radar had sighted a doodlebug, and to be ready. Then you would hear the drone of a doodlebug approaching. You could spot the doodlebug by the flames coming out of its tail. The guns would begin to fire – pow, pow, pow! If they scored a hit, the doodlebug would come down in an arc like a shooting star, and then explode as it hit the ground. It was all very exciting. Lastly, the green flares would go up to let the gunners know that no more doodlebugs were coming, and then the 'all clear' siren would sound.

Next morning, if there had been a hit near us, we would go out to see the remains of the burnt-out doodlebug and pick up pieces as souvenirs. Once, I found a shiny black nose-tip, and I kept that for many years as a prized possession. If a doodlebug came down in a cherry or apple orchard, it would plough through and uproot several trees. This was an awesome sight to see. But that was nothing like the damage they did in London.

Occasionally, a doodlebug came over in daytime. We were drilled to get under something as soon as the warning siren sounded. I remember once, we were walking along the road, coming home from school, when the siren went off. Susan quickly pushed Joan, Guy and me into a ditch under the hedge. She told us to put our heads down and to put our hands over them. A doodlebug came right over us, so low that we could see its markings. I think it had already been hit, as it was flying lop-sided. When the guns fired, we heard the shrapnel pattering down in the road. As soon as the 'all clear' sounded, we scrambled up out of the ditch to find the shrapnel. It was still too hot to pick up! I collected a big tin full of shrapnel bits. They were good for trading at school for sweets or cigarette cards.

I never heard of a doodlebug coming down on any buildings in Kent, but I am sure there must have been some. As a child aged nine, I had no idea of the danger. It never occurred to me that a doodlebug could crash down on our house. Mr and Mrs Goodricke must have been very worried about our safety, but they didn't show any signs of it to us children, and that helped us youngest ones get through what could have been a terrifying experience. It was probably quite difficult for the three older children, Ursula, Susan and John. They must have needed a lot of reassurance from their parents.

But Martin could not be comforted. He was most upset by the doodlebugs. He would go and hide, and he wouldn't talk about it. I feel ashamed now of how we teased him. He would be trembling and shaking, and our teasing must have made it much worse for him. For us younger three, Joan and Guy and me, the doodlebugs were just exciting fun. If you want to see what these flying bombs looked like, you can see one in the main hall of the Imperial War Museum in London. It reaches all the way up to the fourth floor terrace.

Martin found it much more difficult than me to settle down in the Goodricke family. In fact, he didn't really settle down at all. For one thing, Martin would argue if he thought something was not right. We children argued a lot among ourselves, but Martin argued a lot with Mr Goodricke. You weren't supposed to argue with grown-ups, and I simply accepted that, even if it felt unfair. I told myself that one day I would be a grown-up and then I would decide what was fair or unfair.

Martin didn't join in much of our playing. He even had to be persuaded to take part in the Sunday fun. He preferred reading and 'doing science'. Mr Goodricke didn't like some of the books Martin chose to borrow from the public library, but he was very tolerant on the whole.

Martin was allowed to have chemicals and carry out experiments. He used to make carbide bombs in tins and set them off in the garden. It was quite amusing to watch the tin blow its lid high into the air. Once, one of his experiments in the scullery went wrong and produced clouds of stinking black smoke, which penetrated through the cracks round closed doors and spread all over the house. It was most unpleasant and took a bit of time to clear up.

Then there was the business of the radio. Martin's interest in science took him into electrical shops, and he would be given scraps from their waste bins. He built himself a crystal radio from these scraps, which he could tune in to many more radio stations than the normal wireless. Mr Goodricke became alarmed when he heard Martin listening to German on his crystal set.

It should have been obvious that Martin was homesick for his original language, his mother tongue that represented his mother to him, and only natural for him to seek it on his radio when he couldn't sleep at night. But during wartime, things were different. People had to be suspicious for their own and other people's safety.

Mr Goodricke reported Martin's interest in German on his radio to the police because he thought that a German spy ring might be using Martin for getting secret information. Martin and I were called to the police station and questioned. I had no idea what it was all about. They asked me if I knew any communists. I didn't even know what a communist was! After that, we had to report to the police station every six months.

When Martin became seriously upset by the doodlebugs, Mr Goodricke decided again to report him, as he feared that Martin was going mad. This time, he took Martin to a psychiatrist. I didn't go with them, so I only know what Martin told me, years later. The psychiatrist talked with him for a long time, and asked him a load of questions. Then he told Mr Goodricke that there was nothing wrong with Martin. He had been upset by the doodlebugs coming from where he knew his mother to be.

The psychiatrist recommended that he be moved to live where there were no doodlebugs coming over. The refugee committee found a place for Martin at Midhurst Grammar School, where the headmaster was known to be very good at helping boys who were upset.

So Martin had to leave Westenhanger and the Goodrickes, and live with a family near the school. I just accepted this, and had no idea that there were long-term plans for me to move too.

After the war was over, the whole Goodricke family emigrated. They were fed up with all the wars in Europe, and wanted to go to a country where there had never been a war. They chose Tasmania. That is about as far away from Europe as you can get. Joan and I stayed in contact and we often wrote to each other. One winter, which was summer in Tasmania, while visiting the Goodrickes, we went to a museum of Aboriginal Culture. I learnt that the first settlers had killed them all – and that is worse than war!

I visited the house at Westenhanger in the 1990s. It had been beautifully redecorated. The disused oast house where we used to play had been refurbished as a little mini-cottage, and it had become a listed building.

Westenhanger

CHAPTER 10

The End of the War

The war lasted six years. That is a very long time for a child between four and ten. It seemed to go on forever. I didn't understand that much about it, because the grown-ups believed that children had to be protected from hearing the truth about horrible things. So I picked up fragments.

I knew that we had to flee Germany because Hitler wanted to kill us. Hitler was a very bad, wicked man. I heard the BBC radio broadcasts, which told us all about the terrible cruelty of Hitler and the Nazis. And I learned things by chance. Once, when I was in the holiday hostel in Hastings, I was taken to the cinema. The Pathe News came on and showed some very frightening war scenes.

I was surprised that the Germans did not look like monsters. The German soldiers, mostly ones that had been captured, looked like ordinary men. They were not any different to Allied troops. I had imagined them to be huge, evil creatures with enormous teeth and at least six arms, each carrying a gun.

I was concerned about spies. I knew we were not supposed to ask questions. There were posters at bus stops and in stations saying, 'Don't speak to strangers' and 'Walls have ears!'. Anybody might be a spy. If they were, they might pass information to the Nazis and then the war would go on longer, and we might even lose. When the war dragged on and on, I used to wonder who had been telling things to the Nazis.

Then one day, May 8th, 1945, the war in Europe ended. The Germans stopped fighting and unconditionally surrendered to the Allies. All the Goodrickes cheered when they heard the news on the wireless.

I asked Mrs Goodricke, 'Can I see my daddy now?' She was very sweet and explained that he was very far away in China – it would be difficult to travel to see him because the railways, ships, and planes, had been destroyed in the war. She said that all the soldiers would have to be brought home first. So it might be a long time before my daddy could travel. We hadn't had any letter from him for a long time, and I began to wonder if he was dead – like my mummy. Nobody mentioned her, not even Martin.

When I grew up, I discovered that I had imagined far more horrible things than had really happened. Sometimes I think, if I had been told the truth – that nobody knew if my mother was surviving the war or not – then I could have learned to deal with the uncertainty of not knowing if she was alive or dead. Children are intelligent and, if not told the truth, will decide it for themselves. So it really is better for adults to share what they know, even if the news is bad. Sometimes, children imagine it is the adults, who might fall to pieces, if made to speak the truth. Then children dare not say anything for fear of the consequences, afraid that maybe there will be no-one capable of looking after them.

On VE Day, the day the war ended, crowds came out into the streets in London and all over the country. They hugged each other and danced with joy. They celebrated the end of the war with street parties. Long trestle tables were set up outside and everyone sat down to tea and cakes and music. Anyone who had a musical instrument played in the streets. I learned all this later on from films.

Mr Goodricke said that it was disloyal to our brave soldiers to go to parties until they were all home again. But, of course, lots of them never did come home, at least not alive. Mr Goodricke told us that there was more to be sad about than to rejoice about. But most people felt like rejoicing and thought it was the right moment to celebrate. It was certainly good that the killing had stopped.

The Kent Education Committee thought VE Day (Victory in Europe) was something children should remember and arranged for every schoolchild to go to the cinema. It was a huge treat to have a half-day out of the classroom. We marched gaily in a crocodile along the road from school to the cinema, where we were each given a bar of chocolate and four threepenny bits. Threepenny bits are no longer currency. They are collectors' items now. With their twelve sides, they were unusual coins even then. Four threepenny bits made a shilling. That was quite a lot of money. It was six times as much as my pocket money then. It would be worth around five pounds now, given the rise in the cost of living. We were quite awed at such a present. Someone from the education committee talked to us, from the stage of the cinema, about the ending of the war and told us to keep the four threepenny bits as a souvenir. Sadly, I didn't keep mine and I can't remember what I spent them on. Joan Goodricke kept hers and she gave two of them to me when I visited her in Tasmania many years later.

After the speech, came the film show. It was the film *Bambi*. It was 70 minutes of pure enchantment. I knew the story because I had read the book in school, but we had no TV at that time and I had never seen a Disney film before. It had a powerful effect on me. After seeing the film, I had to read the story again and again. I became obsessed and persuaded the Goodricke children to act out *Bambi* every time we had a chance to play. We were always dressing up in old clothes, acting make-believe stories, and we were quite ingenious at inventing plays. It was a very satisfying thing to do. Joan, Guy and, sometimes, Susan and Ursula, joined in. It was just fooling around for them, like any other game. But for me, it was vital for survival.

It was only later, when I was a grown-up studying psychology, that I understood that *Bambi* was my story. I was Bambi, the little child whose mother was shot by the evil hunter-Nazi. Bambi's father was my father, who said I mustn't give up, but should now learn to live without my mother. I had already been living without my mother for six years. Like the imperial stag, Bambi's father, my father was far away, 'on important business'. Now he was telling me that, whatever happened, I mustn't give up. He would be there when I needed him.

The combination of the end of the war and seeing the film *Bambi* had stirred up something deep inside me. The war was over and that meant that things were going to change. However, the only thing that had really changed was that Martin had gone to live somewhere else. He telephoned often, so that I knew he hadn't abandoned me, but it must have made me anxious. I wasn't really a Goodricke. I once had parents, but where were they now? What would become of me?

Strangely, nothing seemed to happen. Life went on just the same as before the war. After a while, I stopped asking Mrs Goodricke when

I was going to see my daddy. And then the summer term ended and it was holiday time. It had been arranged that I should go to the farm where Martin was living with the Halting family. I forgot about the end of the war. It was going to be good to be together with Martin again.

CHAPTER 11

Arriving at the Halting's Farm

W hen I went to the Halting's farm to be with Martin, I thought it was going to be a similar summer holiday to the one I had enjoyed the previous summer. I just accepted it as I always accepted things on the surface. Besides, now that my big brother was with me, everything felt OK – even when it wasn't.

I remember the long train journey from Tunbridge Wells, and then being met at Rogate station by Mrs Halting, her daughter, Lavender, and Martin. Mrs Halting's car was a rickety, bumpy, old Austin Seven that smelled of animals and animal feed. She stopped several times on the way to pick up sacks of feed, bags of dog-meat, and other things, until the little car could hardly pull away with such a load. She chatted to us most of the time, but I was feeling tired and carsick. I just wished the journey would be over.

When Mrs Halting realised I was feeling carsick, she made me come and sit in the front, instead of Martin, and told me to look away as far as I could see. That helped. And then I saw it! A beautiful range of hills with gentle, rolling curves on the horizon. A strange feeling of excitement stirred in me. We drove onwards, until there was only a row of fields between the road and these hills. I could hardly believe it when Mrs Halting told us these fields belonged to the farm. She stopped the car, and I jumped out and looked longingly at them, rising above me, so close, just as the sun was setting. It was a picture to paint – and I actually did paint it, many times, later on.

That was my introduction to the South Downs. They never lost their magic for me. They became a very important part of my life on the farm. Mr Halting grazed sheep on these downs and, later on, I would ride up on horseback regularly to count them and check they were all right. Riding horseback on the Downs was a huge, exciting pleasure. Every December, we would set off with several spades and a pickaxe over the back of the Downs to the woods, where we uprooted a small conifer for a Christmas tree. After Twelfth Night, we re-planted it, but not always in the place it came from, because that was hard to find. I loved the Downs, like I loved the farm animals.

Even then, I did not understand until several decades later the significance of the South Downs as Mother Earth for me. That first time I saw them, I was only 10 and I had not seen my mother for six years. I was convinced she was dead – otherwise she would have written letters or something. I didn't understand that, during the war, letters wouldn't get through. But that first time I saw the gentle curves of the South Downs in the distance, they looked like the curved outline of a woman lying down – my mother in bed on a Sunday morning, when I would climb up and lie down beside her. Later, while riding on the Downs, I would dismount and lie on the grass, looking up at the ceiling of blue sky and clouds. Something deep inside me was excited by the South Downs and their huge protective presence. I only worked out why, decades later.

When I was about thirteen or fourteen, I wrote a poem about the South Downs, which I called 'Mother Earth'.

Mother Earth

Majestic your hills roll to seaward,
Roughly caressed by the breeze;
Where the wind blows your tussock in ripples
And sighs through the gnarled yew trees.
Where many a time I rode horseback,
And the thunder of hooves on your turf
And the silent hills soothed my heartache
With the comforting surge of the surf.

And the curving brow of the headland
Rises up clear in my mind,
As I gallop again the wild stretches
And leave all my troubles behind.

Majestic your hills roll to seaward,

> Gently caressed by the breeze;
> Your bounteous bosom that lures me
> Can always restore me to ease.

Much later, when I finally understood the symbolic meaning for me of the Downs and Mother Earth, I added another verse:

> Majestic your hills roll to seaward,
> My green-robed mother of earth;
> Your scent fills the yawning absence
> Of the mother that gave me my birth.

That summer holiday was truly wonderful. There was so much to see and do which was new to me. Mr and Mrs Halting were lovely people. I adored them. They were not cruel like the Steads had been, nor were they very strict like the Goodrickes. There were four children; Jack who was 16, Lavender (always called Luvvy) 15, Kevin 13, and little Robin, who was 8. I was allowed to run wild with the four Halting children and that was fun! We ran barefoot everywhere. That was never allowed at the Steads or at the Goodrickes. I can't describe the delicious pleasure of deliberately plonking your foot in a still-warm, newly made cow-pat and watching it ooze up between your toes! Of course, we had to wash our feet before coming into the house. There was a scrubbing brush and soap for that, beside the cold water pump in the washhouse.

Running barefoot over the stones and fields causes you to grow an extra thick layer of skin on the soles of your feet, so that nothing hurts. We used to laugh at children who picked their way gingerly in bare feet. We used to call them 'timid townies'. To prove you were not a feeble timid townie, you had to run across a stubble field just after it had been harvested. It would be all prickly with thistles, as well as the short corn stalks, so it was quite a feat.

It was such a brilliant summer holiday that I didn't want it to be over. I was sad when it ended and I went back to the Goodrickes. The day before the new term was due to start, Mrs Goodricke took me into school, where a teacher explained to me that I needed to sit exams, to go to a new school a year early. I didn't really mind. I liked schoolwork and I didn't find the exams hard. In fact, the teacher remarked that I finished each of them well before the time allowed.

I had hardly started back at school, when Mrs Goodricke suddenly told me I was to go back to the Haltings and join Martin. She said that they were moving to a smaller house. The Goodrickes actually did move but, when I visited them later on, I realised it was actually a bigger house, and it was right in Tunbridge Wells, near the school.

Changing foster parents was thought to be in my best interests. It would enable me to be with Martin. Mr Lucas, a headmaster who specialised in helping disturbed boys, had taken Martin into Midhurst Grammar School and had asked the Haltings to billet him. Mrs Halting, wisely, did not think it right to separate two siblings who had been together for six years without their parents. She would only take Martin if I could come too. The summer holiday had been a sort of trial period.

I had been convincing myself that I had become a Goodricke and that I was part of that lovely family. It was a great shock to find out that I wasn't considered part of the family, and I felt that they were sending me away. I supposed that I was too bad and unattractive for them to want to keep me any longer. This seemed to be the pattern of my life. As soon as I had got used to a place, they didn't want me any more and moved me on.

CHAPTER 12

Living in a Farming Family

When I went back to the Haltings in the autumn, aged 10, this time as their foster child, things were not quite the same as the previous wonderful summer holiday. Robin, the youngest Halting, had died from a very nasty accident. He was only eight. He had been wearing a cowboy hat and was swinging a lasso around, when he got too close to the threshing machine. The lasso caught in it and pulled him in. He died in hospital after a few days. After that, children were not allowed anywhere near the thresher.

Threshing machines did not have safety devices. They were powered by a steam engine driving a big moving belt and were very dangerous. Over the years since then, farm machines have been designed with built-in safety precautions. For example, tractors now have to have little cabins where the driver sits. The cabin keeps the tractor driver dry when it rains and protects the driver from being crushed if the tractor rolls over. A tractor being driven along a steep hillside can easily roll over and, if the doors don't open, there can be a nasty accident. There were often accidents on the farm, but usually they were minor ones. I saw tractors topple over several times, but each time the driver was thrown clear and was not hurt.

Mr and Mrs Halting were distraught over the loss of their little son, Robin. I don't think they ever got over it. How can you get over the loss of your child? Parents are supposed to die of old age before their children, not the other way round. In those days, people didn't understand the need for time to grieve and mourn a loss. The doctors would advise parents who lost a baby to have another one as soon as possible, instead of encouraging and helping them with their grieving. It didn't work for Mr and Mrs Halting. Mrs Halting was probably already too old to conceive. They both got back into their old routine and worked very hard, but something of their brightness and cheerful patience had been lost permanently. Mrs Halting became rather sharp and often scolded, and Mr Halting spent more time alone in the fields and barns. He was hardly ever in the house. I often took meals out to him in the fields.

I felt very bad about what had happened. That lovely summer holiday, I had played a lot with Robin, and I had been jealous of how everyone loved him. He seemed to get on with everyone and do everything much better than I could. I envied his easy happy-go-lucky way of doing things. Once, we were both given some seeds to plant in the garden. I followed the instructions carefully, preparing the ground very nicely before planting my seeds and watering them regularly. Robin just poked his finger in the ground a few times and dropped a seed in each hole. I was furious when all his seeds came up and thrived, while insects or birds ate most of mine, leaving only a few scrawny shoots.

Because I had been so envious and angry, I believed I had had something to do with Robin's accident – even though I wasn't even there at the time and knew it could not be my fault. I just felt bad. Whenever Mrs Halting scolded me for some minor misdemeanour, as she often did, it proved to me how bad I was. Children often feel responsible for things that happen around them, and need someone to take notice of them and encourage them to talk about their feelings.

So, although the Haltings treated me as one of the family, I always felt different, however hard I tried to be like the Halting children. I was keenly aware that Mr and Mrs Halting were their parents, but my foster parents, who could pass me on to other foster parents if they became fed up with me. All the others at school lived with their parents; mine had sent me away. I could not get rid of the feeling of being different. Many children feel different from others. Unfortunately, like me, they usually don't tell anybody, so they never get to know that others feel just like they do. I never dared to ask what the three Halting children felt about sharing their parents with me. I just imagined that they didn't really want me taking up time in the family, and I tried not to be greedy for attention although I was hungry for it.

As the youngest of the children, I came in for a lot of teasing and even a bit of bullying. I used to bite my lip and pretend it didn't matter to me. That was the way I dealt with it, because it is no fun to tease someone who doesn't react, and they usually stopped after a while. But it still hurt inside. It made me feel different and lonely. It is very important to most children to be like everyone else.

I desperately wanted to be a normal child and be just like the others. But that was not possible. The Halting children, and all the other kids at school, had parents. I had guardians. Every time there were forms to fill in, I had to put guardian instead of parent. Other kids used to ask me where my mum and dad were. I could proudly tell them my dad was in China, but then they wanted to know why I was left behind. I didn't want to tell them about the Nazis driving us out and wanting to kill us. I simply told them my mother was dead. At that time, I really believed she was dead. As no-one contradicted me, I took that as confirmation that she was dead.

I am sure none of the Haltings realised how I felt. I simply didn't tell them. I was confirmed in my sense of failure as a person. But I was determined to survive. All the children on the farm, including me, had daily chores. I was always asking for more. Not that I liked the tasks in the house, although I genuinely wanted to be helpful. Doing extra chores was a way to make up for being bad and feeling like a failure. Most of all, I wanted to become indispensable, so that I would not be sent away again.

So I didn't mind helping around the house, be it cleaning, ironing, peeling potatoes or preparing vegetables. I felt I was making a contribution. Whether it was a school day or holidays, there was always something to do on the farm. I got to know about the fields, and when to plant, hoe, harvest, or to muck-spread and plough in.

I began to help look after the animals on the farm. The horses, cows, pigs, rabbits, and poultry all needed tending and feeding, and their stalls and coops had to be kept clean. They soon became a big part of my life.

Recognising each animal comes naturally for those born into farming. It was something I had to learn. I remember the first time I saw a herd of Guernsey cows coming in to the milking sheds; they all looked the same. Later I recognised each one, knew her name and all her little personality foibles. It was the same with sheep. They, also, all looked the same at first. There were too many to name each one, but

I soon learnt to recognise the troublemakers and the stragglers. It was good practice for later in my life when I was a teacher. It took time to learn each student's particular characteristics, but very little time to recognise the troublemakers and the stragglers.

Kevin and I used to make scarecrows to put in the fields at sowing time. Jack would go out, now and then, with an airgun to scare the rooks and we would tag along to watch. These birds were a real menace to the crops, eating every kind of grain. The rooks would fly up in the air squawking like mad, as if every single one had been shot. They usually came back all too soon, and needed watching for several weeks, until the seed grains had grown into little plants and were of no more interest to them.

Mr Halting was very pleased when Kevin raided the rooks' nests for eggs, as it cut down the rook population. I would sometimes go and help him. This was not an easy task. Rooks build their nests high up for safety, as they lay their eggs before the trees have enough leaves to hide the nests. They made their homes in rows of tall, spindly trees around the farm. There used to be at least six or more rooks' nests, right at the top in March and April.

We went barefoot in order to get a good enough grip on the slender branches and, as it was very cold in springtime, I would get frozen. I stayed in the lower branches with a cloth bag round my waist, so that I had both hands free. Kevin went right up near the top. Then, with a bent spoon fixed to the end of a long stick, he scooped up the eggs from the nests above his head. He then put the eggs in a little sling and lowered them down to me. We would go home with twenty, thirty or more eggs.

Kevin would keep the eggshells, as they were collectors' items. Rooks' eggs are only about a quarter the size of a hen's egg, but they are a pretty, speckled, pale blue-grey. He 'blew' them himself – by extracting the inside without damaging the shell. They were very good for baking cakes and delicious as scrambled egg on toast. Using rooks' eggs meant that the hens' eggs could be saved for selling and getting coupons for animal feed.

We caught rabbits and pheasants a different way. They used to come out into the cornfields at dusk and dawn, so we would lie in wait for them and then, when they were busy eating, we would jump up very suddenly, banging dustbin lids and blowing gym whistles. The rabbits and pheasants would be so startled they would run helter-skelter straight into the wire netting and get their heads caught. If we were quick enough, we would catch a rabbit or pheasant before they could untangle their heads from the wire netting. One of us would hold open a sack, ready for the others to pop our catch into it. Then we would sling the sacks over our shoulders and sing songs like 'Waltzing Matilda' or 'Run Rabbit Run', all the way home.

It was always very welcome when we caught rabbits, or a pheasant, or some fish, as we ate meat rarely so that we didn't lose animal feed coupons. Usually, there would be a Sunday roast joint, and then thinly sliced cold meat on Mondays, and the leftovers would be minced with vegetables the next day. The rest of the week would be without meat, unless there were visitors, in which case a chicken might be killed.

On hot summer days, we would go and cool down by the stream under the willow trees. Lying on the mossy bank was delicious; damp earthy smells rising up from underneath, the fragrance of wild flowers, a gentle breeze and the sound of birds twittering. It was heavenly. I would swim in the old mill pool. As I swam, fish would nibble at my feet.

Catching fish was something different. We didn't have proper fishing rods. They didn't make things like that during the war, or for a long time after. You are supposed to be able to tickle trout and then, when they are ecstatically enjoying it, scoop them up in a net. We tried lying on the banks of the trout stream but, if we saw any trout at all, they never came near enough to be tickled.

Jack made a fish-trap out of wire netting. One end was the open end of a netting funnel and the other a box. The narrow end of the funnel was only just big enough to let a fairly big fish into the box. As fish are not as intelligent as birds or mammals, once a fish was in the trap it could not find its way out again. But you may well ask why the fish should want to go into the funnel in the first place. Like nearly all animals, including people, fish can't resist the smell of aniseed. One of the few kinds of sweets we could spend our sweet rations on was aniseed balls. So I would tie a couple of aniseed balls in a scrap of the muslin used for making cheese, and would suspend it over the narrow end of the funnel. Then Jack lowered the whole trap into the water and waited. We never did see a fish go in but, when we left it overnight, there would be at least one or two fish in the trap the next day. Then there would be fried fish for high tea!

Most necessities would be delivered from the bakery, butcher or general store in South Harting. Once a week, Mr or Mrs Halting would drive the little, green Austin Seven car to Petersfield, to get raw meat from the knackers' yard for the three or four working dogs and, sometimes, for their puppies. Only condemned meat and offal, unfit for human consumption, was allowed for dogs. There was none of the fancy tinned meat you get nowadays for pets. Otherwise, most things we needed were produced on the farm, and there was always so much to do that we didn't think about going anywhere else. Letters were few and far between. There was no telephone until the 1950s. We had an old radio that crackled and the News Chronicle, a daily news-paper, to keep us in touch with what was happening in the world.

CHAPTER 13

Petersfield High School

My new school was in Petersfield, a twenty-minute bus ride away. I went to Petersfield High School, a grammar school, having passed the eleven plus exam that I had taken a year early, when I was still at the Goodrickes. Martin and the Halting boys, Kevin and Jack, went to a boys' school in another town, Midhurst, and my foster sister, Luvvy, went to a ballet school in London. She became a ballerina and danced for the Ballet Rambert. We all went to see her up in London, as one of the cygnets in *Swan Lake*. I admired her enormously and desperately wanted to be like her. Sadly, later on she grew too big and had to give up ballet.

Petersfield High School, affectionately known as 'PeFe Hi', was always a bit ramshackle and dilapidated. It was a big, rambling building that used to be an inn, with stables, before it was converted into a school for girls with a tarmac playground and an orchard. The orchard was our favourite playground, but the tarmac was better in wet weather and essential for netball.

It was a small school of about 230 girls. There were only seven classrooms and a science laboratory. As there were eight classes, one had to have its home base in the science lab. I was the youngest in my class, right through my schooling at PeFe Hi. But I felt at home very quickly, as the other girls in my class were friendly. Because it was a small school, the teachers came to know me well and they took notice if I was absent or upset. They were all dedicated to the school and our welfare.

My favourite was the geography teacher. She once stopped the class from laughing at me, when I didn't know what a banana was. I had never seen one, let alone eaten one. Bananas were hugely expensive, and could only be bought in the big towns or on the illegal black market. Somehow, she got a banana for me and gave it to me one day after the rest of the class had gone home. She had a blind and swollen

eye, and some children made rude remarks about her appearance behind her back. One day, I told them, in front of the class, that they
were better looking outside but ugly inside, because only ugly people
make rude remarks.

Along with some other girls, I used to tease one or two of my classmates, not always playfully but nastily. Once, we kidnapped a girl in
the playground and threatened her with all sorts of things if she did
not do exactly as we dared her to do. We stole her knickers off her and
she had to go to afternoon lessons without them. Her parents complained to the headmistress and we got into trouble, and I had to write
apologies to the girl and to her parents. Another time, we conducted
a terror campaign against a new girl, Dorothy, by collecting spiders
and creepy-crawlies and puting them in her desk, because we discovered she was petrified of them. She screamed and ran away, until
teachers put a stop to it.

I feel slightly ashamed of these pranks, but I was proud of the
homework syndicate I organised with five friends. We each did one
homework subject we were best at and then gave copies to the others.
Each girl's task was to write the homework out six times, each time
with a different tiny mistake, so that the teacher would not realise one
person did them all. It took us just as long as if we had each done our
own version of each of the homework tasks, but it was much more enjoyable.

I was once sent out of my lesson to stand outside the door, and I
was furious, because I thought it was unfair that I had been sent out
when it was someone else's fault. I needed to go the toilet, where there
were six cubicles in a row in the washroom. I locked myself in the first
one, climbed over the divide into the second one, locked that too, and
climbed over to the third, and so on, until I was locked in the last one.
This last cubicle had a small window out into the road. I managed to
squeeze out of it, drop into the road, and come back in the side door.
When the bell went, I was calmly standing outside the classroom door.
All my rage had gone in the activity of climbing over divides. But
there was chaos. The whole school had to queue up to go to the teachers' toilet. No-one had any idea that it was my doing. That spoiled it
a bit, because I couldn't talk about it with anyone.

The teacher who made the greatest impression on me was the headmistress, Miss Chadwick, or 'Old Chad' as we called her affectionately. I was sent to her quite often for doing naughty things and she would speak with me gently. She told me sensible things I could understand. She didn't shout at me or try to make me ashamed. She made me think about my responsibilities, and would tell me to channel my mischievous initiatives and energies into doing something creative. Once, after I had persuaded a classmate to hide in a cupboard during a boring Latin lesson, she made me stay after school and polish all the sports trophies. It was actually quite enjoyable and she praised me for doing a good job. She said that punishment never really works and everybody who does bad things should do something good to 'repair the damage'. I never forgot this and would always ask for something useful to do in detention instead of 'lines'. If a teacher insisted I did lines, I would write something like 'Miss X is a silly old fool' diagonally across the page, hidden in the lines. I was disappointed that no teacher ever discovered this.

Once or twice when a teacher was away, Miss Chadwick would take our lesson and it would always be fascinating. I remember one particular English lesson when she read Francis Thompson's *Hound of Heaven* to us and then explained what each phrase meant. I sat wide-eyed, listening to her reading it with passion, and then it was even more beautiful when she explained the difficult words. She stirred in me a love for literature that has given me immense enjoyment throughout my life. I recall all my teachers with great affection, even the ones I didn't like so much at the time.

But even Old Chad was not immune to our girlish shenanigans. Once, when it was raining, we had to stay in our classrooms at break, and we amused ourselves by cutting up some paper in the waste basket into confetti. Our classroom was at the very top. It overlooked the front door of the school and opened straight into the high street. We pretended that the headmistress was getting married and we showered down confetti while singing at the tops of our voices, 'Here comes the bride! Fair, fat and wide!' The astonishment on the faces of the passers-by made us howl with laughter. Of course, someone complained, and we had to go down in the rain and pick up every piece.

But we had had our fun. There was a serious side to this. We were well aware that as many soldiers had been killed in the war, not all the young women would be able to find one to marry. We really liked our headmistress and wanted her to get married. Years later, I found out that she never did marry and nor did many of our teachers. But our very pretty French teacher got married while I was at school. She was nice and included us in her celebrations. She brought us all sweets before her wedding, and cakes when she came back from her honeymoon.

At first, dinner was eaten on trestle tables in the library in three sittings, served and supervised by teachers and sixth formers. As we didn't have a proper dining room, it was later arranged that we had to walk half a mile, in a supervised crocodile, to a canteen hut, half-way between PeFe Hi and Churcher's College, the boys' school. A lot of bartering used to go on. When we had jacket potatoes, I always traded my 'middle' for two people's skins. Of course, that was when you could get potatoes again. Through the war, and for some time after, we had 'pom', which was made from dry, powdered potato. It was all lumpy and sometimes a bit greenish-black. Nobody liked it, but you couldn't have seconds of anything else, if you hadn't eaten up all your pom.

Because I was always watching the animals, learning their shapes and movements, and studying their personalities and behaviour, I very quickly learnt to draw animals. It was a joke among my classmates that, whatever the task we were given in art classes, I would find a way of adapting the theme to include animals, mostly horses. Even when we had to make potato cuts to print on textiles, my potato cut was a horse's head! Most of all, I liked to doodle and make little pencil sketches, which I then went over in black Indian ink. Sadly, most of my paintings got lost. I did hundreds of them as, on rainy days, we could paint instead of going out in the playground.

So I discovered a way to please teachers with my drawings. They were not so pleased when they caught me drawing instead of listening or doing the exercise they had set in class. Usually, I had finished the task and I told them, truthfully, that I could listen better if I was drawing. In general, I got off lightly with teachers. They seemed to understand, that when I did things I knew were naughty, it was because I was bursting with energy and found it hard to sit still in lessons.

I was never good enough at acting to get a part in school plays. So, my role was always to design and organise the painting of the scenery and backdrop. One year, there were scenes in a railway carriage. The backdrop was the inside of the carriage. I painted a very long roll of paper with landscapes and villages and, of course, plenty of horses and other animals. This roll was scrolled behind the windows of the railway carriage, and very effectively gave the impression of the train moving, especially as the actors were directed to keep gently rocking, like a train makes you do.

In my last year at school, in 1951, we staged our school play in Pe-

Left: One of my farm scene paintings.

Below: My painting of a workhorse

tersfield Town Hall, with a whole week of local audiences. The Town Hall stage was huge and it had to have a very large backdrop. The play *The Zeal of Thy House* had a religious theme and the backdrop had to be the inside of a cathedral. First, we had to sew strips of hessian together to make a vast sheet, which we hung from the gallery rail that overlooked our school hall. Next, a team of sixth formers had to paint it with 'seize' to fill the gaps between the warp and weave of the hessian. Then I had to draw the pillars and arches of a cathedral interior on it. Finally, the team had to paint it to look like stone. I even managed to get permission to make out of painted cardboard, a horse and cart loaded with building stones that was pulled on stage at one point!

That year we had country dancing lessons, which we performed on stage at Petersfield Town Hall. First, there was a competition between classes in our school and then an inter-school dancing competition. That too was enormous fun. We didn't have TV to watch the professionals in *Strictly Come Dancing* type programmes. Instead, we watched the live programme in which we took part ourselves.

Where the London to Portsmouth road crosses the top of the High Road in Petersfield, there is a modern block of flats. These flats have been built where Petersfield High School used to stand on the corner. The first time I motored past, long after I had left the school, seeing the flats gave me a shock, and I felt quite disorientated. A chunk of my life in England had vanished. I knew my life in Berlin was gone forever, but I had imagined my life in England would stay intact permanently. I had not yet realised then how nothing is permanent; only that some things remain a bit longer than others, before they change and then disappear.

Farm Life

CHAPTER 14

Basher

Perhaps we had something in common, Basher and I. Just as I had come to the farm a displaced person, vulnerable, unable to get by without the help of others and wanting to be accepted, so Basher was also reliant on others. He was one of the farm hands. He lived with the family in the farmhouse because it was his first time away from his parents and, as he was almost blind, he needed looking after. I can't remember his real name. He was already nicknamed Basher when I first came to the farm. Because of his blindness, he would 'bash into' gates and things, and sometimes into people. He had glasses but he didn't like wearing them while out and about on the farm. As they could easily get lost, nobody encouraged him to wear them. When the school's optician discovered I had very long sight, I was given glasses too. They did not stay on my nose very long. Because of all the active things I did, I kept losing them. The third pair of my glasses went through the chaff-cutting machine and ended up as a mangled mess in a cow's manger. Then it was decided that I could see perfectly well without them.

Not being able to see properly must have made life hard for Basher. Sadly, we made it even harder for him by teasing him. All of us children used to call to him, even offer him sweets, to try and make him bash into things in his way – just for a laugh. Basher was over-weight and ungainly, so it could look very funny. He used to hide a lot, behind doors or in dark corners, and we would be sent by Mrs Halting to look for him, as there were jobs to be done.

Mrs Halting told us he was lazy and it was good for him to be chased out of hiding. She said he needed to be more active to make him lose weight and be more sociable. She even encouraged us to tease him. When no adults were around, we were sometimes downright cruel to poor Basher. Looking back, I think the teasing probably made him depressed and tired. Of course, it wasn't good for him.

Although he was not out of his teens, Basher was a big strong fellow. Whenever there was a job to be done that needed a strong pull or something had to be heaved up, Basher would be called in. Then he came into his own. As long as you made sure he was holding on in the right way, he could pull up a root nobody else could. He would make light work of heaving sacks up to the granary loft. Even people in the village would ask to borrow Basher for such jobs. Basher would then be very proud to help villagers, especially as they would give him cakes or chocolates as a reward.

Dealing with manure or dung is an all the year-round task, and muck-spreading was Basher's main job. I sometimes did this with him. There was always a huge pile of cow manure in the front yard outside the cowshed. Every day, the cow stalls would be cleaned out. First, the horse cart would have to be loaded up. Basher did the heaving up of forkfuls of dung, while I guided him and kept the horse and cart in the right position. Then we would both sit on the front ledge of the cart with our feet on the shafts, and I would drive the horse into one of the fields. The dung would be dumped in suitable corners of the fields, for spreading fertiliser during the winter.

When we got to the chosen place, I would jump down and Basher would climb over the front onto the load and start chucking forkfuls down. Again, I would guide and encourage him. We would also chat about all sorts of things. When no-one else was around to tease him, he would become quite chatty and tell me all about what he had heard on his radio the evening before. He felt safe with me, as I wouldn't tease him. The first time I did, I got a forkful of muck on my head!

I used to marvel at how sensibly Basher could talk and discuss things. Much later, when I worked as a therapist with people who had relationship problems, I learnt how some people pretend to be stupid so that others will not expect much from them. Basher would come out of his protective shell when he felt safe. I realise we could have made it feel much safer for him most of the time. Teasing was the worst possible thing for him.

But he had a reasonably good life on the farm. In spite of all the teasing, he was part of the family and he was included in everything. He came to all the farm events and village celebrations. He even came to the cinema on the rare occasions we went. Even though he couldn't see much of the picture, I knew he was following the story, because he would talk about it the next time we were muck spreading together.

Basher would be sent to muck out the large hen house. That was a job everyone hated doing. Cow dung and horse dung have a smell that you can easily get used to, and then it's not unpleasant. Pig dung takes a little bit more getting used to, but duck and chicken dung smells vile, and we all hated clearing their mess. Basher didn't seem to mind and he quite liked working on his own. I happened to go into the hen house to see how he was getting on. I saw him bending down stroking what looked like the rooster. I wondered what the rooster was doing in there anyway. Then Basher said 'It's OK, little Cocky, I'll get you out.' Before I had realised that the rooster had its head stuck between two of the wooden floor slats, Basher yanked it. The rooster's head came off in his hands. The look of pained surprise on Basher's face was comical. Then he realised what he had done and burst into tears. Later, when I read about Lennie, in Steinbeck's story *Of Mice and Men*, I thought of Basher. Lennie was a big, gentle giant, just like Basher, who didn't know his own strength.

CHAPTER 15

Washing Day and Other Chores

Monday was washing day on the farm. When I came home from school, it was my job to go up into the garden and bring in whatever washing was dry after the morning wash. Martin, Jack and Kevin had jobs to do in the barn after school. When I had fed the animals and made a big salad for high tea, I would go and bring in the rest of the washing. After high tea, I would do an hour of ironing before I started on my school homework.

I liked ironing, especially if there was some good music on the radio. In cold weather, ironing was a nice warm job. Sheets and shirts had to be ironed, and there were always lots of them. There were one or two striped shirts that made me feel dizzy when I ironed them. The stripes would shine in a strange way that made them look as if they were moving and crawling with worms – like the worms you keep in a tin for fishing.

In holiday times, Monday's wash took up most of my day. I used to think it was very unfair that the boys didn't have to do any of it. They would disappear out into the farm, and I was told they had just as much work to do on the farm. I didn't believe it and, anyway, anything outdoors on the farm was fun and not work! Luvvy was mostly away at her ballet school.

Before breakfast, after I had already been a good hour out in the barns feeding animals, I had to light the fire in the wash-house – even on school days. First, the big copper boiler had to be filled with water from a bucket filled by a hand pump. That was heavy work, pumping the handle up and down and then lifting the full bucket to empty it into the boiler. Then, the previous Monday's ashes had to be raked out of the ash pit in the brick casing surrounding the boiler. Next, I had to put paper, twigs and kindling wood, in the ash pit, correctly placed, so that there would be enough air to keep it burning once I had got a flame going with matches and a little paraffin. Only when the flames had turned the kindling glowing red, could I put on a log or two, and leave it. I had to make sure the big wooden lid covered the boiler, before I could go in to breakfast.

If I was too slow, the porridge would have already been poured out, and mine would have become cold, and there were no microwave ovens to warm things up quickly. Toast was plentiful, but butter and marmalade were in short supply, and might have run out before I got there. Breakfast was usually a bit hurried. On school days, I had to be down at the bus stop to get the 8.15 bus to Petersfield. There wasn't another bus till 9.15, and then I would be dreadfully late for school.

During holidays, I also had to hurry to get back to the washing. While the water was heating, I would go upstairs with Mrs Halting and sort the washing. All the beds had to be 'clean-sheeted'. That meant the bottom sheet and pillowcase of each bed were put in the wash basket, while the top sheet became the bottom sheet and each bed got a fresh, clean top sheet and pillowcase.

There were five bedrooms upstairs and Basher's room downstairs. In all, two double beds and seven single ones had to be changed, and I had to lug around heavy basketfuls of dirty washing.

Once the water in the boiler began to boil, all the bed linen and white shirts and hankies were stirred in. While waiting for the whites boiling away in the copper, all the muddy overalls had to have the muck scrubbed off them. Then it was their turn in the boiler. At the end of the wash, everything was fished out with a big, wooden paddle and put into big zinc tubs filled with water from the pump, and rinsed through a couple of times, and wrung out each time before drying. Basher's job was to wind the handle of the wringer. You had to be careful feeding the washing between the two rollers, otherwise you could get your fingers caught in the gap, and that could be very painful.

Sometimes, it was well into the afternoon before all the washing was hanging on the line. Often, there was not enough room on the line. Some had to be hung on wires under a large corrugated iron cover over the back door of the kitchen that reached right to the washhouse. We called it the tin roof and it protected bicycles and gumboots, and other odds and ends, from the rain.

In very wet weather, the washing would stay under the tin roof for several days before it was dry enough to fold and iron. Even in the winter on frosty mornings, or when there was snow and ice, washing day still went ahead. I remember hanging up the 'stiffs' on such Mondays when the washing would freeze stiff before I could peg it to the line. Amazingly, when the stiffs were brought in and thawed, they were dry enough to iron.

By the time everything had been washed, rinsed and hung up on the washing line, it was dinnertime. It would be a very simple dinner of cold meat and leftovers from Sunday lunch. To make up for it, there would be a more substantial, cooked high tea later, at about 6pm. There would be something nice to eat, such as fried egg and potatoes, bubble and squeak or toad-in-the-hole. Also, there was that nice, satisfied feeling, of a big job well done.

I loved the bubble and squeak, the leftover mashed potato and greens fried in lard from rendered pig fat. Later on, I used chicken fat, which was even tastier. I would watch Mrs Halting make the toad-in-the-hole. Again, the lard made it tasty. She would be quick and got it just right so the batter rose and the sausages/toads were all hidden in their holes when they came out of the oven.

Mrs Halting seldom let me cook anything but porridge. Everything was scarce and, if I had made a mess of things, there wouldn't have been enough to go round. But I had to peel potatoes and pick vegetables from the garden to make salad for everyone. I enjoyed making the salads, which I put into huge dishes and decorated with slices of tomato and cucumber, or spring onions and parsley, all from the garden.

One of the jobs I hated most was Saturday chores. I had to dust down all five bedrooms in the farmhouse, the long passage connecting them and the two staircases, the back one leading down steeply into the kitchen, and the front one straight down to the hall and front door. All the floors were wooden and, after dusting them, they all had to be polished with special floor polish. There was only one radio, a huge one, about the size of a small fridge, so there was nothing to listen to, in order to relieve the boredom.

I felt resentful on these Saturday mornings, because I was doing chores while the boys, Martin, Jack and Kevin, went to school. My school had hockey and netball matches, but I wasn't very good. I didn't enjoy these games and was never picked for any team. Although Jack and Kevin also had chores to do on Saturday afternoons, theirs were outside on the farm. Mucking out stables and stalls, carting dung out and bringing fodder in, were all things I loved to do. I often chose to help the boys doing these things. They hardly ever appreciated my help and used to tease me, and sometimes it ended up in water fights or slinging dung at each other. Somehow, I was always the one who got into trouble, not them. Boys can be horrible creatures when they are thirteen or fourteen!

I was never deliberately naughty at home on the farm. Yet I was repeatedly scolded or teased for things I got wrong. That hurt a lot, because I was desperate to get everything right, so that I would never be sent away again. Every time I was scolded, and it was probably very mild scolding, I experienced it as my failure – failure to be good enough not to be sent away!

I usually hurried to get my chores done when the sun was shining. If I got finished in time, I could go out on the farm and see what was going on, help a bit, or even go for a ride on one of the ponies. I couldn't hurry too much, otherwise Mrs Halting would find dust when she came to inspect and then I would have to do it all over again. I would have to find her when I was finished and ask if it was all right to go out. If she was in a good mood, or if she was very busy with something, she would let me go without inspecting. But, if she thought I had been too quick or she was not in such a good mood, she would go round the bedrooms, running her finger over ledges and skirting boards. Then she would hold her finger up with dust on it, and say, 'My dear child, what is this?' I would have to do that room over again. If I was unlucky, or Mrs Halting was in a downright bad mood, she would give me extra chores, and there would be no time to go out till after lunch.

CHAPTER 16

Village Life

Town people usually don't know much about their neighbours, maybe not even their names. In villages, people living near each other will know a lot more. There is a web of 'who knows who', that, more or less, includes everyone. News, especially gossip, travels very fast. Your enemies get to hear all the gossip, as well as your friends.

If you have ever played the game of 'whispers', you will know how quickly gossip gets distorted. The funniest example I remember was 'send reinforcements, we're going to advance', which, by the end of the row of whisperers, had become, 'send three and fourpence, we're going to a dance.'

One of the silliest bits of gossip that went round Harting was that Mary, my best friend at school, and her family, were going to move out of their farm in Nyewood, which was near to where the Haltings kept some horses. Of course, the gossip went full circle as it usually did. Someone asked Mary's mother, 'Well, when are you actually going?' Mary's mother replied that they were not moving. The gossipmonger retorted, 'Oh, yes you are! And I know where you are moving to.' 'In that case you had better tell me where, because we have no intention of moving anywhere,' responded my friend's mother. Needless to say, that was the conversation that became the next piece of gossip to go round the grapevine.

Harting was a group of villages. South Harting had a church, vicarage, primary school, two pubs and a few shops surrounding the village square. The square was little more than a crossroads but, on summer evenings, a gypsy band would sometimes come and play for square dancing.

The Haltings' farm was in East Harting, where other farms and cottages were scattered around. There was a tiny shop just up the road. West Harting had a similar group of scattered farms and cottages. To the north, a bit further away, was Nyewood.

Winning the Young farmers' Club milking machine competition – this photo appeared in my local paper!

Because of the very quick and efficient grapevine in Harting, everyone knew about upcoming events and it was easy to find helpers. There was a village fair in summer and a Christmas party in winter.

The first summer fair I went to in the village was in 1945. The war had only just ended. Everyone was tired from the stress of living through six years of war and uncertainty. We had little money to spend, but the mood was happy and joyful. It was a small affair in the gardens of the vicarage, with stalls selling bric-a-brac, home-made jams and cakes. There was red jelly and white ice cream for the children, and we played games where everyone joined in.

It was a rare treat for us at that time, because food was still rationed. In 1945, there was so little that the taste of everything lingered on in your mouth and in your mind, and the pleasure lasted a long time.

What I enjoyed most of all was the tea tent. Everyone sat round folding tables in the sunshine and talked and talked. It was the first time for years that people could sit out all day without fear. We could relax, and do and say whatever took our fancy, without worrying about whether enemy planes would come over and drop bombs.

The following year, the fair was held in the field behind the church that belonged to Church Farm. The Bickfords, who ran Church Farm, had a beautiful herd of cream-coloured, curly-coated Charolais cows. Charolais cattle originated in France and were rare in England.

This fair was bigger; there were more stalls and a little roundabout for the children. The village blacksmith, who was a gypsy, had borrowed it from some gypsy friends. I took Copper, a little Exmoor pony, for the younger children to ride on. We made a lot of money for the church to distribute to war widows and their children. The year after that, we needed a bigger field, out in the valley between South Harting and Tarberry Hill.

That year and in following years, there was an array of big marquee tents with competitions for local grown vegetables and flowers. One year, I won the competition for making a decorated vegetable salad. Another year, Angelina, my creamy-brown coloured doe rabbit won a prize. The Haltings donated a weaner piglet each year for the competition to guess the weight of the pig. There were not only pony rides, but donkey races, where the money collected was spent on necessities, like clothes and food parcels for the poorest families. The gypsies brought in the donkeys and it was tremendous fun. I made myself a jockey outfit by sewing pieces of shiny scarlet taffeta onto a white shirt and fishing cap. In one race, my donkey refused to face in the right direction, and we covered the whole course backwards! We came in second, because all the others, except for the winner, fell off their donkeys and were disqualified.

In winter, Lord and Lady FeatherstoneHaugh would invite the whole village to a Christmas party in their huge manor house called Uppark. He was a lord, because his family tree went right back to feudal England, when his ancestors were Lords of the Manor of Harting. Lord and Lady Featherstone Haugh would welcome everyone. An enormous Christmas tree stood in the stairwell, some 20 feet high. It was a wonderful sight, decorated with shiny silver balls and red candles, with flickering red flames.

There were lots of big rooms, and all of them were needed to seat the whole village. We tucked in to elegant sandwiches and shop cakes with cream, at trestle tables, and chattered away. Everyone was on their best behaviour, which meant being very polite and considerate. Nobody would take a second sandwich or cake without making sure everyone on their table had already had at least one. No-one stretched out to grab anything. We asked our neighbours to pass the sugar.

After we had tea, we sang carols. It was a tradition that little groups of five or six members of the church choir went from room to room to lead some of the more difficult carols, by singing the descant themselves or organising four-part harmony singing. I still go into raptures of memory when I hear four-part harmony. On the way out, every child was given one of the little parcels from the huge mound round the tub of the Christmas tree. It was quite a long walk from Uppark, through its grounds and down the steep hill, to South Harting. Sometimes, it would be snowing and we would joyfully sing carols all the way down.

Other wealthy families in Harting, such as Squire Hawthorn, Captain Blackmill and the Wallaces, would have their own Christmas parties and invite the Haltings. There was always lots of entertainment with music and dancing, games for the children and, as the years went by, a wider variety of cakes and fancier ice cream. At that time, records the size of dinner plates were played by a needle on a turntable. I often found myself with the job of turning the handle, between records, to wind up the spring on the turntable. It was very funny if I forgot and, in the middle of a record, the music would get slower and slower and lose its pitch.

The Haltings' farmhouse wasn't big enough to have such a big party, but the last party at the farm that I remember was a huge one and it was a barn dance. It took weeks to plan and prepare. The big double barn had to be emptied of straw and hay. Two lofts were completely cleared by filling up the third one. The floor of the barn had to be cleared of everything and swept extra clean. A dais was erected for the band and a dance floor laid down. The eats and drinks were fantastic: hot food at one end of the barn, cold food at the other end, and the band and dancing in the centre. Drinks were up on the middle loft, with one ladder for climbing up and another for coming down. I don't know how Mrs Halting organised all the food. She cooked a lot herself and lots more came in vans. There must have been at least two hundred people and everyone had a good time. The third loft, which was stacked high with hay, was also full of people. You could tell who had been up there by the bits of straw and hay sticking to their backs! We carried on till daylight the following morning. I won't go into the clearing up, but we did it willingly because it had been so much fun.

We were always invited to the big events, as Mrs Halting was considered a very important person in the village because she was leader of the Women's Institute, the WI. She specialised in basketry, millinery, canning and a few other things too. She held classes in the nearby town, Petersfield, and travelled all over England teaching people, who would then hold their own local classes.

I used to go with her to collect bundles of green rushes and yellow willow from down by the river, and red dogwood and clematis from the hedges. We put everything growing around us to good use. There were no craft shops to buy from. Clematis, or 'old man's beard' as we called it, had puffs of feathery seed pods in the autumn, and that was when it was best for making baskets. We peeled the skin from the strands of clematis, down to the white cane underneath. The strands were soaked to make them supple before we could weave them into baskets. I liked the green rushes best. They were good for platting and then sewing the plaits into tiny dolls' cradles or baskets.

Mrs Halting held mammoth canning sessions on the home farm. People from around the village would bring fruit and vegetables, and Mrs Halting hired a canning machine and bought a huge stock of cans. The fruit and vegetables all had to be washed and prepared, filled into cans, put in boiling water to drive out the air, and then sealed by machine. In summer, the canners sat out on the lawn, working at trestle tables. People had to pay so much per can they used and donate a proportion of their cans to the WI. Mrs Halting ran a WI stall in Petersfield market. All the profit went to helping others in need. Sometimes in summer, I got up early on market days, at about five in the morning, when it was getting light, to pick watercress from the stream across the fields. The water was icy and my fingers would go numb. But it was worth it. Bunches of watercress sold out quickly on the WI stall. I got half and the other half went to WI charities.

One time, we had to can a whole cow! The boys, including my brother Martin, were making an electric fence for the kale field. Electric fences had become all the rage just then. Everywhere, cattle were being penned in and, every few days, the fence would be moved to give the kale, or grass and clover, a chance to grow higher in the fenced off part. Martin designed the transformer that was needed to control the current, and the two Halting boys put up the fence in a field of kale. Cows like kale, which is a kind of cabbage on thick, juicy stalks. They tend to overeat if they are not rationed. Kale had to be cut and carried to the barn and the cows were given it in their mangers. The boys put the new electric fence in the kale field, to save the labour of cutting and carrying it. It worked very well for a long time.

Then they moved the electric fence, so that it ran right over a large pile of dung that had been put in the field, ready for the next muck-spreading time. All went well until Buttercup trod her way up onto the dunghill – goodness knows why, as it was a stupid thing to do – and slipped. She fell right onto the electric fence and was electro-cuted. It should not have happened, because the current was sup-posed to be only enough to put her off trying to get through, but not enough to harm her. By electrocuting Buttercup, the fence short–cir-cuited and went out of action. The rest of the herd soon found out and pushed through. They gorged themselves sick on kale and spoiled a lot more of the field by trampling around, looking for the juiciest stalks.

When Buttercup was brought home on a wagon, we could see where she had fallen, by the piece of wire buried deep in her side. The wire fence had been cut to get her off the dunghill. It was in the late 1940s and food was still scarce, so Mrs Halting got out her can-ning machine. (She had bought her own machine by then.) She gave cow meat to the farm hands in the cottages for their families. Then it was 'all hands on deck', as the Halting family and farm hands gathered to can the rest of Buttercup. The catch-phrase was 'Eat what you can and can what you can't!'

In those days of restrictions, we were allowed to kill one of our own pigs, every so often, for the family and sell the rest for meat and, in return, we got ration coupons we could use to buy a variety of things. We gave up meat coupons to do this but it was worth it. Some-times, Mr Halting would select a pig and let it get a bit bigger and fatter than the preferred size for market. He would slaughter it, quickly and cleanly cutting the pig's throat. I watched him do it once.

He deftly distracted the pig's attention and then, with one slice, it was all over. In no time after that, he had the pig hanging by its hind legs. To get edible meat, all the blood has to drain down to the cut and into a bucket under the dead pig's head.

Mr Halting was a very gentle, considerate man who loved animals. He treated them with kindness and respect. He never killed a pig in the same part of the farm buildings twice. This was so that there would be no smell of pig's blood before the pig was dead. Slaughter-houses are not so considerate. As soon as the pigs arrive, they smell the blood of the pigs that have gone just before them. I visited the bacon factory in Reading, as part of my dairy technology course. I saw a lorry load of pigs arrive at the slaughtering department. I will never forget the squeals of terror, as they were unloaded and imme-diately smelled pigs' blood.

The first time a pig was selected for family use, it walked onto the local slaughterhouse's pick-up lorry on its four trotters. It came back in pieces, with six trotters. Some of the pieces seemed too small to have come from our big pig. Mr Halting said we had been cheated – the two extra trotters made up the weight lost in the smaller meaty pieces. After that, he decided to slaughter the pigs himself. Each time, the pig meat had to be dealt with quickly. Some pieces, especially the pig's buttocks, would be packed with salt and a curing concoction, and put into a metal tray in the farmhouse dairy, which was a large larder room. Much later, these pieces would be hung up to smoke in the chimney-breast of the wash-house. A fire would be lit there, every washday, to boil water.

I used to ride over the Downs to find juniper bushes. Juniper berries were thrown in the ash, as the fire burnt down, to give the ham joints a very nice flavour. You sometimes still get that flavour in ham joints that pubs buy from local farmers. You never get it in preserved supermarket ham. The remaining pig meat, after we had eaten some and the cottagers had taken their pieces, had to be canned. The dogs would get gristly, fatty bits.

As well as the two main fairs, there were annual county shows. Mr Halting sometimes entered Suffolk Punch horses or heifers in the show classes. Sometimes I was allowed to help get them ready and

The Haltings' farmhouse

On the Downs, with Mrs Halting (in front), farm hands and friends

At the farm, holding a puppy

Ruth at Haltings' farm with yearling calves

lead them in the ring. I felt proud, as our show animals never misbe-
haved, though some of the others did. County fairs, like the Bath and
West Royal County Show, which we often went to, had a lot more
competitions for the best of everything: the best animals, vegetables,
flowers, and sacks of different types of corn. Big firms showed all their
latest models of tractors, and other farm machinery and equipment
for sale.

The Taro Fair was held every autumn on Petersfield Heath, a piece
of natural common land. Gypsies would come from all over England
to buy and sell horses. They would trot their horses up and down for
buyers to admire, and there were funfair amusements, candyfloss and
toffee-apples to keep the children amused. The blacksmiths in South
Harting were a gypsy family. I got to know them well, through taking
the Haltings' horses and ponies to be shod there. Gypsies were part
of the rural community in those days, and their way of life, moving
around the country, was simply accepted. Some village folk grumbled, but they grumbled much more about town people buying up
houses for weekend use. The townies considered the gypsies, and
many of the villagers, 'a bit common', and the villagers accused the
weekenders of 'putting on airs and graces'.

We would also go to the heath at other times in the year. In summer, our art teacher would take us there to draw and paint landscapes.
We even persuaded the biology teacher to escort us there to catch
frog-spawn and various creepy-crawlies.

When I was older, I liked to take part in competitions run by the
Young Farmers' Clubs. I usually did well in two disciplines. One was
to be the first to correctly harness a working horse into a cart and drive
it to the other end of a stretch of field. The contestants had to carry
the harness to a horse tied to a post by a rope on its headstall, and
then reassure the horse that it was in the hands of friendly strangers
who were in charge. Some people missed this stage out and had difficulty putting on their harnesses. After fitting the harness, we led our
horses to sniff the cart. Some horses would object strongly to being
strapped up to a strange cart with a smell they were not used to. Then
we had to jump up and drive to the finishing tape. We could get our
horse to trot but we would be disqualified if it went into a canter. A

horse 'trots between the shaft', which means the shafts remain level while the horse goes up and down just a tiny bit. If the horse canters, it bounces up a lot more, and that can wear out the shafts and joints of the cart and, eventually, a shaft will snap.

Assembling a milking machine was the other competition at which I did well. Each contestant had a trestle table on which lay the parts of a milking machine and had to fit them all together accurately. The first to finish was the winner. Most people were disqualified because they got the fiddly bits of tubing muddled up. In both these competitions, I was usually the only girl. I had made up my mind, at that time, that I was going to be a farmer. There were, of course, competitions to attract girls but they didn't attract me. Who wants to be fastest to iron a man's shirt?

One year, I entered a national model competition. I can't remember who organised it. My entry was a model farm with a farmhouse, barns and sheds, fences and horses, cows, pigs and sheep, all made out of matchboxes, matches and coloured felt. I had to pack it in a little box and send it to the competition master. I won first prize, which was announced in the *Farmers' Weekly* magazine. Sadly, I never got my model farm back, because they lost it. Mr Halting wrote them a stern letter and they compensated me with money. I would have preferred my model farm back. After that, I used the patterns I had designed to make little animals to sell in the WI shop.

I was a member of the Young Farmers' Club based in Elstead, a tiny hamlet, but nearer than the club in West Harting. We used to meet weekly in a community hall and listen to a speaker on some relevant subject. I don't remember the lectures, I only remember it was fun to run things ourselves, without anyone interfering, and when the only person older than 21 was the speaker. It was a properly constituted club with a chairperson and a secretary. Ordinary members were encouraged to get up and speak about their experiences.

That was my introduction to public speaking. I discovered my peers were interested in my stories about my pigs and ponies – the kind of stories I have included in this book. I never rose to be the chairwoman, but I was secretary for a time, and so I wrote lots of letters to get speakers and learnt how to gather information from people.

The Young Farmers' Club also helped to organise the annual summer fête, and we had hayrides and picnics.

We held a club dance every winter. Adults had to be invited by a club member, who was then responsible to see they behaved! Mr and Mrs Halting never went to these dances but encouraged us children to go. My friend Mary's whole family went. I used to enjoy dancing the Gay Gordon with Mary's father. He really knew how to dance. Most of the young farmers would shyly stand round the walls. When they asked you to dance, they would stumble around, looking at their feet, and tread on yours. Mary's dad held his head up high, as he whisked me around the dance floor, cracking jokes all the time.

In 1947, when I was twelve, Princess Margaret attended the Royal Sussex County Show. A big parade passed in front of the stand where she was sitting with the other VIPs. The local Young Farmers' Clubs provided a float for a section of the parade and lots of members were in charge of animals. I was given a cute little calf to lead. When I came to the VIPs' box, Princess Margaret stepped down and stroked the calf. I can't remember what she said, because I was too surprised and embarrassed.

HARVEST TIME

CHAPTER 17

Winter, Summer, Haytime and Harvest

L iving felt so much easier in summer on the farm than in winter, even though there was a lot more work to do. But most of the farm work did not seem like work. As a child, I used to think that work meant peeling potatoes or laying the living room fire. Feeding the animals or joining in haymaking just seemed like fun.

But winters were hard. I remember them as wet, muddy and freezing COLD. The farmyard was always mucky. I wore wellies all the time outside. Walking across a ploughed field was exhausting because so much sticky, wet earth would cling to the wellies, so that I could hardly lift my feet! My feet would get cold, even with thick socks, and then I would get chilblains on my toes that itched and kept me awake at night.

My hands also suffered in winter. It was impossible to wear gloves around the farm. They got sodden wet very quickly. Gloves were no good for picking grass or herbs for the rabbits; or for mixing bran with water for bran-mash. If gloves got wet, they became hopeless for riding a pony; they would slip on the reins and the ponies would get out of control. I often rode without a saddle in winter, because then I would get warmth from the pony, and I would sit on one hand after the other to stop them freezing. Sometimes, my hands would go blue and numb with cold. As with my feet, my hands were susceptible to chilblains. If you have never had chilblains, you don't know how lucky you are. When you warm your numb hands indoors, they tingle and then swell up in bumps that throb. It is very painful and it hurts like hell. Because my hands got frozen numb every day, the bumps didn't recover all winter. I could hardly hold a pen to do my schoolwork or homework. But the animals had to be fed, I still had to pick rabbit food, mix mash and do other things. Sometimes, the chilblain lumps would split open and bleed. I would stick plasters over the wounds.

Winter wasn't all bad. There would be cinema outings and parties at Christmas. We had a few board games, like Monopoly, but we hardly ever played with toys. Winter evenings round the fire were for telling stories, while Mrs Halting and I darned socks. Mr Halting and the boys told the stories. Fires in other rooms were only lit for special occasions and only ever in a bedroom when someone was very ill.

People were seldom ill enough to stay in bed on the farm. The Aga cooker in the kitchen was on all the time, day and night, and that kept the water pipes from freezing. The bathroom upstairs was just above the Aga, so that it got a little warmth. The bedrooms were so cold that I used to put my pyjamas on top of my clothes, jump quickly into bed and disappear under the blankets, because I was convinced that there were foxes under the bed that would bite my legs if I came close enough. I often read storybooks with a torch under the blankets.

When there was snow and the weather was good enough, we all preferred being outdoors and liked to go sledging. There were no sleds to buy in toyshops, so we made our own sled out of a piece of galvanised iron sheeting. We turned up the front and fixed baling twine to the base to make a handle each side, for the front person to hold onto. Sometimes, four of us would pile onto the sled. It would flatten the snow the first time and, after that, it would go faster and faster on the impacted snow. It went fastest of all on thick frost. You didn't need snow. Up on the Downs, the frost would form much thicker than on the fields in the valley. Once, we were sledding on thick hoar-frost and one of the handles snapped. It was impossible to steer and the sled careered off-course into bramble bushes. The others all fell off before the sled and I hit the brambles. By the time I reached home, I was covered in blood all over! Fortunately, they were only surface scratches and healed very quickly.

Every year, for at least a week or two, the duck pond used to freeze over, hard enough to skate on. We had a lot of fun playing on the ice. There were only three pairs of skates, of the simple kind, that fixed onto the soles of ordinary shoes. We took turns when there was a crowd of kids at the pond. The poor ducks didn't stand a chance. Sometimes, they waddled down the road to the pond in a line, like little soldiers, to look for water, but mostly they stayed around the farmyards.

One year, the big lake just outside Petersfield froze over and we all went to skate there. There was music to listen to and food to eat. People sold hot soup and hot bread on the ice. I got wet, from falling and slithering on the ice, but was having such fun I didn't notice the cold, till sitting on the bus going home, I started to shiver.

You can imagine how pleased I was, when spring came. Snowdrops flowered by the first day of February, then the crocuses and, when the daffodils came out in all their golden glory, winter was nearly over. March, April, and sometimes, even May, were still cold. Sharp winds made the daffodils dance and the cows and horses, if they were in the fields, would turn their backs to the wind. Ponies have thick tails they can spread over their buttocks, but the poor cows would look forlorn with their rope-like tails.

Occasionally, there was a last fall of snow before the buds opened on the trees, and every twig would have a sugar-white coating of snow that sparkled in the sunshine. I can remember how beautiful it all looked from the top of the bus going to school, but it would be gone by the time I went home.

In April and May, the fields and hedges suddenly burst into leaf and the flowers began to bloom. Winter-hungered sheep, cows and horses would have a feast. But the new growth was rich, and it was easy for them to get too much. Many animals developed 'gassy-stomach', which was quite painful for them.

The more it rained in April and May, the better it was for the hay to grow and the ears of corn to swell. By the end of May, we would look anxiously at the weather. Plenty of hot sun was then needed, to dry the hay and ripen the corn. The second week in June was the best time to cut the hay. The grass would be at its best to make good, sweet, nourishing hay. If it was left longer, as we had to do if the weather was wet, the grass and clover would go to seed. The seeds would blow away, and the hay would lose its sweetness and not taste good to the animals the next winter.

Hay-time required a good ten days of fine, sunny weather. First, the long grass was cut with a horse-drawn mower. Once the sun had dried it enough, it would be turned by a tedder. A horse pulled the tedder, which neatly turned over the lines of mown grass, to dry the damp underside. If it rained, the grass would need to dry and be turned again. When the grass was dry right through, it was hay.

Then the hay harvest began. The horse would pull another machine that had a big, fork-like grab at the rear. It acted like a rake. Every two or three yards, the driver would pull a lever and the grab lifted, leaving a pile of raked-up hay. The farm hands would be out in the hayfield with pitchforks, shaking the piles of hay and making them into tiny haystacks, called haycocks. That protected the hay from rain and dew. When all the hayfields had been raked up and piled into haycocks, the horse-drawn wagons would come into the fields, and the haycocks were loaded onto them.

The horses pulled the wagons down the road, back to the farm, where the hay would be unloaded onto a hayrick, by farm hands using pitchforks. For about ten days, every evening, everyone on the farm, including children, would work to get the hay in, until it became too dark to see any more.

No time was wasted when there was daylight. I would sometimes be out in the hayfield for an hour or so before school, and another five or six after school. Meals went out to the fields, and every meal was a merry picnic, with everyone sitting round laughing and joking, in a sunny corner of the field. It was my job to drive a horse and cart out to the fields, full of jugs of cider, orange juice, Cornish pasties, bread and cheese, pickles and scones. Everything was homemade, except the bread, which came from the village bakery. Our farm mill could only grind corn roughly, for animal feed. You need very fine-ground flour for bread. The pickles and cider were made on the farm in the autumn, after the harvest. Cottage cheese, butter and clotted cream were also made regularly, and had to be eaten fresh. Sometimes, I was allowed to help bake the scones and pasties. When the hay was all safely gathered in and stored in ricks, the tops of the ricks had to be thatched, just like thatched cottages, but with the previous year's straw, instead of thatching reeds.

In July, there was still plenty of work to do, hoeing and weeding the root crops in the fields, and picking soft fruits and vegetables in the huge farm garden. There were peas and beans, carrots and onions, and plenty of tomatoes, strawberries, raspberries, gooseberries, red-currants and blackcurrants. Some would be pickled or canned, and some would go to be sold in the market. I would climb the big walnut tree in the orchard, to pick the green walnuts for pickling. When the walnuts were ripe enough to eat they would fall, but then they would be no use for pickling, as the shells would have hardened.

The Goodwood races were held in July, so that the local people could come, as it was between hay-time and corn harvest. Few posh people came to Goodwood in those days, and it was quite a small affair. The racecourse was on a little plateau with rolling hills on three sides. It was a beautiful setting and unspoiled by the commercialisation that ruined it later.

There was one small grandstand for the better off and one general enclosure for locals who wanted to bet with the bookies. Families, like ours, could cross the racecourse and picnic on the far side, where there was no grandstand and there were no bookies. I don't know why, but the horses always ran to that far side. We could almost touch them as they galloped past. We had a wonderful day out each time, without betting, and it cost us nothing but a little petrol to get there.

I used to read the back page of the *News Chronicle*, which was always about racehorses. I collected the pictures of horses racing and stuck them into an exercise book. I had about ten of these scrapbooks by the time I went to university and lost interest. I used to read all about the horses. I would check how they were doing, whether they liked soft turf or ran better when it was harder. I wasn't allowed to place bets; that was really frowned on, especially for children. So I wrote my bets on pieces of paper, and looked up the winners the next day. I only bet a shilling each way and regularly made a profit of a few shillings every week. Of course, I hid it all from the grown-ups. If I had been found out, I would have been in trouble. Thinking back, if somebody had realised how much I knew about betting, that person might have made a fortune using my tips!

Sometimes in July, we would drive to the coast, which was only about 20 miles away, and have a picnic and a swim. We always went to West Wittering, where there were huge stretches of sand dunes that were difficult to walk over to reach the sea. Most of the beaches were spoiled for bathing by huge concrete tank traps that were built during the war, when everyone thought Hitler would invade Britain.

August was corn harvest time. It usually rained sometime in the month, so it was difficult to pick the right moment to cut and stack. The corn had to be ripe, but if it was too wet when gathered in, the ears of corn would start growing green shoots. Then it would be useless.

There were many different kinds of wheat, oats and barley. The secret of good farming was to plant the fields with different corn, to ripen at different times throughout August. But it always depended on there being enough hot sun to ripen the corn, gentle wind to dry it, and enough dry weather to get it in safely.

First, the horses would go in with the binder, a machine that would cut the corn and, at the same time, tie it into bundles or sheaves. Then everyone would be there in the fields, stooking, which meant arranging the sheaves close together, upright, so as to dry them.

Pitchforks were not used, as when making hay. One had to pick up two sheaves by hand and balance them together so that they stood upright, and put them next to two other people's pairs of sheaves, to make a stook of six upright sheaves. We worked together in threes. There was always a bit of competition as to whose team could make the most stooks. The sheaves were always scratchy, and sometimes they were prickly too, if there were thistles growing in among the corn.

If it rained, the water would run down the sides of the stooks and the corn would quickly dry again. But a storm could blow the stooks over. When the stooks were dry enough, they were brought in on wagons. Here, we would use pitchforks to hoick up the corn. One person would be on the wagon, building up the sheaves in secure layers, and two people would pitch the sheaves up to that person. Again, teams of three were needed.

One time, I was on the wagon and I was using my hands to stack the sheaves, until I reached for a sheaf, just as the person below thrust it up. One spike of the pitchfork stabbed into the palm of my hand, just at the base of my thumb. It hurt like hell, but, strangely, it didn't bleed much at all. A piece of skin was torn and a lump of fat poked out. I ended up in the casualty department, where it was stitched back. I was back next day in the harvest field, but I always used a pitchfork after that.

I used to lead the horses back to the farm with their full loads of corn sheaves. It was dangerous to sit on top of the load and drive a horse, as the sheaves might slide and the load was over ten feet high. Besides, the load alone was heavy for the horse to pull, without a person on top. Back at the farm, the sheaves were unloaded into a corn rick. Sometimes an elevator was set up, powered by a tractor, to lift the sheaves to the top of the rick, when it got too high to pitch them up. When the last sheaf had finally gone up onto a rick, there were celebrations, including a harvest supper round the ricks. We would have a glorious picnic, and the best time of all was when stooking the last few sheaves in moonlight. A moonlit picnic is magical!

Return to Germany

CHAPTER 18

Repatriation

By the spring of 1949, Martin and I had been living on the farm with the Haltings for four years. This was our third foster family, and I had come to think that I would live there forever. Mr and Mrs Halting were very fond of me and I, of course, adored them. I didn't know at the time, I only discovered much later that they had applied to the Red Cross to trace my parents because they wanted to adopt me as one of their family. That was just what I would have wished. It was four years after the end of the war, and the Red Cross was not able to locate, either my mother in Germany, or my father in Shanghai. We had not heard from my father for a long time, and we had heard nothing from my mother since 1939 – ten years earlier.

Although the terrible war had ended, it did not mean that things were back to normal. The bombing had done widespread damage and used up money, equipment, food and other resources. Everything was scarce and communication disrupted. All over continental Europe, there were camps full of displaced persons. They were called DP camps. Many of the people in them had lost everything and had no homes to go back to, and some didn't want to go back to countries from where they had been driven out or bombed out. All those people, many of them ill and starving, had to be found food, clothes and medical care. They needed help to get somewhere where they could begin life anew. The ordinary people who were not in DP camps were also finding life hard. There were shortages of everything. Soldiers were being demobbed and coming home, many of them wounded and traumatised from all the horrors they had seen in battle. Everybody had more or less to begin a new life. Looking back, it was not so surprising that the Red Cross had not been able to find my parents.

It was a huge surprise to get a letter from my mother suddenly in May 1949, and soon after that, she came to England to take me back with her to Germany. It is hard for me to convey the quality of the confusion I was suddenly pitched into. In my mind, my mother was already dead; I had thought this since we were in our first foster family, the Steads, because otherwise she would have rescued me from Miss Wright's cruelty. While we were at Westenhanger, Mrs Goodricke had kept my father alive in my mind, by telling me how exciting it would be to go to China in a big ship to join him. I longed for the war to be over so that I could go there. But when the war finally ended in May 1945, and the Goodrickes sent me away to the Haltings, I gave up any thoughts of being reunited with my parents. I created a fantasy world in my imagination, in which I was a Halting, and would be part of the Halting family for ever. I convinced myself that I was such an important part of the family economy that they couldn't possibly send me away again, as I had taken on so many household and farmyard jobs.

It was an immense shock to be confronted with a strange woman and told that she was my mother. I didn't recognise her at all. I remember it very clearly. Martin and I went to the station to meet her off a train. What on earth had this big fat woman to do with me!? She certainly didn't fit the vague image of my mother that I had had in my mind since I was four. She couldn't speak a word of English, I couldn't speak German and I didn't want to talk with her. She wanted to pull me to her and hug me, but I couldn't bear her touching me. As I thought my mother was dead, it felt as though she had suddenly come back from the grave. I was not sure whether she was real or a ghost. It was a terrible situation. I was so full of confused, unmanageable feelings that I feared I would explode.

Once we got back to the farm, I couldn't bear to be with her or with anyone. I ran out to the stables to take comfort from the horses. They nuzzled me and it was as if they were giving me the mothering I had yearned for, all along, but couldn't now accept from this stranger that they said was my mother. She undoubtedly wanted to mother me and make up for lost time, but it was too late. If she had come as soon as the war ended, four years earlier, when I was still with the Goodrickes, I am sure Mrs Goodricke would have helped me through the confusion. But the Haltings believed that because my parents had not come earlier, they couldn't really want me. It was not until many years later that I began to piece together some of the difficulties my parents had at that time. Though he never once spoke of it, my father had a nervous breakdown when he first returned to Berlin. And my mother flatly refused ever to set foot in Berlin again. She wouldn't talk about it. Perhaps she had a breakdown too. Many people succumbed to illness just after the war. It is a strange fact of human psychology that you somehow keep going while there is danger or an essential job to be done. Then, when it is all over and you can relax again, you get ill. It is as if you take out a loan of energy, and willpower, that you have to pay back later when the crisis is over.

I became very distressed, rather like Martin had over the doodle-bugs in Kent, when we were living with the Goodrickes. I had completely lost the sense of myself. I wasn't the same 'me' any more, so I didn't know who I was. The Haltings didn't want me to be unhappy and said I could stay with them. After a few days and a lot of tension, arguments and language difficulty, my mother went back to Germany on her own – without me. It must have been awful for her to be so rejected by her daughter. I can see that now, but at the time, I couldn't deal with it. I didn't wish her any harm; I just didn't want her to be there, disturbing my precarious emotional life yet again. I just couldn't cope with it. My father, who by then had recovered and had a job as a lawyer in the court of Mainz, served a court order on the Haltings to bring me to Germany. That meant even bigger confusion for me. The Haltings had said I was part of their family and could stay, yet Mrs Halting was taking me to Germany! I knew she had to obey a court order, but it felt like a monstrous betrayal.

I remember the journey, with Mrs Halting trying to do everything possible to cheer me. I was numb and gloomy with misery and confusion, and unresponsive. It was a terrible, long journey, in every sense, because I was depressed and didn't want to be going on it. Mrs Halting could not add me to her passport because I was not her child. Nor could I have a passport of my own as Hitler had taken away my German nationality. I was not eligible for British nationality because I was under 18. The Jewish Refugee Committee got me a 'travelling paper'. It was a large sheet of paper and had 'PERSON OF NO NATIONALITY' typed in big letters across the top, and then lots of visa stamps and things that didn't make sense to me. At all the check-points, the officers looked at it suspiciously and told us to wait at the side, until everyone else had gone through. Then they called their superiors and, by the time we were allowed to go, we had missed the train. This happened at the Hook of Holland, where the boat docked, and again at the Dutch border with Germany and a third time at the German border. It meant an awful lot of waiting around. I had books and toys but I was far too upset and disoriented to concentrate on anything. It is well known to paediatricians, doctors who specialise in children's health, that the first sign of a child who is unwell is when she or he can't play.

The trains in Germany, in 1949, had slatted wooden seats. They had no upholstery like the English trains, so it was a very uncomfortable journey. Every time we got out at a border, I could feel the ground under my feet moving as if I was still on the train. And it felt as if the wooden seats had made my bottom slatted. I was exhausted by the time we reached Mainz. I think Mrs Halting was exhausted too, as she had given up trying to chat with me. The station where we got out was just a huge shell, with all the glass blown out by bombs. The landscape as we left the station hall was like a film set and I was terrified. There were heaps of rubble everywhere, with temporary wooden planks for walkways. Jagged bits of buildings jutted out of the rubble. I was convinced that there were Nazis in jackboots with Bren guns behind each one. I had been reading the *Beano* and *Dandy*, right through the war, and they were full of stories about 'nasty Nazis' jumping out from behind buildings.

If my brother, Martin, had been there, he would have said, 'Don't be stupid, there are no Nazis any more, they have been completely defeated.' But he wasn't there. My parents wanted him to stay in England because he was studying for a scholarship to Cambridge University. So I went through the original Kindertransport experience a second time, this time in reverse. Overnight I had lost my home, foster parents, language, and everything familiar, and found myself in a strange world, where everything was different to what I was used to. Only, this time, there was no 'big brother' to make meaning for me out of a world gone mad. There was so much fear and rage, inside me, that I felt I was just as mad inside myself as the mad world outside me. I just couldn't cope with yet another massive change in my life. It is unbearable to feel mad inside and outside. I felt I was being punished for being bad and getting everything wrong. I had tried so hard for so long to be good, and it seemed as if all my efforts had come to nothing.

CHAPTER 19

Conflict

Mainz is a city halfway down the river Rhine in Germany. My father was living in a part of the city that was not damaged very much. It was on the outskirts, on a hill overlooking the city centre. We came up that hill in a taxi from the station, leaving behind the horrifying rubble of bomb damage all round the station. I noticed some old, rather lovely, houses and blocks of flats, as we came up the hill. It had obviously been an elegant wealthy suburb of Mainz before the war. All the people who lived there during the war had been forced by the German government to take lodgers in every room, except one bedroom, and one living room, that they could keep for themselves. My father rented a room in a flat owned by an elderly couple; at least they seemed very old to me as I was only 14. They were kindly. I could tell that, even though I couldn't understand a word of what they said. Not only did they speak German, but in Meenzer dialect (Mainz dialect). Every flat in the block had a tiny patch of the garden at the back, to grow a few vegetables in. The old couple had made half of theirs into a pen for two hens. Because there were thieves at night, the two hens were carried up three flights of stairs, every evening at dusk, and 'put to bed' in a cupboard under the kitchen sink.

My father's room was tiny. I think it must have been a boxroom before the war. There was only just room for a single bed, a tiny bedside cupboard, one chair and an open rail for him to hang his suit and jacket. There was no space for anyone else in that tiny room. We all had tea in the old couple's living room. It was very dark, with lots of old-fashioned furniture and cushions, and had a musty smell. I just wanted to rush out and find a train to take me back to England. But the old lady had baked a special cheesecake with eggs from her two hens. I had never seen cheesecake before and I was curious. It seemed daft to me to make a cake with cheese, but it was actually delicious. I ate the cheesecake, but I was too confused and disoriented to talk,

PERSON OF NO NATIONALITY

even with Mrs Halting and my father, who spoke excellent English. In fact, my father used long words in English that I had never heard before. When I felt like being nasty later on, I used to tell him he talked like a stuffy textbook.

There was no room for me, or my mother, in that flat, or even in the whole block. So Mrs Halting had to set off back to England, the same day. My parents, Mrs Halting and I took a tram back down to the station. I had never been in a tram before. Even though there were trams in London, I had only been on London buses. I found the tram unfamiliar and scary, especially going down the hill. Like the trains, it had only slatted wooden seats, which made it bumpy and uncomfortable.

When Mrs Halting's train left the station, I said goodbye without looking at her. I was in a terrible conflict. I wanted to hug her and cling to her, except I felt she had betrayed me. She had brought me to this terrible place: now she was going to abandon me and leave me to flounder. I wanted to plead with her to take me back to England, however I was too confused and angry to say a word. My mother couldn't say anything either, because she didn't know any English. My father scolded me for being rude to Mrs Halting, and for not showing her gratitude for bringing me to Mainz. I was nonplussed. Why didn't he realise that I couldn't possibly be grateful, because the last place on earth where I wanted to be was Germany? Was I being bad again, or was he being silly? I started to feel as though I was falling apart. Was I still me? Was I going mad, or were my parents mad?

My parents desperately wanted their sweet little four-year-old back, the one they had sent off on the Kindertransport. They were in no fit shape to cope with a teenager, and a dislocated one at that. They had no idea what it was like for me there on Mainz station and, at that time, I had no idea what it was like for them. It was like a solid, invisible wall of incomprehension between them and me.

After Mrs Halting's train left, I began to feel that I was lost. Mainz station was strange and eerie and I started to shiver. My father led the way to the platform for the train my mother and I were to take to the South of Germany, where my mother was living. As he said goodbye to me, I turned away. I didn't want to kiss him. I wanted to run away – but where could I go? Everything was strange. My father's last words were, 'Be good and don't make trouble for your mother – she is not very well.' I felt nauseous with rage, and wanted to spew up out of the carriage window.

It was a long journey through the night on a steam train. The wooden seats were uncomfortable. At least it wasn't crowded and I could lie down. I slept fitfully, and I was asleep when we arrived at Lindau, a lovely little island, situated on Lake Constance. The lake straddles the border between Germany, Austria and Switzerland. You reach Lindau by a railway bridge or a road bridge. I came to know Lindau very well; its narrow, cobbled streets and uneven, old, beamed houses with pointed roofs and turrets, rather like the pictures in an old copy of *Grimm's Fairy Tales*.

When we first arrived there, I was too tired and lethargic to notice how quaint and pretty the town was. Anyway, we had to get a bus to take us back over the road bridge and through the countryside to the little village of Unterreitnau, where my mother had rooms in a farm-house.

Although it was only midday, when we reached that farmhouse, I was exhausted, and just wanted to sleep. I found myself in a little room with a wooden bed, and I, more or less, fell into it. Instead of the sheet and blankets I was used to, there was a big fat feather duvet. It felt like sinking into a fluffy, white cloud. I didn't wake up until almost noon the next day. My mother was sitting there when I woke up. She was reading a book. As far back as I can remember, I have always woken up completely, all at once, and alert for any danger. I still do so today. Although everything was strange, it was as if I had not been asleep, but was still on the journey from Mainz. I could feel the rocking motion of the train under me. I had a shock when my mother said, 'Good morning! You sleeped whole day.' I couldn't believe my mother spoke English. The book she was reading was to help her learn English. She wanted to talk with me. But I didn't want to talk with her. I didn't want to be there in Unterreitnau, even though it was a farmhouse and in a very pretty village. It was the wrong farmhouse and the wrong mother. Where was the right mother? Mrs. Halting, like all the others, had betrayed me. How could I trust this one, an entirely new mother – not the one I had lost, when I first came to England?

You simply can't pick up a relationship again after a ten-year gap, which is what my parents expected me to do. It had no chance of working. My identity was completely fragmented – I had left it behind on the Haltings' farm. Here in Unterreitnau I was not at all sure who I was, and I felt completely cut off and lost. Sometimes, when I shut my eyes, I felt I was nowhere at all. I imagined that, if I closed my eyes and tried hard enough, I would be back in England when I opened them again. It never worked. I tried so hard that it gave me a splitting headache. That was when my headaches began. After that, I had headaches at least once or twice a week. I simply drowned them out with aspirin. My headaches only petered out in my 50s, when I began to reconnect my roots and understand what I had experienced.

No matter how much I felt disoriented in Unterreitnau and desperately wanted to escape, I never actually got lost. When my turbulent feelings reached bursting point, or my mother wanted me to do something – anything – I would run out of the farmhouse, and off over the fields and woods. I wanted to be lost. Sometimes, I had the crazy idea of running and running until I came to the coast, and then I would sneak onto a boat as a stowaway and get to England. That was completely crazy, because it would actually have taken three or four weeks, or more, to reach the coast on foot. I even imagined I would find a horse somewhere in the fields to ride. But all the horses were in stables, not out in the fields. What actually happened was that, without planning it or realising what I was doing, I always went round in a circle and came back to the farmhouse. I made sure I didn't go in until long after dark. That was a nasty thing to do and my mother must have been very worried. I felt nasty. The whole world felt nasty to me. How could I cope with so much nastiness?

Soon after I arrived in Unterreitnau with my mother, my father came for the two days of the weekend. My mother told him how I had run out for hours, wouldn't speak to her or eat what she cooked, and that I spent long hours in bed, pretending to be asleep. I think I must have been quite depressed and sleep was my escape after battling with my confusion all day. When I woke up, I didn't want to face the day, so I pretended to be asleep still.

My father was very angry with me. Didn't I realise what a hard time my mother had had all these years through the war and that it had left her health damaged so that she had constant back pain? No, I didn't realise. I didn't want to know about it. It was too difficult to do anything more than cling on to my sanity and exist day by day, with the terrible confusion going on in my head. My parents didn't realise what it was like for me. How could they? I wasn't able to think clearly enough to tell them, and I didn't want to talk to them anyway. I didn't want to be there. That was the only thing I was sure about.

My father came nearly every weekend. He would be very cheerful and pleased to see my mother and me. He brought me small presents of chocolate, or books and pictures, which I accepted rather ungraciously. My parents would talk endlessly together, in German. Quite quickly, their voices would get louder and they often ended up in a full-blown row. I imagined that my mother had told him all about my bad moods and refusal to do anything she wanted of me. I knew I was behaving badly, but I had given up even trying to be good. Trying to be ever so good had not got me where I wanted to be. Why should I bother any more? Yet I felt even worse because I knew I was behaving badly, deliberately.

Later, when I studied human development for my teaching certificate, I began to understand that I had not been behaving badly deliberately – I simply couldn't help it. What I thought was my bad behaviour was, in fact, the way that a normal teenager behaves when she is confused and her feelings are out of control. But, in 1949, when I was only 14, I thought that it was always about my badness that my parents were rowing. After all, what else do parents have to talk about?! What I couldn't know at the time was that my parents, after the long separation, were strangers to each other. They had great difficulty getting their own relationship together again. They didn't know what to do about relating to a distressed teenager. My parents were nice people but I couldn't appreciate their problems when I was with them in Unterreitnau. I only began to understand much later how their own experiences during the war had affected them. They had gone through terrible anxiety and stress. They wanted a happy companionable daughter and didn't know what to do with the unhappy moody teenager that I was.

As the autumn turned to winter, there was thick snow. All the children played at snowballing and skiing. I joined in a bit, but the children laughed at my incorrect German. One of the farmer's sons lent me his skis and showed me how to ski. The children laughed at my attempts. Even toddlers on tiny skis could do better than me. I had learned to skate on the duck pond at the Haltings. So my mother bought me a pair of good boots with skates, and I went nearly every day to Lindau. The lake froze over completely, between the two bridges. That was a huge area, more than fifty times as big as the duck pond at the Haltings' farm.

The lake attracted a lot of skaters but it was so large that it never got crowded. I usually took the bus back to Unterreitnau afterwards, but one evening there was a full moon. It was so lovely skating in the moonlight that I stayed very late, until there were no more buses. I had to walk the five miles or so back to Unterreitnau, but it was magic in the moonlight. My mother didn't appreciate that at all because, of course, she was worried when I was not on the last bus. For once, I had not been deliberately bad. I had just been enjoying the natural beauty of the moonlit landscape. It was a shock that my mother was so upset and angry. It felt so unfair. It seemed I could never get anything right.

After a few weeks, which seemed to me like years, it was approaching Christmas and my brother, Martin, came to visit. My sullen mood suddenly evaporated when my big brother turned up. I was eager for him to arrive, and I actually enjoyed that Christmas with some gusto. I was hungry for everything, not just for Christmas food, but most of all, for companionship. I was starving for a hug and I could hug my brother, whereas I couldn't bear my parents touching me. Martin and I talked well into the night, nearly every night, and got up late in the mornings. There was snow with sledding and skiing. Everything was suddenly great fun. Then the crash came! Martin had to go back to school in England, and he didn't take me with him. I pleaded. It was no use; I didn't have a passport – only that horrid sheet of paper with 'PERSON OF NO NATIONALITY' along the top. After the train pulled out of Lindau station, with Martin on it and not me, I was devastated. I broke down screaming and shouting – a real tantrum.

After that, I became sullen and uncooperative again. My father said I needed to go to school. When he told me he had arranged for a teacher from the school in Lindau to pick me up, and take me to see the school, I ran out of the house and didn't come back for at least 24 hours. After hiding and sleeping in a barn full of hay, I went in a circle and eventually came back, as usual. I feel rather ashamed now, because my parents must have been beside themselves with worry about where I was.

I think that was the moment when my parents realised it wasn't going to work for me in Germany. They said they would let me go back to school in England, on condition I came to visit with Martin, every school holiday. I readily agreed to that. What neither my parents nor I had anticipated was that it would take a long time for me to get a visa. I had been repatriated and neither the German, nor the British authorities, wanted to let me go back to England. It took several months to get that visa, but it seemed to me like forever.

CHAPTER 20

Unterreitnau

Unterreitnau was a very small village of six or seven farmhouses clustered together with a church about five miles from the island town of Lindau, on the Lake of Constance. Thick, dark, coniferous woods surrounded open fields. Farm animals had to be kept in the stables and stalls because of the lack of fences, or otherwise they would have eaten the crops as well as the grass. I was used to hedges enclosing each of the fields on the Haltings' farm. There were relatively few thin deciduous coppices and woods in the English countryside. In comparison, the woods around Unterreitnau were plentiful, dark and gloomy.

I found it unbearable to be in the house with my mother. She would try hard to engage me in conversation or some board game like chess. I showed no inclination to learn German, so she made efforts to learn English - and wanted me to teach her. But Germany, and everything German, was anathema to me. I had picked up a few essential words of German very quickly, to get the gist of what was being said, but because I was so angry, I focused my utter contempt on the German language and deliberately ignored the grammar. I decided German people were quite mad to call things, like tables and chairs, either male or female. It was bad enough that the French did this, as I had learnt at school. German, on the other hand, had many words the opposite gender to the French words. So, when my mother asked me to teach her English, I deliberately taught her incorrectly: 'I is', 'you am' and 'she are'! It was very spiteful of me, but I felt vengeful. That was something else that made my father angry. He taught my mother correct English, and it was not long before I could no longer pretend that I could not understand her.

During the week, my mother worked part-time in Lindau. In spite of my endless raging, I was curious to see where she worked, but she refused to take me with her, or even tell me anything about it. It remained a mystery forever, just like she kept silent about where she had been and what she had experienced in the ten years we had been separated.

It was always a relief for me to get out of the house into the open air. When my mother was in Lindau, I also felt free being on my own. I could push all my troubles and conflicts to the back of my mind. I was more at ease. I would watch the local women, in long skirts and colourful headscarves, in the fields, cutting grass with scythes and loading it onto ox carts. They would lead the oxen back to the barn and feed the grass to cows in the cowsheds. I thought that it was daft to do all that work; instead, they should have let the cows get their own grass in the fields, as Mr Halting did. But, then they would have needed hedges, or at least fences, to keep the cows from wandering. My mother said the strips of land belonged to different people, and were too small to fence in. The farmers, their sons and daughters and wives, had lots of these tiny strips scattered all around and every time someone died, the land was further carved up and shared out between the next of kin.

There were neither tractors nor any other farm implements that would have needed engines. Although it all seemed very primitive and rather stupid to me, I was fascinated. It was so different to how things were done on the Haltings' farm. But then, what we did at the Halt-ings would be considered primitive by 21st century standards. A few years ago, when my family visited Unterreitnau, I noticed that they had caught up, and were using mostly up-to-date farm machinery and the strips of land had been sorted into bigger patches with electric fences. In 1949, on the local Unterreitnau farms, everything was done by hand. There weren't even any milking machines; cows were all milked by hand, as were goats and sheep. That struck me as very funny. It was a relatively poor village because most of its resources had been requisitioned for the German forces during the war. There were few horses and mostly oxen and cows were used to pull the carts that went back and forth, between the farm and the fields.

The farmers in whose house my mother lived were called the Maurers. They had two sons. The younger one, Irwin, was the same age as me. Although I had learnt a few words of German, I couldn't understand anything he said because he spoke with the local dialect. Not only was it a difficult dialect but many of its words were only used by the locals. Even my parents had difficulty talking with the Maurers. I sometimes played with Irwin when he wasn't in school, and he taught me to ski in the winter. The farmhouse was bigger than the Haltings' farmhouse. It had three storeys. My mother rented half of the top floor, another refugee family had the other half at the top, and the Maurers lived below, on the middle floor. The animal stalls were underneath, on the ground floor. They made a lot of heat that kept the Maurers' home warm. Even the top floor was warm, because there was a big loft. Everyone hung up washing to dry in the loft. The washing was done by hand. My mother had a big bedroom, a kitchen with a bench and a table in the corner, and there was a small room for me. We had to share the bathroom with the other family.

The house was sturdily built, mostly out of timber. The part where my mother and I lived was made of new, light-coloured, seasoned wood. The Maurer family had built the whole house themselves. I learnt that it was traditional for families to do this. Mr Maurer had inherited the house when his parents died. He was the eldest of five brothers and three sisters who had left to get married. Two brothers had died in the First World War. Mr Maurer, and his two remaining brothers, did well with the farm. Between the wars, the whole family, with the help of other villagers, raised the roof to build extra rooms for the families of the two younger brothers. Sadly, both brothers died in WWII, before they could marry or have children. That is why the rooms were available for my mother and the other family. There were many refugees, who had lost their homes in the war and needed somewhere to live. All over Germany, every house owner had to give up some of their rooms to refugees.

In the winter, the farmhouse was warm and even cosy, but in the summer, the smell was pungent and the flies were a menace. There was no modern sanitation. The animal stalls were cleaned out onto a dung heap at the back, and the liquid was channelled into a huge cesspool underneath the human quarters, so that the toilets in the house could also feed into the cesspool. There was a proper lavatory seat, like I was used to, but there was no U-bend. A dead straight pipe took the urine and faeces, 'plop-splosh', straight down into the cesspool, and the stench came right back up. Primitive but effective! Every few months, a pump would be brought to empty the cesspool into a closed tanker, which was drawn by two oxen into the fields, and the soupy liquid was then released onto the soil to fertilise it. This equipment was shared; it went round the farms in rotation. You could smell which farm's cesspool was being emptied! However, the Maurers' farm had running water and electricity. Not all the farms had this.

The woods were interesting, as well as gloomy. There were lots of birds, rabbits, moles and voles. Sometimes, when I crouched silently for a long time, I would see deer. There were varieties of mushrooms and toadstools that looked unfamiliar, so I didn't touch them. Then I found a spot where there were mushrooms that I recognised, because we used to pick them on the Downs, near the Haltings' farm.

When I brought them back to the house, my mother tried to throw them away. I wanted to cook them. My mother said we couldn't be sure they were edible. She thought I was trying to poison her! Anyway, she let me cook them for myself, but she wouldn't try them. I made a delicious, thick and creamy mushroom soup followed by fried mushrooms with an egg on toast. I was still alive next morning, and none the worse, for eating mushrooms, so my mother said she would try them if I got more. She came to like the mushroom soup and asked me to make a big pot to give to the Maurers.

Because I missed riding the ponies on the Haltings' farm, my mother made an arrangement with a farmer in Oberreitnau, the next village. He had a horse I could ride on Sundays, when it wasn't needed for work. The farmer had a fancy saddle that looked like it was borrowed from a circus. The horse was thin and bony, and tired from working in the fields. I don't think it had been ridden before. When I clicked and said, 'Walk on!', the horse turned its neck right round and looked at me in surprise, as if to say I was crazy getting on its back, when I should be in a cart, slapping it with the reins. The farmer shouted at it and made it trot off with me. This was boring. I was used to ponies that got excited about being taken out and wanted to trot and gallop. This poor, dull, old horse just wanted to dawdle.

My mother tried all sorts of things to keep me occupied and make the time go by while we were waiting for the visa that would allow me to go back to school in England. Most of them were a dead loss like the horse. She found a lady living a few villages away, who was an artist. She spoke good English and was supposed to give me drawing lessons. I didn't like her as she reminded me of Miss Wright. However, I did like to use a paint box and pencils, and I drew and painted on my own. I also wrote letters, especially to Martin, and to my geography teacher. She was interested in all I had to say and was fascinated by the different farming methods in Unterreitnau and England. When the weather got warmer, I found two freshwater lakes nearby and went swimming. I had already learnt to swim at the Goodrickes and loved the water. So it was not all bad while I lived in Unterreitnau.

The most difficult times were weekends when my father came. I was scared of him, because he was quite terrible when he was angry. When he was in a good mood it was interesting going for long walks with him. He talked about his life in China and told many fascinating stories.

There had been refugees from many different countries in Shanghai when he lived there, but there was only English law as the city was in British hands. He had to study English law books and pass exams before he could get a job there. While he was studying, he contracted malaria and nearly died, but he pulled through, and charities in the international community looked after him until he passed his exams. After that, he did quite well. He told me about some of his legal cases. There was a couple that had come to him for a divorce. As refugees, they had lost their marriage certificate. Without it, they couldn't get a divorce paper. My father had to marry them before he could give them a divorce. Then there was the Chinese tailor who made him a new shirt. My father had taken his old shirt for the tailor to use the measurements. The new shirt was identical to the old one including two patches on the elbows!

Though he told me of the hardships, there were gaps in his stories, which I pieced together later. He never mentioned that, after war broke out, the Japanese invaded China and put all the Jews into a ghetto in a run-down, disease-ridden area of Shanghai. Recently, I discovered a photo of him, in the Jewish Museum in Berlin. He was in a queue of workers seeking permission to leave the ghetto to go to his work. It must have been a frightening experience.

I quite enjoyed being with my father alone, but, sadly as soon as we got back to my mother it would develop into a row. Sometimes we would all go out for a meal in a restaurant in Lindau before he had to take the train back to Mainz, where he worked in the court. That was interesting and special. Unfortunately, nearly every time, one of the waiters would upset my father, with anti–Semitic remarks. That spoiled it as he would get very angry and shout at the waiter or call the manager. I didn't know it at the time, but my father was right. The German people were not suddenly cured of their anti–Semitism by the ending of the war. There were denazification programmes after the war, but not everyone was included, especially not out in the country.

On one occasion, we went to church for Easter, and the priest, in his sermon, said that the Jews had killed Jesus, and that was why Herr Hitler sent them 'up the chimney'. I hadn't fully understood what had been said, but my father was incensed, and shouted that he was going to report the priest and walked out. My mother and I followed. That was a terrible thing, that the priest said, but obviously, he had been brainwashed by Nazi propaganda. The Nazis had told lies about the Jews, so often and so loudly, that most of the German people believed them. We had propaganda in England too. We were told how bad Germany was, and that all Germans were bad. I found out, gradually, that there were good things in Germany too, and there were many very nice German people. During the time I lived in Unterreitnau, however, I was too suspicious to trust anybody, even my parents.

One of the interesting good things in Unterreitnau was Horse Blessing Sunday. Horses from miles around, were brought, once a year, to be blessed on Holy Horse Hill. It was a great sight. Hundreds of horses were ridden or led up the hill. Up till that day, I had seen only a few horses around Unterreitnau. I couldn't imagine where they had all come from. They were lined up on the top and, when the last horse had arrived, the service began. I didn't understand the service but I enjoyed watching the horses. They are such wonderful, noble creatures. They were of every colour and size. Some got very excited and tossed their heads, snorted and pawed the ground with their hooves. There was a lot of neighing right through the service. Then they re-formed in a procession down the hill, led by numerous church ministers, who looked quite a sight, in long black robes over their riding britches.

CHAPTER 21

Back to England

Martin was 18 in 1949 and had become eligible for British citizenship. As a British citizen, he was able to go back to England, as that was his permanent residence. But my permanent home was supposed to be in Germany. So I had to obtain a visa to get back into England. It was a very frustrating business, which took several months because my identity papers didn't constitute a proper passport. You can only get a passport if you are a citizen of a country. I was not a citizen of anywhere. I desperately wanted to belong somewhere, but not in Germany!

Finally, when my visa arrived, I was allowed to go back to England. I still couldn't get a passport because I was neither a German citizen nor a British citizen. The Nazis had taken German nationality away from all Jews, and I was not eligible for British citizenship until my eighteenth birthday. Twice, I had to go to the Passport office in Ravensberg, a city about 50 miles from Unterreitnau. The passport officers were suspicious about that miserable paper stating that I was a person of no nationality and wanted to ask me questions. But, at last, I had the visa.

My parents arranged for me to stay a couple of days in Mainz, where my father lived during the week. My mother and I could not stay in the tiny room my father rented. We stayed in a Pension, a cheap boarding house. We had one dismal dark room and it was very uncomfortable. The toilet was one floor down and there was no bathroom in the whole house. Because we needed a bath, my mother took me to the municipal bath house. Anybody could go there and pay to have a bath. We were given a towel, soap and a bath-tub full of steaming hot water. My mother told me I could have just ten minutes. I didn't take her seriously about that. I was lying relaxed in the nice, warm water when a buzzer sounded and the door flew open! A woman was standing outside with her towel and soap, waiting to go in. She was very cross and started shouting at me, until my mother came and calmed her down. I didn't think much of the public bath system!

Four years had passed since the end of the war, but there had been hardly any rebuilding in the city of Mainz. It had been flattened by incendiary bombs and the city had been in flames for a whole week. Thousands of people, hiding in their cellars, had been killed by heat and smoke. Mainz was a major centre of wine and beer making. Every house had a big cellar. During the war people used these cellars as air raid shelters and, during the firebombing, they became death traps.

The people of Mainz were, understandably, utterly demoralised. They had lost relatives and friends, and a lot of their property had been burnt. It takes a long time to recover after surviving such a shocking experience. Germany was split into four zones after the war. Unterreitnau and Mainz were both in the French zone. The Russian zone was the worst, where German people were treated very badly. The French and British zones were a little better. Only the U.S. forces treated the German population generously and people recovered more quickly in the American zone. America had not been bombed or occupied by the Nazis during the war and their response seemed less angry than that of their European allies.

What I saw of Mainz, in those few days in 1950, was very depressing. My mother took me shopping to get me some new things for going back to England. There was not very much of anything in the shops dotted around the most damaged part of the city. Some of them were only makeshift huts. As my German was not good enough to understand very much of what people were saying, I was very frightened. I imagined they were saying horrible things about me.

There were few cars at that time, and not many clear roads for them to run on. A few main roads had been cleared. They had been made out of cobblestones but now, in their place, every few yards, there were potholes. There were a few buses, and it was very bumpy to ride in them, because the roads were so bad.

Mainz was not only famous for wine – there was a huge beer brewery in the centre. It had been renovated and the brewhouse was working flat out when I was there. The *Mainzers* needed their beer because they had little else in 1949. Most of the beer was exported. The brewery had no lorries. Instead, they had floats and huge transport barrels, all pulled by horses. A full transport barrel needed four big cart-horses to pull it. The horses were very important, so they were well looked after. Their coats were sleek and shiny and they were very powerful. Once, I saw them getting their beer ration. The horseman lifted each horse's chin, in turn, and poured a bottle of beer down its throat. The horses seemed to like beer. After drinking some, they shook their heads and set off prancing, merrily.

Finally, the time came for me to catch the boat train to Hook of Holland. I wanted to do some last minute shopping. Not that I wanted anything really. I was in a state and I couldn't bear waiting ages with my parents on the platform. I dallied for so long at the shops that I almost missed the train. I had to run back to the station. I got terribly anxious and jittery. My parents thought I was frightened of the train. They didn't know what was going on for me and couldn't understand the state I was in. I was in a quandary. I didn't want to hug them to say goodbye and, at the same time, I knew that was what they wanted and expected me to do. I was in an impossible confusion. I can't even remember what I did in the end. I was overwhelmed by some vague memory of my mother saying goodbye, and then disappearing, when she brought me to England at the age of four.

For the first time, I was going on a long journey all on my own. I was only 15, and I was a bit scared, as well as very determined. My trunk had been checked in through to London and I had only a backpack with me. Again, it was a very long train journey on uncomfortable, wooden slatted seats. Again, I missed my train because the officials were suspicious of my miserable sheet instead of a passport. That meant I had to get a later boat, too.

I got anxious again on the boat when a man seemed to be following me. I shook him off by diving into the women's cabin room where he couldn't follow. I didn't have a booked bunk. I told the cabin stewardess that I was alone and a man was following me. She was very kind. She let me have a bunk, and got me a drink of water. There were long rows with high bunks, and mine was a top one of four. I was supposed to get the night boat but the delay meant I had to wait for the 5am boat. I was very tired, but grateful to have somewhere to sleep.

The cabin stewardess had to shake me to wake me up. She told me we were just docking in Harwich. I was only half-awake as I stumbled down the gangplank onto the quay. It was another long walk through customs. This time I was waved on and not stopped. Another long walk and I was on the London train. I was still so tired that I fell asleep in a corner as soon as I had heaved my backpack up onto the rack.

When I woke up, to my horror, the man who had been following me was sitting opposite me in the carriage. The compartment was full and, as there were people standing in the corridor, I guessed I would not find another seat. I craned round and checked that my backpack was still on the rack above me. The man opposite watched what I was doing. Then he leant forward towards me and whispered to me – Would I have room in my backpack to put some stockings in it, to take through the customs for him? He pulled a package out of his pocket and showed me. It was a pack of two pairs of silk stockings.

During and after the war, silk stockings were in great demand on the black market. They cost a lot of money because, even in wartime, women like the latest fashion. The man whispered that he would give me one packet to keep, if I took 20 packets in my backpack. Even though he whispered, I noticed that he had a German accent. I felt anger rising inside me. I said in as loud a voice as I dared, 'I don't want your filthy Nazi stockings!' All the people in the carriage looked at us. The man was obviously furious, but he just got up and left the carriage. A woman came in from the corridor and immediately took his seat. 'I 'eard that, Ducky', she said, 'You done right by him, an' all!' She fumbled in her handbag and offered me a sweet. 'It ain't a German one, me lovey', she said when she saw that I was looking doubtful. She smiled at me reassuringly and so I took the sweet. My anxiety dissolved away as the sweet melted in my mouth, and I smiled back at her.

Fear came back with a rush and overwhelmed me when I got out of the train at Liverpool Street Station, in London, and realised there was nobody there to meet me, as I had been delayed and come on a later boat and a later train. I didn't have a clue how to get to Peters-field, which was the nearest station to the Haltings' farm. Then I realised in panic that I had forgotten my backpack. I turned to go back into the train, and there was the kind woman holding my backpack out to me. 'Do 'ee knows where you's go'in, me lass?' she said kindly. I told her I had to go to Petersfield. She didn't know where that was, but told me there would be someone to ask and we would find out. So I walked confidently along the platform with her. There at the end of the platform, behind the barrier was my brother, Martin. Was I glad to see him! All my fear and anxiety burst into a hug that nearly crushed him. 'Reckon 'ee's awright now,' said the woman, 'I bes be on me ways.' I was too overcome to say thank you but we smiled at each other as she left. Martin had worked out what had happened when I wasn't on the right train and had waited for the next one.

I have never quite forgotten those childhood journeys. All my life I have felt a rush of anxiety whenever I have had to set off from a big railway station.

A British Citizen
at Last

CHAPTER 22

Back on the Farm

My repatriation back to Germany had lasted less than a year. When I finally got back to England, it was not so easy to settle down. Nothing was quite the same as when I left the previous summer. The world doesn't wait for you, it simply carries on and things change. Perhaps I had changed most of all. Before I went back to Germany, I was still a child even though I was 14. I trusted people and believed what they said. Then, after being made to go to Germany and all I experienced there, I felt confused and betrayed by everyone and everything. Parents are supposed to keep you safe. I certainly didn't feel safe in Germany. Nor did I feel safe in England when I came back to the farm. If the Haltings could pack me off to Germany once, they could kick me out again. I had been forced to leave Germany at age four and three lots of foster parents had sent me away. The Haltings took me back but it was never quite the same. My trust was completely shattered. I was no longer a trusting child but a very suspicious adolescent. I had learnt that making a huge effort to be good and trying to please everyone didn't work. I had become wary and all the time I was looking for signs of things going wrong. In Germany, I had become confused and angry. That was all still there, just under the surface, and I often hid away in the hay loft, or, at night when I couldn't sleep, crying with the horses in the stable. The horses accepted me just as I was. They didn't criticise or tease and didn't give me the brush off with 'Not now – I'm busy.' They had all the time in the world to nuzzle me when I needed comforting.

At Petersfield High School, all the teachers and my classmates were pleased to see me and welcomed me back. But they had moved on in the months I had been away. It was May and my class were about to take the School Certificate exams in July. I was just in time to do the mock exams with my class. It was a horrible shock for me. A friend, called Kitty, and I had always come top and second. This time I did very badly in everything, except English language and art. I even did badly in English literature, which I loved, because although I had been reading lots of books they were not the set books the class had been studying. I had some ability in art, and I had been drawing and painting in Germany, but I had missed months of school, and some of my earlier school work had got lost.

I was devastated when the headmistress, Miss Chadwick, said I would have to repeat the year. From the teachers' point of view, that would have been fine because I would still have been 16 by the time of the exams the following year. But, can you imagine being told you have to join the next class down in your school? I felt humiliated at the suggestion. I was angry as well as upset. I was lucky to have very sensible, thoughtful teachers. I think the headmistress was concerned I might go off the rails if she put me down a year. She was right; I probably would have created mayhem in the younger class. That is what angry adolescents do, if they feel they are being treated like young children.

Miss Chadwick treated me with respect. She discussed the possibilities with me and I really appreciated that. She said I could go up with my class into the sixth form but I could take only three, not four subjects, as I would have to repeat the School Certificate maths I had failed. She wanted me to study English, which I had passed, and which was her subject. I wanted to learn botany and zoology, to become a farmer!

I opted for botany, zoology, geography, literature and maths. It was a mistake. I did very well in all five subjects, but English and history would have been much more appropriate for the interests I developed later. It is difficult to protect young people from mistakes. Miss Chadwick was very wise not to try to make me take her subjects. I had to find out for myself. Parents and teachers who try to persuade adolescents to do something are quite often right but their pressurising may have the opposite effect. It is no good telling a teenager that you know better than her. If she were to believe you that would make her feel useless, so she has to stand and fight. Sensible adults give teenagers the information they need and leave them to make their own decisions.

Entries for the School Certificate exams were made on a special form. I had to put my date and place of birth on the form too. I had spoken English without an accent since elocution lessons at the Steads. Having no accent made me think I was truly English, which I wanted to be. It was a big slap in the face to have to put 'Germany' on the form as my place of birth. What was worse was that it made it possible, I think, for someone in my class to find out that I had come from Germany. A small group from a younger class started calling me a Nazi and made 'Heil Hitler!' salutes at me. My friends were shocked and couldn't believe I was German. I didn't consider myself German, as I knew I had been sent away for not being a 'true German'. I remember screaming in the playground that I couldn't be a Nazi because I wasn't even German – I was a Jew!

The teachers very quickly stopped that nasty group, and it didn't happen again. But being taunted once was such a shock that it was burnt into my memory. I had to realise that I wasn't really English. However well I spoke the language I would never be fully English, because I wasn't born in England. I was very confused. I couldn't even become British for another two years, when I would be 18. So what was I? Who was I? Not English, and certainly not German; there was only Jewish left. I had to be Jewish. The trouble was that I had no idea what it meant to be Jewish. I asked my favourite teacher, Miss Sadler, who taught geography. She didn't know, but she comforted me by explaining to me how I could become British at 18, whatever else I was or wasn't. She told me the only test was that two professional people who knew me well had to write a reference for me, to say that, in their opinion, I would make a good citizen. She said she would certainly do this for me. She told me I was a good citizen already. That made me feel quite a bit better, but I was still very confused.

By chance, a Jewish lady came to stay with the Haltings. As it was a huge farmhouse, and to make a little extra money in the hard times during and after the war, the Haltings took in lodgers. Mrs Simeon was one of these lodgers. She arrived soon after I had decided I was not German or English, but Jewish. I liked her because she had a lovely, warm smile, and was plump and cuddly. She invited me into her room, which was full of Jewish things: shiny silver and gold candlesticks, ornaments and pictures. She told me all about what they meant and read me Jewish stories. That excited me and made me feel truly Jewish. Then she told me I couldn't be Jewish because my mother was not Jewish. That was another slap in the face. I thought that, because my father was Jewish, I was at least half-Jewish. Mrs Simeon told me you had to have a Jewish mother to be Jewish at all. I thought that was crazy. She explained to me the reason was that you could be certain of your mother's identity, as there were almost always doctors or midwives as witnesses. However, nobody could prove who your father was, least of all the father himself. He had to trust that his wife didn't have a secret lover. That seemed to me even crazier.

I started having daydreams that my father might have been a king or a film star. One day he would find me and take me to Hollywood. Then I had nightmares that my father was a Nazi and I was German after all. That was horrible and confusing. When I told Mrs Simeon, she reassured me that the Nazis would not have persecuted my family unless my father was Jewish and so I was half-Jewish. The Nazis counted anybody as Jewish if they had one Jewish grandparent, and I had two. She also told me that, when I became a grown-up, I would be able to convert to Judaism, if I really wanted to. So I began to wonder if I was Jewish after all. This business about Jewishness was getting very complicated! Why couldn't everybody just be accepted as whatever they wanted to be?

Not long after, in 1951, I came to London to see the Festival of Britain with a group from school. The Festival was intended to cheer us all up, after six devastating years of war and six years of post-war austerity. There were some interesting installations and huge pieces of architecture; some were permanent like the Royal Festival Hall; others were just for show, like the Skylon, an unusual, cigar-shaped steel tower, and were dismantled after the exhibition ended, much to my regret. There were entertainments and fun rides. Everything was lit up at night and looked marvellous. It was a dazzling contrast to the blackout curtains of wartime. I had a great time that day. It was a terrific experience and, by being a part of the Festival, I felt very British.

CHAPTER 23

British Citizenship

I couldn't wait to become a British Citizen. It became my fervent dream. I would be a British citizen, a real British citizen, and then they would never send me away from England, even if I would never be fully English. Two and a half years of waiting is a very long time for an adolescent. I was impatient, but I worked hard at my school studies and I worked hard on the farm too and I did my chores like everyone else, and that was something else real British people did.

I would concentrate for up to an hour and a half on my studies and then do something active. My schoolmates used to waste whole evenings going out with boys or hanging around in groups doing nothing much at all. I found boys boring. Either they were tongue-tied with shyness, or they wanted to kiss and grope. I wanted to talk about interesting things to do with animals and science, the world and the universe, and discuss interesting storybooks I had read.

I kept studying well and I passed my Higher School Certificate exams in summer 1952 with good grades, but I didn't want to go on to university. Only one other girl in my sixth form class passed with high enough grades for university and she was planning on going to America to study there. I just wanted to work on the farm.

My father put his foot down. He said I could choose any subject I wanted but I had to go to university. I remember him saying that if times got bad again, enemies could take away everything you possessed – your money, your home and even your clothes - but they couldn't take away what you had collected in your brain. That really made an impression on me. I knew what it was like to lose everything overnight. I had experienced it twice: when I came to England on the Kindertransport and again when I was repatriated back to Germany. I decided my father was right; it would be a good idea to stuff my brain as full as I could, so that, if another disruption happened to me, I would be well equipped. Besides, I thought that going to university was what real British people did, and I would do it too.

The compromise was to apply for a degree course connected with farming. Reading University was famous for its agriculture and horticulture courses. Mrs Halting got the prospectus from Reading University and it looked exciting. The first disappointment was that I was not entitled to a grant because I was not a British citizen. I was told I couldn't be a British citizen until my 18th birthday. That I had lived in England three times as long as I was in Germany didn't count. What was there 'un-British' about me? It was as crazy as the Nazis saying that I was un-German because I was half-Jewish. I was told I would have to apply to my local authority for their support. Mrs Halting helped me write a very nice letter to the Chairman of West Sussex County Council Education Committee, applying for a grant. My father had to write a letter too. Miss Chadwick, being my headmistress, also had to send a supporting letter. The council called me up for an interview. It was the first interview I had ever had. I didn't know what to expect. I had a bath, to make quite sure that I would not smell of horses and pigs, and I dressed up in a smart woollen costume that Mrs Halting had made for me. She was very good at dressmaking.

I had to wait in a corridor with several other young people. They didn't look any more British than me. We were all a bit too nervous to talk to each other. When it was my turn, an usher called me in. There were three men sitting behind a huge shiny mahogany table. They were leafing through sheaves of paper on the desk in front of them. I stood and waited until they looked up at me. The middle one, who I presumed was the chairman of the education committee, invited me to sit down. Then he said to me, 'Miss Michaelis, you are a very pretty young woman, so I expect you will get married in a year or two. Don't you think we would be wasting our money if we sent you to university, when you, most likely, won't even finish the course after you get married?'

At first I thought he was paying me a compliment – then I realised it was a sexist insult. There was no such thing then as equal opportunities for women and sexist remarks were commonplace. I was furious. I told the chairman that I had no intention of not completing my degree, and that anyway I would only marry a man who could appreciate an educated wife. I was so enraged that I no longer cared about getting a grant. The chairman hummed and ha-ed and mumbled something. The other two then asked me some sensible questions.

Anyway, I got my grant, although it was only a partial grant. My father said he would pay the rest of what I would need. So I sent off all my documents to Reading University. The dean of the agriculture faculty invited me for an interview. He saw me on his own in an untidy, musty-smelling study. There were books and papers piled up on his desk and on the floor too. He had my application in his hands, peered at it through his glasses and then at me. He asked me why I was only 17. I was puzzled and said I was born seventeen and a half years ago. He laughed and said most people were 18 when they applied. Then he noticed that I was not a British citizen and he asked me what my nationality was. I told him Hitler had taken away my German nationality, and I didn't want it back because I only wanted to be British. He said they couldn't let me begin until I was 18 and British. Once again, I had that awful feeling that I didn't belong anywhere.

The dean must have seen I was upset and he promised that I would definitely have a place the following year. 'I'll put you down for horticulture', he said. 'No. I want to learn agriculture', I replied. He shook his head again. 'We don't take women on the agriculture course', was his reply. 'Why not?', I said. 'I have been living and working on a farm for seven years and I can do anything the boys can do.' 'I'm sure you can,' he said kindly. 'But the degree in agriculture is to prepare young men for running a farm. No farmer is going to employ a young woman as a farm manager. Do you have enough money to buy your own farm and manage it?' I had to admit that I didn't think my parents or my foster parents had enough money for that. I was very disappointed, but I could sense that the dean was not being sexist. He was actually quite thoughtful. He asked me why I didn't want to learn horticulture. I would be able to do research work afterwards. I told him that I wasn't so keen on plants because I liked animals more. He then said I should do dairying.

I came away feeling very miserable. My father said it didn't matter which subject I studied as long as I got into the university. Once I was there, he said, I would probably be able to change to another field of study. As usual, my father was right, but I didn't understand that at the time. The world seemed to be a very unfair place. After a struggle, I had got used to the idea that I was going to university, but now they wouldn't let me just because I was too young. I didn't feel too young. I had gone right through school and passed my exams. I could do things like milk a cow and drive a horse and wagon, things that not every adult can do. I was fed up with not being allowed to do things that only grown-ups are permitted to do.

CHAPTER 24

Gap Year

In 1952, most school-leavers went straight into full-time jobs because their families needed the money. The idea of a gap year to travel abroad had not been thought of. Only very rich families could pay for their adolescent offspring to go abroad.

I had expected to go straight to university from school, but as I wasn't allowed to be a British citizen till I was 18, even though I had spent 13 of my 17 years in England, I was stuck with a gap year between school and university. I went to Germany when the summer term ended, as I had done before with Martin, every school holiday. He was already at university by the time I left school. Cambridge University had allowed him to begin before he was 18, which I thought was very unfair and I told him so. His answer was that he would have to spend two years in the armed forces on national service, which I would not have to do. He thought that was even more unfair.

We argued for a long time about that. During the war, young women had voluntarily joined the forces, and they were an important part of the army, navy and air force. There was even a Women's Land Army, which came to work on the farms as the men were away fighting. The land army girls had a uniform of corduroy breeches, green shirts and jerseys. They usually looked a bit scruffy, like everyone who worked on a farm. But the Wrens, the Women's Royal Naval Service, looked very smart in blue-grey costumes as their uniform. Princess Elizabeth, the future Queen, served as a WREN in the war and that made me want to be one too. So it seemed to me unfair that, after the war, girls were not wanted any more in the forces. Women had 'kept the home fires burning' during the war. They had kept Britain functioning by working on farms, and in factories, as well as in the forces. As soon as 'the boys' came home from the war, women were told to 'go back to the kitchen'. I thought that was the most unfair of all.

My parents wanted me to stay in Germany with them for the

whole of my gap year. I didn't like the idea of that at all. There was no way I could get a job. I spoke only a few words of German. Even those few words were all higgledy–piggledy because I had deliberately learnt the grammar all wrong in my protest at being repatriated to Germany. My parents wanted to get me into a German school, to learn German properly. I was still very anti-German, and I thought going to school in Germany was like going backwards. I had had enough of school. I wanted to go back to England when my brother went back for his university term. I didn't feel safe in Germany without my brother.

I think my parents didn't want a repeat of our upsetting reunion in 1949. They did not pressurise me to stay in Germany and allowed me to go back to the Haltings' farm until I could go to university.

Working on the farm full-time made me feel very grown-up. For the first time in my life, I had a weekly pay packet, just like all Mr Halting's other farm workers. This felt much grander than getting pocket money from Mrs Halting or, since 1949, pocket money from my parents. Although I had enjoyed school, it felt good not to be going to school any more.

Farm work was tough. Working hard physically, all day, was different to doing it only on weekends and school holidays. I still had to do my household chores and I had to look after my own pony, pigs and rabbits. I was nearly always up before 6am, and was often still working out on the farm at nine, or even ten, in the evening, in the summer and autumn. We never downed tools until the job was done. There was no knocking off time and Mr Halting himself was usually the last person to finish work for the day. Once a job was started, it had to be finished. Mr Halting used to say, 'If a job is worth doing at all it is worth doing properly'.

I never complained about the work being tough on the farm but I found myself getting very tired. After a farmhouse dinner midday, with lots of potatoes with gravy and stodgy pudding with custard, I just felt like sleeping. I would have to drag myself outdoors and back to work. Once or twice, I actually found a hiding place and had a snooze. I felt very ashamed of doing that. I probably would not have got into trouble if I had been caught. I felt ashamed, because I considered it a weakness. I wanted to be big and strong, and hated it when

I had to admit something was too much for me. The farm workers would carry huge sacks of grain, or meal, or something else heavy on their backs. I couldn't even get such a sack up on my back. Even the two Halting boys, Jack and Kevin, could do that. But I had a way with animals. I made friends with them all, and they would come to me. They would sometimes be very awkward with anyone else, especially the horses and the pigs.

Although the long hours in summer made farm work tough, it was good to be outdoors. It was not such fun in winter. The animals had to be looked after, even if it was pelting with rain or sleet. The work-day was shorter because it got dark early, but I found the cold and wet very painful. I never complained because I considered feeling the cold another weakness. I wanted to be like all the others who didn't seem to mind the cold. I learnt later on that I was not really cut out to be a farmer, but in 1952 that was all I wanted to be.

The winter of 1952 was a particularly cold and foggy one. There were always foggy days in the winter. Quite often, a thick mist would come down at sunset and it would still be there next morning. Usually it would clear by 11am or midday, and then there would be three or four hours before the fog set in again. Sometimes this pattern would last for a week or more. It was dangerous to go up onto the Downs when there was fog about. Up on the hills the mist would gather into fog very quickly, and one could get caught in it. I used to ride up on horseback to round up and count the sheep. If the fog came down suddenly, the pony could stumble and, sometimes, we would get lost. Then we depended on the sheepdog to nose the way home. Patrick was a very well trained sheepdog and knew what he was doing. I couldn't see him in the fog, but he would give little grunts and yelps whenever I called him, and the pony would follow the sound. A man once turned up at the farm in the fog. He had completely lost his way on the Downs. Of course, he was invited in for a hot drink, and to warm himself by the Aga cooker.

One day during that winter, I went to London with a friend. We bought tickets to see Peter Ustinov in *The Love of Four Colonels*. We went to Lyons Corner House for lunch before the show. When we reached the theatre, there was a newspaper boy selling papers and shouting that fog was forecast. We argued about whether to go straight home or see the show. My friend was scared, and insisted on making for the train home. I went to the show. I remember it very well.

I completely forgot about the fog until I came out of the theatre at about 5pm. It was dark. Visibility was about three yards. It was not too difficult to find my way to the station and catch the train. By the time I reached Petersfield and got off the train, it had become smog. First, I had to find my bicycle and then I had to ride the four miles back to the farm. My bicycle lamp was not much help, but just a little. I crashed into the bushes several times. I was lucky no car came past the whole journey. When I reached the farm, they were all surprised to see me, as they thought I would have stayed overnight in the YMCA hostel in London where I had stayed before. But I was a proud and stubborn teenager who was not going to be beaten by smog!

In the middle of that dreadful winter, on the 23rd January 1953, I became 18 years old and I could become a British citizen at last. I gathered all my documents together beforehand, with letters of recommendation and sent them off to the Home Office. When the reply came, it contained a paper with an official stamp saying that I had been 'naturalised'. I was now a British citizen. I immediately applied for a passport. That was the best birthday present I had ever had: a big, blue and gold British Passport. I tore into tiny pieces the loathsome paper with 'Person of No Nationality' written across the top. Now I had British nationality, I didn't need it any more. I had had to use that wretched sheet for four years, instead of a passport. Now I had a spanking new, real passport!

Sadly, it so often happens that you don't think of the consequences your actions might have in the future. I wish I had kept that humiliating document. It could have been an item in an exhibition of original documents telling the story of the Holocaust and the Kindertransport, if only I had not destroyed it! By making *Person of No Nationality* the title of this book I can, at least, recall it and tell others of its significance.

CHAPTER 25

Coronation Day

The people of Harting greatly admired the royal family. King George VI was loved and respected, because he stayed in London during the war, and spent time visiting people to cheer them up when their homes had been bombed. He didn't flee London to somewhere out of danger. He had stayed with his subjects and shared the hardships and dangers with them. When he died suddenly in 1952 everyone was shocked and saddened. Their daughter, Princess Elizabeth, at age 25, was just eight years older than me. She could have been my older sister. Perhaps I imagined she was. I had three older foster sisters, and I admired all of them. I admired Queen Elizabeth most of all, as she was a WREN during the war. Now that I was a British citizen at last, I was her subject and she was my queen.

The village people liked the new queen, because she had been in uniform doing her share in the war. So the village put on a huge show to honour her coronation on June 2nd 1953. The usual summer fair became Coronation Celebration Day. Everything was bigger and better than usual, with more stalls and more ideas. For the opening of the event there was to be a procession through the village to the fair. Every family was expected to provide a float or something else that was special. It had to be in fancy dress, and there was a big prize for the best turnout.

It was my idea to create a 'Saint George and the Dragon' entry in the procession. Everyone thought it was a good idea, but expected me to organise it. I was only 18. Organising it and getting it all ready took a lot of work and imagination, but it was great fun. Mr Halting had to be Saint George on one of the Suffolk Punch horses, as no-one else would be able to control a Suffolk Punch in all the excitement.

I bought lots of knitted dishcloths and some silver spray paint to spray on them. Luvvy helped me to make a suit of armour for Mr Halting out of these silvery dishcloths. Over the suit of armour, he wore a short white tunic made out of a sheet, with a red cross painted on it. We made a magnificent helmet and shield for him out of thick cardboard, all painted silver. He also had a thick, leather belt with a silver-painted, wooden sword hanging from it. I even painted his oldest pair of shoes silver.

We chose Damsel, as she was a quiet mare. I used another sheet with a large red cross painted each side to cover Damsel, with the saddle on top of it. On the day, I got up especially early to groom Damsel until her coat shone, and I brushed and curry-combed her mane and tail with a bit of oil until they too glistened. She looked a picture.

The dragon was a magnificent beast. It took several weeks to make. I organised several local children to help paint scales made of cardboard, in all different colours, but mainly green. They had to be fixed with twine onto a wire netting body, about 25 feet long, that would sit on the backs of eight children. The head of the dragon was big enough for Luvvy and I to be inside, and to look out of the dragon's eyes to see where we were going. The dragon had huge, long jaws, rather like a crocodile. Luvvy pushed the top jaw up and down with a short broom handle, while I lifted and dropped the lower jaw with a piece of rope. Everyone in the dragon contributed to the roaring.

Colin, the village doctor's son, volunteered to be the lovely maiden whom Saint George had to rescue. He made his own costume: a long, yellow dress and a sort of dunce's hat, painted yellow to match, on top of his flowing, golden wig. He put lots of lipstick on his cheeks as well as on his lips. He was fantastic, walking coyly round the dragon! Damsel took a very poor view of the dragon, snorted louder than the dragon could roar, and refused to go anywhere near it, however hard Mr Halting tried to bring her round.

We had to take up our position at the rear of the procession because Damsel didn't like the loud 'oom-pa-pa' band that led the procession. It made her dance and snort. The crowd lining the route of the procession loved it. Damsel didn't think much of their cheering and snorted at them too.

By the time the procession got to the fairground field for the judging, the dragon was completely exhausted and laid down and died of its own accord. The onlookers cheered and howled for Saint George to rescue the maiden. But the maiden had to rescue Saint George. Damsel was showing her displeasure by rearing up and so the maiden ran up and held her bridle to calm her. She knew Colin well and calmed down. There were two reporters from the local paper. They wanted a photograph, and insisted on giving Colin a leg-up to sit sideways, behind Saint George, on the horse. It made a lovely picture. By now, Damsel was tired, and it was a job to get her to lift her head and look proud.

It was a wonderfully colourful procession, with everyone dressed up as characters on every kind of transport you could think of - from pony traps to penny-farthing bicycles. One farmer's wife, dressed as Boadicea, drove a dung cart as her chariot, pulled by two beautiful, black ponies. I think she got second prize. A Little Bo-Peep shepherded along six sheep with little coloured jackets on them. Villagers dressed as soldiers rode on tractors that had

Coronation horse

turned into tanks. Everyone waved Union Jack flags, and some children wore them as outfits. Because we had given the crowd such a wonderfully entertaining performance, our Saint George and the Dragon won first prize.

The most important thing was that everyone enjoyed themselves to the full. The dragon remained in the field and the children had fun all day playing with it. I rode home on Damsel and came back again with three ponies, so the children could have pony rides, organising them was my main job at the fair. In the evening, a hillbilly band came and there was square dancing. We carried on till well after midnight.

After the excitement of the day, I watched the coronation in the cinema four times. In those days, the cinemas had a running programme, all afternoon and evening. You could go in any time, even in the middle of a film, and leave when it came back to the point where you had come in. There were always two films, a feature film and a shorter 'supporting film'. The news came on every time between the films. So, by seeing the whole programme twice, I managed to see the coronation four times. It was just the same magic for me the fourth time as the first. She looked so poised and lovely, just like a queen should look. The procession, with the queen and her consort, the Duke of Edinburgh in the golden coach, was just like a fairy tale come true. I certainly fancied myself in that coach with a handsome prince at my side, waving serenely to the crowds. All in all, it had been a memorable gap year for me.

CHAPTER 26

Visits to Germany and France

My parents let me go back to England in 1950, on condition that I would visit them in Germany in the school holidays. I agreed to that because I so badly wanted to get back to England, where I could feel safe. It was bearable to go to Germany for school holidays, because, each time, I had a return ticket in my pocket and, most holidays, my brother came with me. I felt safer when Martin was there. It was through these school holidays that I gradually got to know my parents and Germany.

Returning refugees, like my father, had top priority for new houses. As a result, my parents were able to move to a brand new house in Mombach, a suburb of Mainz. They made the house very nice inside, but the outside was unattractive. Brunnenstube, 11, was one of about 50, all exactly the same, in a vast, new estate that had been part of a huge factory. The factory, or Waggonfabrik in German, was still active making buses. I imagined that, during the war, it had been making the wagons, or cattle trucks, that carried the Jews to the concentration camps where they were murdered. It could have been true. My brother said I was silly to think about that. But that was what came into my mind every time I had to walk past the factory.

Every holiday, things changed a little. The residents on the estate planted trees and bushes, which made their gardens look prettier and not so alike. My parents planted three silver birch trees in their back garden, and five peach trees in the front. The trees grew tall remarkably quickly and looked lovely. To insulate their house against losing heat in winter they put wooden tiles all over the outside. This also helped make the house look better, and gave it more character.

My parents had got to know, and make friends with, neighbours on their estate. There were two families, in particular, who lived nearby, and the men worked in the same court as my father in Mainz. Every holiday I was there, these two families would come for drinks or a meal; or call at our house for one thing or another. I liked the Bessfelds. Frau Bessfeld would talk about music and other interesting things. Her husband was charming and their daughter was friendly. The other family, the Lockners, I didn't like. Herr Lockner talked very loudly and I was a bit scared of him. He had a scar down his face, which was a war wound. Frau Lockner was strikingly beautiful, but was moody, and only interested in fur coats and jewellery.

The Lockners had three children and I used to play a lot with the youngest one, a scamp aged about five and nicknamed Bubi. Once, I was playing hide-and-seek with Bubi, when he ran into his house to hide. I tracked him down in his parents' bedroom, under their duvet. Then I noticed a big photograph of a handsome man in full Nazi uniform. I was shocked, and asked Bubi who that was, as it clearly was not Herr Lockner. Bubi said he would have to ask his Mum. She was just coming in as we went downstairs and so he asked her. Frau Lockner said he was her first husband, a high-ranking officer in the SS, who was killed in Russia, during the war. She went on to say that Germany should never have been defeated, and we would all be better off now, if the Nazis had won the war. I was horrified and told my father. He didn't believe me. He said I didn't understand enough German, and must have got it all wrong. I knew I had heard correctly. It was just too difficult for my father to accept that his close workmate's wife was a confirmed Nazi sympathizer.

Through living with three country families, I had come to understand country ways and love the countryside. My parents, however, were not very interested in the countryside. It was as unfamiliar to them as town life was for me. Their interests were in reading and going to lectures, discussions and theatres. I had no experience of those things. My mother was very keen on music and took me to concerts and operettas. A new world opened up for me, the world of classical music. We often went to Wiesbaden. The opera house had not been destroyed, like the one in Mainz. At the Wiesbaden *Kurhaus* there were concert halls and gardens. My first experience of opera was Mozart's *Magic Flute*, which was delightful. The magic of the music and singing made the event a real live fairy tale. I lived it with the performers. I began to associate Germany with some nice things, as well as the bad things to do with the war. And I have some fond memories.

My father was soon promoted to the rank of judge in the Mainz court. Martin and I sometimes went with him. We would sit in the public gallery. I was disappointed not to see my father in a wig, but German judges don't wear wigs. I couldn't understand very much German, so I was very quickly bored. But I liked to listen to my father telling stories about his work. Some of his cases were fascinating. Once, he kept asking me questions about horses, because he was working on a case about racehorses and I knew more about horses than he did. How did horses respond to strangers, and could the colour of their fur be dyed? How could you steal a horse or swap a horse with another one without making a noise? I was very proud to discuss these things with him.

He told me more about his life in Shanghai and the hardships there. I only learnt about the bad things when I read some books about refugee life in Shanghai much later. My father didn't want to talk about having no money, no food and being restricted to a slum area in a ghetto.

My father was in this daily queue of workers leaving the Shanghai ghetto.

Martin and I were unable to share our experiences of the war years with our parents, just as they were unable to tell us about theirs. I found out, later on, that most refugee families that found each other again after the war also found it hard to communicate. Parents wanted to protect their children from hearing shocking things, and children sensed that it would be too painful for their parents to relive the experiences. What they mostly didn't realise was that they were really protecting themselves while thinking they were protecting the others.

Each school holiday, from 1950 onwards, things became different in Germany. Rebuilding was much faster in Mainz than in British cities, because the Germans used their Marshall Aid from America more sensibly than the British did. I noticed that the German people had posh, new clothes, while the British were still mostly wearing worn and patched clothes. Mainz was in the French zone, but Wiesbaden, just across the river Rhine, was in the American zone. We often went there with our parents. We also went on boat trips on the Rhine and for walks in the Taunus Mountains overlooking the Rhine.

Martin and I would also go on our own to Wiesbaden. Everyone spoke English there – or rather, American English. Most things were cheaper and more plentiful in the American zone. The American soldiers were much friendlier than the French ones in Mainz. The U.S. soldiers would give us American chocolate bars and tickets to the American club cinema, where the films were, of course, exciting American films.

My parents didn't like us going around with soldiers, because they had heard awful stories about what the allied armies did to the German people when they defeated the German army and took over the land. Russian soldiers committed the worst atrocities because Hitler and his armies had been cruel to the Russian people earlier in the war. Hitler's forces caused a lot of misery in France and Britain too, but nothing like what they did in the USSR. America was not directly damaged by Germany, but thousands of American soldiers lost their lives fighting in Europe. By the 1950s, when I was going for school holidays in Germany, the war was long over and the soldiers could be friendly. They were probably bored and were always ready to chat with us.

Martin and I used to go for long bicycle rides through the Wispertal valley in the Taunus. After a very steep climb for about two miles out of Wiesbaden, it was about twenty miles gradual downhill through the valley to Lorch on the Rhine, and then flat along the

Rhine bank back to Mainz; perfect for a cycle trip.

One day, we cycled along the Rhine bank to Koblenz and up the Mosel valley. This was not as good, as it was gradual uphill, all the way from Koblenz to the Mosel source. It was a hot day and we were soon exhausted, so we stopped for a rest in a village. We didn't have much money so we decided to have wine instead of lunch. My father had said we must try the Mosel wine. It was delicious! We were so thirsty we drank a whole bottle between us. When we got on our bikes to press on up the valley, my legs wouldn't work and I rolled off into a ditch. It was soft and damp, and I fell asleep. Martin, my responsible, big brother endured my snoring for two hours before I woke up. We were starving, rode on to the next village in search of food, and then we came across a farmer's wife. It was difficult to understand her dialect, but we managed to communicate that we were hungry. She was willing to cook us something. Never have fried potatoes and a fried egg tasted as good as that day!

Once I went on a cycle ride on my own. I noticed signs saying 'Umleitung' so I decided to go where they were pointing. After a while, I lost the *Umleitung* signs and found myself completely lost. Then I found an *Umleitung* sign again and followed them once more until they stopped. Again, I was lost and I had to ask for directions to get home to Mainz. When I asked my mother about this elusive town, Umleitung, she laughed and told me *Umleitung* meant 'diversion'. That's what happens when you don't know a foreign language very well. It was the point at which I began to take an interest in learning German seriously. Unfortunately, though I was now ready to learn the language, after all my objections, I found it difficult to master and struggled to become fluent.

One summer holiday, for some reason, Martin was not able to go with me to Germany. Mary, my best friend at school, came with me instead. As Mary and I used to ride the ponies together on the Haltings' farm, we pretended our bikes were ponies and had a lot of fun riding across fields. We just rode where we fancied, being careful not to go on the crops. We learnt that you are not supposed to do that in Germany. There were very few, if any, public footpaths like we were used to in England. People working in the fields shouted at us, but we couldn't understand. So we made GB plates out of cardboard, like you have for your car when you go abroad, and put them on our bikes. People then just shooed us away.

While we were out cycling one day, two American soldiers in a jeep stopped, insisted on putting our bikes on the back and took us for a drive. We were treated to wine and ice cream but we were too worried about their intentions to be able to relax and enjoy ourselves. I don't think they meant any harm, they were probably just bored and having some fun. They took us home. Only we insisted that they drop us a little way off. I tried to scare them by saying my dad was the county judge and would arrest them if he saw them. I think they were amused.

One summer holiday, I visited my father's cousin, Georges, and his wife in Paris. Georges was a director of Polydor Records. I was only 16 and I had a very romantic image of Paris from novels I had been reading. I spent three wonderful days there. Georges was impressively well-dressed, compared to my father, and his wife was very elegant. They were absolutely charming and drove me round Paris to see the sights, and again after dark with everything lit up. It was breathtaking! I was very excited and I think they enjoyed my joyfulness. Perhaps they were missing their two children who were away camping. On the final evening, before I left for England, they took me to a very posh restaurant, near the top of the Eiffel Tower. That was mega-magic! The restaurant had glass walls, so that it felt as though you were floating above Paris, looking down on all the twinkling lights. I was so thrilled I couldn't sit still. Georges ordered all sorts of delicacies, most of which I had never tasted before. I can remember all the tunes the dance band played, and the sheer delight of dancing with cousin Georges to 'La Vie en Rose'! I still love going to Paris, but nothing quite compares with the magic of that first visit. That's what being 16 is all about!

Two days after I got home to the Haltings' farm, I received a surprise parcel from cousin Georges. Inside were 10 brand new gramophone records from Polydor – the old 78 inch type you don't get any more. They were my favourites that the band had played that night at the Eiffel Tower.

CHAPTER 27

Reading University

I had mixed feelings about going to university. I sensed it was going to be a major change in my life, but I had no idea just how much I would be affected. I didn't realise then that it is normal, and even to be expected, to have mixed feelings about a big change, like leaving home for university.

At 17, I was happy with the animals on the farm and I simply wanted that life to continue – forever. I didn't want to leave. But childhood has to end sometime. My father talked with me about university life, and suggested interesting opportunities and encouraged me to read books.

I read widely – history books and biographies, novels and poems. A very different world to that of the farm began to emerge in my mind. My father had a way of reading that I admired. He would 'top and tail' and browse a book by reading the introduction and conclusion and flicking through it. Within an hour, he would know more about its contents than I did after reading the whole book. I never learnt to do this as well as my father, but it was a useful skill I developed, to see if a book was really what I wanted to read. Gradually I realised that, although I would miss my foster family and the animals, I was looking forward to going to university, and to embarking on my studies.

When it was time, in October 1953, to go to Reading University I was sad to leave the ponies, pigs and rabbits that were my friends, but I knew they would be well cared for by others. I promised them I would not forget them and I would come and see them in the holidays. As always, they were very understanding and made no fuss! Mrs Halting drove me to Reading, with my cases and bags, full of all the things I would need, and helped me find my room in Wessex Hall, my hall of residence.

As a first-year fresher, I had to share a bedsitter room with another new student. My room-mate turned out to be a mousy, quiet, rather small and babyish girl with short, straight hair and a bit of a squint. I was disappointed and I am pretty sure she was too. I wanted to talk about everything. She was shy and didn't want to talk at all. We couldn't agree on whether to have the lights on or off, or to have the windows open or closed.

I soon made friends with other freshers and spent very little time in our room. I wasn't nasty to my room-mate, but I could have been more helpful. I was too busy with my own adjusting to notice how much she was struggling. I felt rather bad when she didn't come back after Christmas. But I enjoyed having the big double room to myself for the rest of the year, and inviting my new friends for pyjama parties. We would gather in one person's room in our pyjamas, drinking coffee and talking into the early hours of the morning, and then we would just fall into bed.

I was lucky enough to spend all of my three years in the delightful environs of Wessex Hall, where four large, beautiful, old houses had been converted into student rooms, and a stately old cedar tree lorded it over a beautifully manicured lawn. There were tennis courts, and a maze of little gravel paths, around flowerbeds and vegetables. The warden of Wessex Hall, Miss Wiseman – nicknamed 'The Wizz' – was very proud of her garden and its upkeep. There was a tale that one year she overspent on bulbs and seedlings for the garden, and some of the students had to lend her money for their food till the next budget!

The campus was half a mile down the road with all the university's facilities and classrooms. There was also the buttery, which was open all day for coffee and snacks. That was where I arranged to meet friends, where all the socialising and politicking went on, and where I first learnt the important skill of networking. no-one took offence if you breezed up and started a conversation. It was an extremely friendly campus, and as there were only about 1,000 students, I quickly got to know most of them, at least on sight.

Some of the laboratories, research departments and sports fields, were a mile away, in Whiteknights Park, among an enormous stretch of beautiful trees and meadows with a lake in the middle. (Sadly, some years after my time in Reading, the university built on the grounds, and many of the beautiful trees were swallowed up in concrete.) Then a couple of miles in the other direction, on the River Kennet, there were the boathouses for rowing and sailing.

I signed up for the rowing club, where I spent a lot of time over the next few years. I went from being a rookie, learning how to make a stroke without 'catching a crab', to being in the women's first eight by my second year. We had a very good eight and won several competitions. I still have two cups from that time, one for an eights race and one for a fours race. Our cups and shields were kept in a cabinet at the boat club by our proud boatman, Happy, whose friendly encouragement helped us all enjoy our rowing.

For extra training, and for the sheer pleasure of skimming over the water, I loved to go out alone in a single skiff either before, or after, the hurly-burly of a rowing session. The scent from the dew-covered meadows in the misty silence of the early morning, the twitter of birds in the reeds, and the rhythmic splashing of my oars, were peaceful and refreshing. I loved the closeness of the skiff, as if we were slipping through the water as one entity. It was rather like galloping over the Downs on my pony back at the farm. Every boat had its own name, like the ponies did, and each boat had its own little quirks.

Freshers from each hall had to produce a concert and a review at the end of the first term, which was a wonderful way of making friends. I was just a scene-shifter, as I didn't have enough stage talent to be a performer, but I didn't mind, because I could enjoy watching, and drinking up all the excitement. I often went as a guest to concerts in the other halls during my student days. They were great entertainment and I loved best of all, the satirical sketches. It felt like quite an honour to be selected for, and to perform in, *Jantaculum*, the university's annual review.

Every hall had a Christmas party and a summer dance with a cabaret. There were boat club dances too, and rag day, every February, with floats and pranks, as we collected money for charity. My father was right; there were so many opportunities. I was meeting people with different lifestyles and idea. A whole world I had never before imagined suddenly opened up: I was mixing with artists and musicians and joining in debates about politics and learning all the time.

Have you noticed that I haven't yet mentioned my studies at university? I was used to studying at school, with lots of homework squeezed in between the household and farm chores. I simply applied my study skills to dairy technology, and found that interesting enough to keep me from getting bored or slacking. I got a good enough second class degree in dairying.

I know I could have done much better if I had changed to literature, history and psychology. Those were the subjects I became interested in, much later in my life, and would have studied earlier, if I had listened to my father and my headmistress. But I had to learn for myself and, besides, it wasn't so important what I was studying as long as I got a degree. I was far too proud to contemplate failing!

The most important thing I learnt at Reading University was that there was a whole world outside the farm. The best teachers for that were the friends I made. However, I did not abandon the farm. I had unlimited energy and sometimes cycled on Saturdays, some 50 miles home to the farm, after a morning of classes and an afternoon rowing, and back again Sunday evening. And, of course, I was on horseback on the Downs on Sunday morning!

Ruth

One of the hurdles to overcome in adjusting to university life was the freedom to choose, most of the time, what to do and not do; what risks to take, and what regulations to keep. It was a problem to manage my responsibilities and have fun without jeopardising my future by getting into big trouble. If I was caught breaking rules, such as staying out late without a pass, I could be rusticated, which meant being sent home for a time. We had alcohol available, but most students, like me, wanted to spend their energy and limited money, on other

Bernard

more important things. I didn't drink more than a glass or two of wine. To have drunk more would have spoilt the enjoyment of events and discussions.

There was an ongoing feud between two of the men's halls, Wantage and St Patrick's. This provided endless high jinks. Pats' boys took the front wheels off Wantage boys' bikes and came down the hill to the campus one morning, bowling the wheels, like hoops, in front of them, to cheers from the women's halls as they passed. Wantage boys returned the compliment by capturing half a dozen Pats' boys and shaving a large 'W' in their hair. Then, when the warden of Wantage proudly proclaimed he had put a stop to all the nonsense, by making Wantage hall impregnable against anyone entering at night, there was the best gag of all. Some Pats and Wantage boys got together to hatch a plot. They collected a lorry load of sheep from one student's home farm and hoisted them on a pulley, one by one, up and through a Wantage window, one Saturday night. When the warden looked out of his window on Sunday morning, he saw a flock of sheep grazing peacefully on the quadrangle lawn of his impregnable castle! It was an unwritten and unspoken rule that all these practical jokes never caused any irreversible damage.

One especially memorable event was 'scratch fours', a knock-out rowing competition with mixed crews. The atmosphere was exuberant and high-spirited. When you are very excited, it is much harder to keep a boat balanced and row in time. Many rowers caught crabs and there was a lot of splashing. Several boats tipped over, even though only clinker boats were used for this event. I met Bernard in one of these scratch four crews. We didn't win even our first heat, but we had a great time laughing. Our boat sprung a leak and the cox tried to bale out water with a plastic cup! We rowed like mad and got back to the landing jetty just as the boat was about to sink. That was our first outing together and neither of us has forgotten it. It was not very romantic, but it was full of laughter.

Bernard invited me to a film, soon after that, called *Blackboard Jungle*. We had coffee afterwards in a café called the Palamino, where students used to hang out. We were so engrossed in discussing the film (and in each other) that we didn't notice all the other students had gone until the manager told us he was closing the café. As the Wessex Hall gate was always locked at 11pm, and I hadn't booked a late pass, we had to walk around for ages, until it was safe for me to climb the back fence, without being seen by the warden on his rounds.

After that, we went to lots of parties and played tennis together, which we both loved. Bernard doesn't look Jewish and so I had no idea he was, until we started talking about our families. He was very moved by my family history and I wanted to find out more about Judaism from him. I was thrilled that he was Jewish, but disappointed that he had not been brought up in Judaism. He knew almost as little as I did. I was even more disappointed when he explained that I could not be recognised as Jewish, unless I went through a conversion procedure, because my mother was not Jewish. After all I had been through it was upsetting to feel that the Jews, too, did not accept me as belonging.

The ending of my third year at Reading was very emotional because it meant parting from a lot of friends living in all parts of the country. We knew that we couldn't possibly all keep in touch with each other. There was also the problem that some of us were happy to have passed our exams, whereas some were depressed, as they hadn't passed and would have to re-sit some of them before they could be awarded their degrees. Those who hadn't passed went home early, and missed the finals ball and the graduation ceremony, so these events were bitter-sweet.

Some of my friends chose to stay at Reading for a fourth year, to get a Certificate in Education, and they tried to persuade me to do so, too. I had absolutely no interest in becoming a teacher at that time. I thought it would be irresponsible to take up a university place, and a grant, just to enjoy myself, when I had no intention of teaching, as some of my friends openly admitted doing. After ten years of school exams, and three more at university, I didn't want any more studying and exams – at least not for a while. Life takes its twists and turns, and things often don't turn out as you imagine.

Graduation was a very big event in the main hall on the campus. Everyone had to dress up in gowns and hats and it was all very formal. When my name was called out by the clerk, I had to go up on the stage and bow to the vice-chancellor, who shook my hand and gave me my degree scroll. The clerk had a lot of difficulty, stumbling as he read out my name in full: Ruth Emma Clara Louise Michaelis. I nearly died of embarrassment and stumbled on the steps up to the platform. The vice-chancellor said to me, comfortingly, that there would be many more stumbling blocks in life and he hoped my achievement of a degree would see me through! He was right. There were to be many more stumbling blocks in my life, and my degree served me well.

I had wanted both my parents and foster parents to be at the ceremony. My mother was able to come, but my father wasn't able to leave his court responsibilities in Germany. Mr and Mrs Halting also came but it was a very tense occasion; they had thought they would be taking me back to the farm afterwards, but I had already made a decision to go to Germany with my mother. The Haltings took it very hard, as hard as I had taken it, when my father had served the court order on them to bring me to Germany.

Bernard persuaded me to try rebuilding relationships with my family before I entered the world of work. He was able to talk me through the upset afterwards and console me, as he has been able to do throughout our lives together. He was horrified at what I told him about my foster families and the hostility between my parents and my third foster family. He found my relationship, or rather lack of one, with my parents, puzzling and disturbing.

He was an only child and very close to his parents. His family had survived the bombing raids on London during the war. His father was in the London fire service, busy putting out fires caused by bombs and doodlebugs. They had stayed in London, so as not to split up their family - unlike my own, split up in three places, in different countries.

The hardest part was saying goodbye to Bernard on the day after the graduation ceremony. As he had done his national service before starting at university, he was a year behind me, and still had his final year to do.

CHAPTER 28

Mainz University

I felt very torn, and alone, going off with just my mother. She was still very much a stranger to me. We both spoke English and German, but not really well enough to talk about anything in depth, in either language.

She had planned what she intended to be a treat for me: a fortnight's holiday on the coast of Holland at Scheveningen. She was excited, and wanted to tell me all about what we could do there, but it was difficult for us to understand each other.

I think she may have arranged the holiday in Holland as a neutral break, because she understood my mixed feelings about Germany. I was 21, but still unresolved in my feelings about being repatriated at 14, against my will. Though Martin and I had begun spending holidays in Germany, she must have been disappointed at how morose and unenthusiastic I appeared. I thought at the time that I was simply too tired to talk or take much interest in anything. I had been burning the candle both ends for the last two weeks of university. When the exams were over, there were loads of parties, and I had gone to as many as I could, and I had lost out on a lot of sleep.

When we arrived at our boarding house in Scheveningen, I didn't want any supper. It was late in the evening, and I flopped into bed with all my clothes on. This was more than just an ordinary tiredness. I just slept and slept. I was still very much a teenager in my development, and I hadn't realised this was a sign of depression. My mother must have felt very rejected. But sleep was my respite from reality, when it became more than I could cope with.

When I woke up from that sleep in Scheveningen, my mother was sitting beside my bed. I jumped up and said I was hungry. She had obviously been very worried and she looked very relieved to see me up and about. She told me she had been listening every hour or so, to see if I was still breathing, and feeling my forehead, to see if I had a fever.

She was afraid I had taken an overdose of sleeping pills. I told her I had never taken sleeping pills in my life as I always slept very well.

I was cross. I could see it was only just morning from the sun streaming in through the window, so there seemed no need for her to make a fuss. I was flabbergasted when she told me that I had actually slept through a whole day, as well as two nights! I had never done that in my life before, and it has never happened to me again.

After a big breakfast, I was in a much better mood. Obviously, the deep sleep had done me good and lifted my depression. I was then able to cope with taking in the new surroundings and made the effort to talk with my mother. The fortnight was very enjoyable. Our boarding house was near a wonderful long beach, of some two kilometres, and the weather was good for swimming and boating. As it was windy on that coast, instead of deckchairs there were basket chairs. You turned them, with their backs to the wind, to protect yourself. There were donkeys and other amusements on the beach, and evening entertainments.

My mother took me to an art gallery that made a big impression on me. I had never seen a rotunda before, a building circular in shape. I found myself looking outwards from the centre at a vast, panoramic, circular painting, a seascape in oils, a massive 14 metres high and 120 metres wide. What impressed me about Mesdag's painting was that the mood of the sea changed, as you walked round, from brightly sunny and glistening blue, through dull grey-greens to dark and choppy, into a violent storm with lightening and lashings of rain. Then the storm died down, gradually, into sunshine again, and you could keep on going round. The various boats and ships, and people on the beach, made it very realistic.

Years later, my husband and I happened to go to a conference in The Hague and we drove to Scheveningen beach nearby, to look for the Mesdag Rotunda. We walked the length of the beach, searching for it. Eventually we found the rotunda, about five miles away, in the town centre of Scheveningen. That brought home to me how memory gets condensed. I began to understand what my father had told me about the unreliability of witnesses in court, even when they thought they were genuinely telling the truth as they knew it.

My father joined us for the last two days of the fortnight, and then things started to go wrong. I didn't understand enough German to grasp why my parents were getting angry and upset. I immediately thought it was my fault, as always. I still hadn't realised that my parents were having as much difficulty getting their own relationship back together, after eight years separation due to the war, as I had relating with them. I was bewildered and panicky. I said I had better go back to England. That made things worse! The upshot was that my mother decided to go back to Mainz and my father stayed for the week with me in The Hague.

As soon as my mother had left, my father calmed down and we had a very good week together. The Hague was fascinating. My father had to do some work, attending a conference and looking up documents in the archives of the Peace Palace. So, some of the time, I went around town alone, but I would meet him at restaurants, and we went to theatres and museums together. There was a wonderful dinner dance as part of the conference, in a restaurant with tables around a lake. My father didn't dance, so I danced with some of the conference participants. One was a very handsome Indian prince in a gorgeous traditional costume but, sadly, we couldn't talk very much; he knew very little English and I did not even know what language he was speaking.

Once we got to Mainz, after the week was over, difficulties set in again. I wanted to get a job, and earn my own money and not depend on pocket money from my parents. I didn't know enough German for most jobs, but I wanted to be a waitress, so I could get to know both German and German people, by serving and observing them, without getting too involved or having to speak a lot. My father wouldn't hear of it. 'A Landgerichtsdirector's daughter can't be a lowly Verkeuferin', he said. A Landgerichtsdirector is one stage below a judge in the German legal system, and a Verkeuferin is a person who sells something. My father was a bit of an intellectual snob, but he also wanted me to do something that had prospects. I flew into a rage at his denigration of sales people. My mother tried to broker the peace, by getting me a job in a fashion boutique. That didn't satisfy my father either. I got even angrier, and said I didn't want to just bum around. It ended up with my father arranging a place for me at Mainz University. In the meantime, I put out some advertisements to attract private pupils who wanted English coaching.

I found two private pupils. One was a boy of 12, who was soon to move to England where his father had a job. The boy's parents wanted him to be able to settle quickly into an English school, so I chatted with him about what schools were like in England. His parents were lovely and hospitable, and invited me to have supper with them after lessons. My other pupil was a university student writing her dissertation on English Literature in English. She wanted me to help her with the finer nuances of the English language. We met in her flat and chatted over coffee. This was the enjoyable part of my attempt to come to terms with Germany. It kept me going. It was something to look forward to, twice a week. I earned a little money, which helped my self-esteem and prevented my confidence from hitting rock bottom, as Mainz University was a disaster for me.

My father had helped me choose some courses, in German and English literature, out of a large, complicated prospectus. I was looking forward to studying literature. I went eagerly to lectures at first. They were huge classes of a hundred or more students, in tiered rows of seats. I felt completely over-awed. This was nothing like Reading University, where the first year classes were almost as big for some lectures, but then there were smaller classes and tutorials. I made friends easily at Reading. At Mainz University, I felt isolated from the start. The students piled into the lecture hall in groups of friends, but no-one noticed me. I was too ashamed of my minimal German to attempt starting a conversation. I knew far too little German to follow the lectures on German Literature. I got the relevant books from the library, but I couldn't read them, so I gave up going to the lectures. I went to the English Literature lectures for a while longer. The professor lectured in German at a level which I couldn't understand at all, and, when he read extracts from books, I found his English almost as hard to understand. His heavy accent was ugly and off-putting, so I gave up on those lectures too.

I went to a compulsory class for all students whose first language was not German. This could have been a home base where I might have made friends, but, sadly, it too was a disaster for me. I was the only female joining an established group of about a dozen students, mainly from Arab countries. The teacher, Frau Poeschmann, was a feisty, domineering woman, whom the male students obviously liked, and she liked them.

I was very nervous, especially as I could not understand the banter going on between the students and Frau Poeschmann and among each other. I tried to respond when Frau Poeschmann asked me questions, but the others laughed at my attempts, and it developed into what felt like deliberately nasty teasing to me. I held my own, until I began to realise that there was an anti-Semitic flavour to the teasing, and that Frau Poeschmann was even encouraging them and egging them on. I promptly left the room, never to return, after saying (in English, of course), 'I am not wasting my time with you, Frau Hitler, and your Nazi troupe.' I expected trouble, but none came.

So I abandoned all my classes. I did not dare tell my parents. I should have told them, but I felt too ashamed. Even though I wrote long letters to Bernard, I didn't mention anything about Frau Poeschmann and her anti-Semitic group.

Then I happened to be eating lunch in the university refectory, a vast impersonal hall, nothing like the cosy, friendly Reading buttery, when a student asked, in English, if I minded if he sat at my table. My eyes lit up at hearing English but even that did not come to anything. He came from the American south and spoke with a slow monotonous drawl. I found it impossibly irritating; I wanted to finish his sentences for him. It was a shame, because he was a really nice guy. But he did introduce me to his American literature classes.

I sneaked into the back row with him. It was a relatively small class of about 30 students. Professor Galinkski was an excellent lecturer and I was fascinated and started putting up my hand and asking questions. He accepted me as one of his class. He lectured in English, and with much better pronunciation than that of the German professor of English Literature. He made the books he chose to talk about so interesting that I spent most of my time between his classes reading Huckleberry Finn and other classic works by great American writers, such as Poe, Melville and Whitman.

Then, suddenly, the bombshell came! My father received a letter from Mainz University to say that, unless he could explain why his daughter had attended no lectures for the last three months, she would be taken off the register of students. I had not been aware of any attendance records being kept, so I was as surprised as my parents, who had seen me go off every morning and come back in the late afternoon. My answers to their questions about how I was doing at university had been minimal. They had seen me bringing back books to read at home, and had presumed all was well. Of course, I then told them everything. My father was furious that I had not told them before. He didn't realise how hard it was for me to tell them about something I experienced as shameful and demeaning.

My father, Robert Michaelis

I explained that I had focused on Professor Galinkski's American Literature lectures. My father hit the roof! He said it was well known that Galinkski was a former Nazi officer who had used his teaching skills before the war to indoctrinate students into Nazi ideology. He had been banned from teaching after the war. My father thought that might have accounted for the relatively small size of his class, and he reckoned that Galinkski hadn't noticed I wasn't on his register, because he probably didn't have a register.

I was very surprised to hear all this. How was I to know that he had a Nazi history? I said I had found him to be an inspiring teacher and there had been no Nazi content to his lectures. My father was still angry, and I began to feel angry, too. I told him about Frau Poeschmann and her anti-Semitic group. He didn't believe me. Frau Poeschmann had a very good reputation for helping foreign students. But she certainly hadn't helped me. My father wrote to the director of Mainz University, to complain about Herr Galinkski – he wasn't even supposed to use the title of 'professor'. I wrote to the director and complained about Frau Poeschmann's class. I don't know if the complaints were taken up, because I went back to England before there was any response.

I could see it wasn't going to work staying in Germany. I had not got any further with learning German; my resistance had been increased by all the failures. Without a working knowledge of German, I could neither take any courses, nor do any kind of job. My parents wanted to get a private tutor to teach me German, but I had had enough and wanted out. I had made no real friends, and how could I trust anyone in Germany, when the one person I really liked in Mainz University turned out to be a former Nazi officer and a cheat?

I didn't want to let my two pupils down. I stayed a few more weeks for their benefit. I had saved enough money from my earnings to be able to buy my ticket to London. I was too proud and too angry to accept anything from my parents. Sadly, my good intention of spending some time getting to know them and Germany better had turned sour.

Bernard met me off the boat train in London. He smuggled me into Pats' Hall, back at Reading University. I stayed a few nights in the room of a student, who had gone home early, for some reason. It was a very daring thing for a young woman to stay illegally in a men's hall. Bernard would have been rusticated, if I had been caught. That was half the pleasure. Bernard was very understanding. We had a few days together, which helped me to recover a bit from the catalogue of failures and unpleasantness I had just experienced in Germany. I really enjoyed sneaking in to some of his lectures on English literature and psychology. It was so comforting to be back in Reading University where everyone was friendly and I didn't have to worry if any of them had Nazi histories.

Work Weddings and Children

CHAPTER 29

Biscuits

I spent a few lovely days at Reading, but I had practically no money and needed to get a job as soon as possible. I had decided to try to get a job in London rather than Reading, because that was where Bernard's parents lived, and where he would go after his graduation. I was unaware that Bernard had asked his parents to make sure I was all right. When they invited me to come to their flat, I was too shy to do so. My confidence had been shattered by my experiences in Mainz University and the rows with my parents. Nonetheless, I went to London with high hopes, to a little furnished room in Maida Vale that Bernard's friends had rented for me, as well as lending me the deposit. There were 72 stairs (I counted them) up to a little room in the garret of a large, old, Victorian house, with space only for a bed, a small wardrobe, chest of drawers, tiny basin and a single gas ring. But it was clean, and the skylight let in the sun, which made it bright and cheerful. That was to be my home, until Bernard and I married just over a year later.

Like most teenagers, I had built an idealistic fantasy of what it was going to be like to be an adult and independent, with no-one telling me what to do any more. When it came to getting a job and actually being independent, I found it was not at all what I had imagined. It was hard and frustrating and, as I was both proud and stubborn, I was ill-equipped to cope. Firstly, I discovered very quickly that my Reading University dairy technology degree was not going to lead me to doing work that would interest me. I could become head of a dairy depot laboratory, and that sounded very grand. But it actually meant working very unsociable hours, from five till nine in the morning, and then again in the evening. At the age of 22, I wanted some social life and I had never been able to stand the pungent smell of the chemicals used for the Gerber fat test on milk in the Reading University laboratory. In the dairy depot, it would be part of the daily routine. Ugh!

The one other job I could apply for was with the Milk Marketing Board. I would be kitted out with a little van, and equipment, to visit the farmers whose milk was not up to standard, and advise them how to improve the quality. Much as I would have liked my own little van and visiting farms, I knew very well that I could not tell farmers how to do their job! Anyway, I wanted a job in London.

What could I do? I scoured the adverts in the evening papers for possible jobs and wrote letters with my CV to all those that I thought might be a remote possibility – about 30 letters in all. One by one, answers came back negative. The job was filled, or I didn't have the right qualification; one said I was over-qualified! I had spent my remaining money on stamps. I didn't even have enough to ring Bernard in Reading and I could only leave him a message. I was hungry and lonely and at the lowest ebb I had ever been in my life. My little store of bread and margarine had almost run out, and a painful boil developed in my ear. I would have been out on the street sleeping rough if it had not been for Bernard's friends, who had found the bedsitter for me and loaned the rent. I couldn't turn to my parents, they were far away in Germany, nor did I feel I could ask the Haltings for help, as my relations with them had become strained, by my going to Germany, after my course at Reading University ended. I felt as though I had messed up absolutely everything in my life. But there was still Bernard – as long as I didn't mess up that relationship too!

Desperate for the sound of another human voice, I walked to the nearest telephone box and dialled numbers at random, one after the other. The person at the other end would say 'hello' but then, because I had put no money in, they would be cut off. I got a little comfort from hearing human voices answering the phone. No-one had told me about the Samaritans, otherwise I would certainly have rung them. One of the numbers I rang was that of Bernard's parents. In fact, I rang them several times. I think they had the calls traced to the Maida Vale call box, suspected it might be me and told Bernard. He couldn't ring me because I had no phone, so he came up to London, to my little room. Was I pleased to see him! He took me straight home to his parents, who put a poultice on my ear and gave me chicken soup, which was out of this world – it is not called Jewish penicillin for nothing!

Next day, Bernard took me back to my room and we read my post together. There was a letter from Scribbans-Kemp, a biscuit firm. It offered me a job as a research and development officer. I was to start straight away, if I was available. It was hard to believe that my world could change so suddenly! There is a saying, 'It's always darkest just before dawn'. Bernard lent me some more money to tide me over and went back to Reading, pleased to leave me cheerful and looking forward to my new job. Although cheerful on the outside, I was full of anxiety and trepidation inside.

It was a simple journey to the biscuit factory from my bedsitter, on the number 16 bus. Someone showed me the way to the research block. In my anxiety, I was very early, and it wasn't even open. One of the secretaries opened up and showed me where to wait. I liked her straight away and, in fact, all the 15 people in that work group were very friendly. I soon felt at home with them, and my fears evaporated.

My main job involved conducting various complicated tests on packaging materials and packets to determine their ability to keep their contents fresh. I also translated German articles about biscuits and packaging, and helped colleagues with their work.

As usual, I got into trouble. We had morning and afternoon breaks for coffee and biscuits, but I had not noticed that there were different tables for graduates and non-graduates. I had, by accident, sat down at a bare table, designated for the non-graduates, for a chat, when I should have gone to one with a tablecloth, for graduates only. When told to move I protested at how silly I thought that was. Later, the director called me in to his office. He explained to me that I had upset several people by my protests. He agreed that the division was undesirable, but he said that it was what most staff wanted and, therefore, as the newcomer, I should fit in.

I felt very chastened, because he had been so understanding about it all. He was a kind and thoughtful man. The next time he called me into his office, he said it had been brought to his notice that I was eating more biscuits at break times than was good for me, and would it help if he got me an advance on my monthly salary? He was right. To make my money last for a month of bus fares, I had not been buying food. The advance enabled me to treat myself to fish and chips, after work!

WORK, WEDDINGS AND CHILDREN

One of my jobs was to help one of the other workers, in a photographic darkroom. In the semi-dark of a red light bulb, I would take out reels of photographic film and develop them in trays of chemicals, to produce negatives. The negative films were hung up to dry and later used to print positive pictures onto matt, or onto glossy, photographic paper. I can't remember what the films were all about, only that I was fascinated by the procedure. After I had become quite skilled at the procedure, I asked the director if I could process some films of my own, after work, and he agreed. In the darkroom, all by myself, I was deeply engrossed and lost all track of time. When I had finished and had cleared up, I realised it was 10pm. The door of the block had been locked. In the darkroom with the door shut, I had not heard the caretaker come and lock it. I tried a few windows, but it didn't seem possible to get out. I resigned myself to spending the night in the block and found a place in a corner to curl up in a bed of all the graduate white coats and non-graduate brown coats. Fortunately, the night watchman had seen lights as I turned them on and off and came into the block. He didn't believe my story, which was the truth, even when I showed him the photos I had made. He phoned the police and, soon enough, two police officers arrived. They phoned the director to ask him if he would vouch for me, which he did. I was then taken to my bedsitter in a police car. The director very kindly told no-one. If he had, I would have been endlessly teased. Even Bernard thought it was hilarious when I told him.

Later, I was given the job of arranging tasting tests. I was given several blocks of similar chocolate, or several bags of the same kind of biscuit, and I had to lay out two small pieces of each kind, on different paper plates, labelled A and B. Sometimes the other workers in my block and sometimes a group that was brought in from the factory had to say whether they preferred A or B, or found them the same. I had to make tables of the results. I became curious as to what it was all about. One time, when I had been sent over to the factory, to bring a group of workers over to the research block, I noticed some large crates labelled 'frozen egg from China'. A corner of one crate was broken. I was able to peel it back and look inside. It was indeed frozen, and had green and black streaks in it! I was horrified. Then I realised what the tasting tests were about: how far could you replace the ingredients of biscuits and chocolate with cheaper stuff without the taste giving it away? After that, I started wondering whether I really wanted to be in that job. They were such a nice group of people to work with that I had not really given a thought till then as to the purpose of what I was doing. But Bernard and I had become engaged. I was up to my eyes with preparations for our wedding. I was not in a frame of mind to question the value of what I was being asked to do.

CHAPTER 30

Weddings and Honeymoons

A s a teenager, I was a closet romantic. Whenever I was sitting on the bus to school, or lying in bed before I fell asleep, I would indulge in a world of fantasy. Handsome, young men and horses figured strongly. I read novels and became addicted to love stories. *Pride and Prejudice* and *A Town Like Alice* were two of my favourites. Gone with the Wind was another. I re-read my favourite romantic passages many times, and mooned over the love scenes. I imagined myself into the stories, usually with a handsome man riding up on a beautiful horse and vowing his unending love for me. So it is very disappointing that neither Bernard, nor I, can remember his proposing marriage to me. And Bernard was not at all interested in horses.

We had spent much of our time as students going to parties and social events, and for walks. We had discussed literature, psychology and philosophy. I think Bernard and I had soon begun behaving like an engaged couple. When he graduated and came back to London, we began to tell everyone we were having an engagement party. Ac-

At our engagement party at Bernard's parents' flat

tually, we ended up having three engagement parties. The first one was organised for us by Bernard's best friends from schooldays, Horace and Louis, with whom we played tennis regularly. All our joint friends came to that one. The second party was in Bernard's parents' flat, for all his family to meet me. And the third one was at my parent's house in Germany.

Bernard started working in a social security office to earn some money while he was thinking about what to do next. He didn't want to take unpaid time off, but I had been over six months at the biscuit firm and could take two weeks paid leave. I went to my parents in Germany before Christmas, and we planned that Bernard would come for the Christmas period. Unfortunately, he suddenly developed chickenpox and couldn't come. It was strange having an engagement party at my parents' house without him.

To my distress, my parents were not at all happy about our getting engaged. They disapproved of my marrying a Jew, and tried to make me promise to remain Christian. I argued that my father had converted and therefore, surely, I could do the same. I assumed he had converted so he could marry my mother, who wasn't Jewish. I didn't know that he hadn't converted till several years later, and it wasn't out of conviction, or for love of my mother, as much as to do with protecting the family from the Nazis.

He got very angry at my attitude, as did my mother. Martin made things worse, by arguing that Christianity was a more up-to-date development from Judaism, and I would be going back to the Middle Ages if I converted. I retorted, furiously, that it was Christians who were still in the Middle Ages, blaming Jews for killing Jesus and spreading anti-Semitism – and, I argued, weren't the Nazis Christians too? That set off a humdinger of a row.

Back in London, Bernard and I looked at what we needed to do and decided that, as he wanted to concentrate on studying, the best thing would be to get married, before he started in October 1958. Having just got through three engagement parties, friends were surprised when we announced our intention to get married straight away. But it didn't happen straight away. We had not reckoned on so many problems. We had not realised how long it would take me to fulfil the requirements for conversion to Judaism.

The Haltings were delighted at our engagement, and offered to host a wedding reception for us at the farm. Bernard thought this would not be right, and that my parents should come first. So I took another couple of days of my holiday allowance, and went for an extended weekend to my parents, where I got an angry reception.

My parents had not taken our engagement seriously. Bernard was the first boyfriend I had told them about and they hadn't expected our relationship to last. They were furious that we were 'in such a hurry' to get married, and took great exception to my expecting them to arrange a wedding for us. When they realised that I had already started preparing for conversion to Judaism, that was the last straw as far as they were concerned! My father said he wanted to have nothing to do with the wedding.

I was so angry and upset that I phoned Bernard, and told him I wanted to get back to the Haltings, and take up their offer. Bernard was against doing that. He said it would make things even worse with my parents. I disagreed, but he won me round (as he nearly always did, when we disagreed) by saying, 'Hey, it's my wedding too!' He was absolutely right to stop me completely destroying ties with my parents. It was not until many years later that I began to understand what our wedding represented, to them. They had not told me, then, that my father's mother, Clara, and my mother's mother, Emma, had been totally against their marriage, and had refused to have anything to do with it. My parents had arranged their own wedding, in a registry office, and had a lunch party afterwards, in a rotating restaurant, high up in the Berlin TV Tower with panoramic views of the city. My father said to my mother, so the story goes, 'Why do you want parents here, when I have laid the whole of Berlin at your feet?' He always had a good sense of humour. Our wedding must have stirred up the painful past. My parents had shut away the hurt and disappointment to the back of their minds. Oma Emma hadn't wanted her daughter to marry my father in 1932 because of the risks of being involved with Jews. Oma Clara had wanted my father to marry a Jewess. Later, when I studied psychology, I came to understand how people are often trapped in repeating a painful situation that they could not bear to think about at the time. My parents, sadly, repeated the role their parents took in their wedding by taking the same stance towards our wedding.

My father's conversion to Christianity in 1938 had made it easier for Martin and me to be raised as Christians in England. That goes some way towards explaining why my parents were so furious that I converted to Judaism before our wedding. Perhaps they hoped I never would, or that I would persuade my husband to convert, as my mother had persuaded my father. Sadly, not even my brother understood that my identity was already Jewish, and the official conversion meant little to me, as Bernard and I intended to study Judaism together, anyway.

My mother always tried to be the peacemaker in family rows. She got my father to agree to buy a wedding dress for me, in Mainz, and pay for a honeymoon holiday as our wedding present. But they were not willing to pay anything towards the wedding. Part of their bargain was that I had to agree to go away for a weekend to a Christian retreat with my mother, which I did. It was a very restful weekend, though my German was not yet good enough for me to understand very much. Why my father did not come too was a mystery to me, as he was so upset about my not valuing Christianity. I now know enough psychology to understand that people mostly do not have the ability to behave logically and rationally when their passionate feelings are involved. Then, I could only see my parents' irrational behaviour, without realising that my own behaviour must have seemed irrational to them.

Bernard and I had to set about organising our own wedding. Bernard's parents wanted us to have a proper wedding, with all the trimmings. They thought it outrageous that my parents were refusing to pay anything. They wanted to contribute but did not have the money. They had spent a lot on the engagement party that they had organised. They wanted us to wait a year, or two, so that they could save up to help us. We didn't want to wait. The next problem was to find a venue that our meagre savings could afford. The two secretaries in my workplace office took me under their wing. The elder one was Jewish, and very understanding. She got her father to give me extra coaching in Judaism, and she found a suitable hall with a Jewish caterer, in the East End, where most things were cheaper than in other parts of London. I still had to borrow some money. I was surprised how helpful my bank manager was. He let me borrow the sum we needed. Bernard couldn't get a loan, because his job was only temporary. When I expressed my anxiety about borrowing so much money, Bernard's parents said it was usual practice with Jewish weddings to give money gifts, rather than actual presents, and we would get most of it back. Sadly, they hadn't realised that all the guests were as hard up as we were, and we did not get very much back. We were young and enthusiastic, and did not let that worry us.

There was such a lot to do, arranging costumes, flowers, taxis and catering menus. Bernard didn't want a stag night and hen nights had not been invented, so that saved some money. The parents of the three bridesmaids and pageboy helpfully organised, and paid for, their own outfits, which were gorgeous. My mother bought my wedding dress. I remember only one conflict with Bernard's family, when one of his relatives said, 'You can't have a proper Jewish wedding without smoked salmon', and I suggested she might prefer to go fishing in Scotland rather than come to our wedding. I don't know how Bernard managed to smooth that one over, but he did. I had never organised a wedding before, and I got increasingly jumpy about it. By the time we organised our daughter's wedding in 1990, I knew the ropes!

There are usually last minute hitches at any wedding that make everyone frantic. It came as a great shock to us when my parents decided, at the last minute, that they would not come and, although my brother and his fiancée decided they would attend, my father had forbidden Martin to 'give me away'. I was devastated. I was particularly disappointed that Martin was not prepared to lead me down the aisle, just because my father had said he shouldn't. Up to that point, I had always relied on Martin to be there for me and on my side. I felt incredibly betrayed.

Bernard did his best to make up for it. His Uncle Morry, who lived next door to the synagogue, was willing to lead me down the aisle, and invited the bridal party to gather in his flat. His wife, Aunty Josie, was the kingpin of Bernard's family, and sorted out all such major problems. At least the conversion service, which we held shortly before the wedding and had feared might cause problems, went very smoothly, and I was, at last, fully Jewish.

The big day finally came. We were married in August 1958. I left my little garret room for the last time and took my few possessions, already packed in two suitcases, down to a double room in the same house, which was to become our first wedded home. I then went to Aunty Josie's flat, where my wedding dress was already waiting, and had breakfast with her and Uncle Morry. I had little appetite; I was very nervous and still very upset about my brother. I had strange feelings of wanting to run out and disappear – as I had done many times previously when I started feeling I had too much to cope with.

My wedding dress was loose – I had lost weight with all the frantic preparations and grappling with the problems, and I didn't like the look of myself in the mirror. Auntie Josie said I looked lovely as a picture and I felt somewhat relieved. Bernard's two cousins arrived with the three bridesmaids and pageboy, dressed in frilly white and blue silk. They looked gorgeous.

As the children looked at me with shining eyes, I began to feel the excitement of the occasion and my panic attack subsided. It was not long before Martin, and his fiancée, Maria, arrived with their suitcase, ready to change into their wedding clothes. Then the photographer, who was another cousin of Bernard's, took some photos: as did Martin, who was working professionally as a photographer. Aunty Josie had made sandwiches for lunch and served cups of tea. Her sandwiches tasted delicious, even though I wasn't hungry, and some of them were smoked salmon – so I didn't get married without smoked salmon after all!

When the time came for the ceremony, we all walked in a procession to the synagogue. Aunty Josie went on ahead to stand under the *chuppah* with Bernard and his parents. The chuppah is a canopy put up over four poles on the *bimah*, a raised platform where the service is read. It symbolises the future home of the couple. The choir sang my favourite psalm, 23, as Uncle Morry led me up the aisle to my place beside Bernard, under the chuppah. Bernard's parents stood on one side of the chuppah and Uncle Morry and Aunty Josie were on the other side, where my parents would have been if they had come. The rabbi read the wedding service. We made our vows and exchanged rings. Then Bernard had to stamp with his foot on a glass wrapped in a cloth to break it. With the sound of the glass shattering, the congregation all shouted *mazel tov*! We could then kiss as man and wife. That was quite a moment! We then had to sign the register and the rabbi gave us our ketubah, a Jewish wedding certificate, handwritten in special script, on a patterned scroll.

Finally, the wedding march was played, as Bernard led me back up the aisle and out of the synagogue. I was surprised to see that the real world still existed outside the synagogue! We had a few photos taken and then got into the taxi, which was all decked out with white ribbons and waiting outside, ready to drive us off to the reception. It was a big enough taxi to take Bernard and me, Maria, the three little bridesmaids and the pageboy. Suddenly, I had a bright idea. I wanted to go through Hyde Park, which was only a few hundred yards from the synagogue, and wave to all the people, like the Queen did. The taxi driver thought this was a great idea; he drove round Hyde Park and thereabouts. The bridesmaids and the pageboy also thought it was a grand idea, and we all waved to the people, who waved back and cheered.

As I had not even been to a wedding reception before, let alone arrange a wedding, it had not occurred to me that the bride and groom are expected to arrive at the reception first so that they can receive their guests. We arrived last! Bernard's parents, Aunty Josie and Uncle Morry received the guests without us and, by the time we arrived, the guests had polished off the canapés and sandwiches, and had already sat down at the dinner tables. They thought we had gone off on our honeymoon! The dinner and speeches went very well, as did the dancing afterwards. Everybody clearly enjoyed themselves.

But we hadn't thought about how we would leave the restaurant. My boss, who had come to the wedding, offered to take us to our digs, and told me not to come to work the next day, until the afternoon. So, we had our wedding breakfast the next day, at lunchtime, in a little pub on the corner of Maida Vale and Randolph Avenue.

A week later, we set off for our honeymoon in an Italian resort. On the way to Italy, we spent a couple of days with my parents, in the Taunus Mountains. Once we were actually married, my parents accepted Bernard as my husband and their son-in-law. They welcomed him into the family and got to like him very much. Their acceptance came as a complete turnaround and seemed weird to me at first, but I appreciated that they were not vindictive.

And then my parents paid for the honeymoon in Italy, which they chose for us. It was a bit of a sore point, as we had wanted to go to

Ibiza. We went by train and arrived very tired in the evening at our resort, Milano Marittima, on the Adriatic. There were miles of golden sand and lovely blue sea but it was flat and treeless, and not very inspiring. However, we were aware that we had no money of our own for a holiday. We would not have had a honeymoon at all if my parents had not given it to us. Milano Marittima was much better than no honeymoon at all.

Our hotel turned out to be a small guesthouse and a young woman was occupying our room. The tour company thought she was our daughter because her surname, Bergfeld, was similar to Barnett! As Fraulein Bergfeld would not budge, we were allocated a new hotel. This time it was a big hotel. We had a wonderful large penthouse suite right at the top on the fifteenth floor, with a fabulous view. So we did very well in the end.

After that, we had a very enjoyable two weeks. One night, there was an almighty thunderstorm. I was frightened that our penthouse in the sky could be struck by lightening and I insisted on finding out if there was a lightening conductor. Bernard found someone who was on night duty who, unfortunately, could not speak English. It took us a long time, through drawing pictures and making signs with our hands, to communicate what we wanted, but we got there in the end. The night watchman made a telephone call, I imagine to the manager, and told us 'biga sticka ona roofa'. After that, we went back to our room and enjoyed watching the lightening flashes until the storm had passed away. I felt safe then and was sure that I had a husband who could solve any problem!

After our two weeks honeymoon, we set off for Bavaria for my brother's wedding. His fiancée, Maria, was one of five daughters of a farmer in a village, deep in a very beautiful part of the countryside. We were made very welcome as soon as we arrived and stayed the night in one of the farmhouses.

Everybody in the village was at least a distant relative of everyone else, and so it was traditional for the whole village to attend every wedding. Those with big farmhouses hosted any guests from outside. The village was very similar to Unterreitnau, where I stayed with my mother when I was repatriated to Germany in 1949. It brought back a whole lot of uncomfortable memories, but I had Bernard with me to tell me everything was going to be all right. I could not help wondering what the adults had been doing during the war. Had they known what Hitler was doing to the Jews? Had they approved or even taken part in it? Bernard persuaded me to stop thinking about these things, or else it would spoil Martin's wedding.

Next morning, we had a leisurely breakfast with lots of people popping in and out, already dressed up in their wedding finery. As they all knew each other, like one huge family, they were used to going in and out of each other's homes. Some time, mid-morning, everyone assembled in the village centre and formed into a procession. Children and single people headed the procession, in front of the bride and groom. As we were the most recently married, we followed directly behind them. After us, came all the married couples, and then the widows and widowers last. We then walked through the village, up to the church, excited and joyful.

Martin had remained Christian, ever since we were baptised, just after Kristallnacht. Maria's family were all Christians. It was a very different wedding service to ours; there was no chuppah, or glass to be broken, but the church was as beautifully decorated with flowers as our synagogue had been. It was a much longer service than ours, because the priest gave a long sermon. Neither of us could understand a word; not only did the priest speak German, but an impossible Schwebisch dialect. There was no register to sign, as, in Germany, state and religious marriage are kept separate. Martin and Maria had had a civil wedding, a month previously, in fact just before our wedding. My father had insisted on this! Back in 1958, no-one could possibly admit to having sex before marriage. Sex outside marriage was not only religiously a sin, it was a terrible social stigma. My father wouldn't hear of his son and his fiancée going to England together for our wedding without them being at least legally married!

After the priest pronounced Martin and Maria man and wife, they kissed and led the procession back down the aisle, and through the village, to the one big *Gasthof*, for the celebration. This time, the children were relegated to last. In fact, everyone just followed the bride and groom, in no particular order. Again, it was very different to our wedding reception. The parents did not have to receive the guests, because they all knew each other, and the few outsiders had been welcomed, and introduced, the previous day.

Everyone sat down wherever they felt like, at the long tables except for seats reserved at one table for the bride and groom and their parents. A delicious and plentiful country lunch was served, and then people moved around, changing places to chat with whom they chose, or went outside for a while. Food was served non-stop, open sandwiches and pastries all afternoon, until it was time for another full meal for supper, followed by more open sandwiches and pastries. Bavarian pastries are not like English ones. Whole cakes, made of layers of light sponge and frothy butter-crème, were put on each table and the guests helped themselves.

I was astonished to see so much food. Germany seemed to have made a stronger recovery from the war than had Britain. This seemed terribly unfair to me. Germany had behaved so badly and had lost the war, yet Britain which had sacrificed so much to defeat the Nazis, was not as well off! And there were still Nazis around, although they did not own up to it.

At midnight Martin and Maria said goodbye as they were setting off for their honeymoon, also in Italy, but in the northern mountains. Next day, it was time for us to make tracks for home. A magical interlude was at an end. It was a long train journey – across Germany from south to north, through Belgium, and then by ferry to Dover, and, finally, by train again, to London.

CHAPTER 31

A Family of My Own

All three of my foster families lived in the countryside so that I grew up to think of town living as something different and strange. I loved the countryside, the trees in all their glorious shades of green, the fields, the streams and the Downs, and the lovely fresh scents. How could I live anywhere without the gentle rolling hills overlooking the farm to keep a protective eye on me? I thought that I would never be able to live in a town, with harsh grey asphalt roads and pavements, where tall houses were crowded together and the air was polluted. Little did I think that I would spend most of my life living in one of the biggest cities in the world, London!

Before we got married, Bernard and I had the idea that we might go to America to study for postgraduate degrees, and we made numerous applications for grants. America was deeply attractive to us; it was the golden land where all wishes came true. We had a vision of a brilliant, new life together. Europe was still scarred by the legacy of the war years; the evidence was there for all to see – shattered buildings and broken lives. Life was still hard for many people. I was also in the process of trying to reconstruct my life, and still trying to work out who I was. America offered a new beginning.

Eventually, I was offered a research post in microbiology at the University of Illinois, while Bernard was offered a scholarship for an MA at a university in Philadelphia, but the two universities were six hundred miles apart and we did not want to be separated. Our dream was over before it had even begun. I had endured a lifetime of separations and I wasn't going to go through that experience yet again with Bernard.

Bernard became interested in becoming an educational psychologist, and the best training course for that was in London. He got a place and a grant. So we stayed in London and I stayed with the biscuit firm. I was bitterly disappointed to give up our American dream.

However, later on, I read in a journal that the microbiology department at Illinois had been developing botulin, a lethal poison, from microbes that could be used in biological warfare. I was glad then that I had played no part in it.

As I was not especially interested in biscuits, apart from eating them, or in a career in scientific research, I decided to leave my job and look for a teaching post. I found a job at Carlyle Girls School, a small grammar school in Chelsea. Bernard had been instrumental in helping me make the decision. He saw, better than I did, that I was best suited to working with people.

It was a huge change, one that reflected where my real interests lay and would, of course, have happened much earlier if I had listened to my father and my head teacher, and had studied humanities and arts subjects, instead of agriculture. I found I was much more interested in children. I liked being with them and teaching them.

I was in charge of biology for the whole of Carlyle school. Not only did I teach, but I also had to create the syllabuses for eleven-year-olds up to sixth formers and supervise the other biology teachers. That meant long hours after school preparing everything, as well as marking my students' homework. I enjoyed working hard at something I could see was important. I had learnt from my father to value education.

I particularly appreciated having my own registration class. They were MY children and I was interested in all they did. I used to sort out their problems. One girl, Naomi, was frequently in trouble. I extricated her from several scrapes, but I wasn't able to prevent her from being expelled for cheating. She had discovered a history test prepared on a blackboard, copied it and passed it round her whole class. The history teacher was outraged when the whole class got all the questions right. I didn't see it as cheating; on the contrary, I praised Naomi for her generosity in sharing it with her class. At least I got permission for Naomi to come back to school to sit her exams, and her parents engaged me to give her coaching at home.

Bernard's training as an educational psychologist had begun, and it meant that we depended on my salary to live on. We thought we would wait three years, till he could get a job, before we could consider having a baby. To my chagrin, Martin and Maria produced a baby girl, my niece Miriam, in 1960, long before we could consider a pregnancy. My brother always beat me and got there first with everything! He was still working freelance as a photographer, in Mainz, and Maria had a secretarial job there.

My niece was a remarkably beautiful baby, and I was very jealous. I visited my brother's family soon after she was born. Maria was beaming, proud as a queen, sitting there being looked after by her mother and younger sister, both of whom had come up especially, from southern Germany. With all the help she had, Maria was able to go back to her job after a few weeks.

The feeling of jealousy was a sharp reminder that there were events that were outside my control. For all my new-found freedoms and responsibilities, there was still a part of me that was insecure and afraid. My self-esteem was unexpectedly shaken by seeing Maria, with her baby, getting all the attention.

Fortunately, this feeling was not to last for long. I became pregnant some months later. I was broody, and Bernard was going to get a grant

At home with Bruce

for his last year of training, so we thought it would be easier to start a family. There was a long, hot summer in 1961. It was hard carrying a big bump around everywhere, which generated heat like a little engine! Going to my teaching job by underground caused me to faint on several occasions. Sometimes we couldn't sleep because our bedroom was too hot and stuffy. We would go at sunrise, to Finsbury Park, armed with pillows and blankets, and sleep under the trees.

Our son, Bruce, was born at 8am at University College Hospital, in October 1961, two weeks late, and just before he was due to be induced. We'd chosen UCH so that Bernard and I could be together to welcome our baby into the world. At the time, UCH was one of the only two hospitals in London that allowed fathers to be present. Nowadays, it is the usual practice.

Bruce looked small and delicate, and we marvelled at his tiny, wriggly fingers and toes, every one of them perfectly formed. His huge mop of fine, dark hair made everybody smile. 47 years later, he still has his thick dark curls and not a grey hair!

I felt like a queen when visitors came in the afternoon, but the next day, things went wrong. My breasts were swollen and hurt and Bruce wasn't interested in feeding. I was in a large noisy ward of mothers and children. I became anxious and depressed. I couldn't eat or sleep. When I did get to sleep, I was woken up by a rather gruff sister, who refused me an aspirin. I was in hysterics by the time Bernard came to see me, the next morning.

I went into hospital, enthusiastically, fit as a fiddle, and came out 10 days later anxious, thin and depressed. Both Bruce and I caught infections, and were on antibiotics. I made a mental note that nothing would make me go into hospital again for the next baby! I would have a home birth.

I didn't want to go back to work. I wanted to enjoy Bruce's babyhood. I didn't want a child carer to see his first steps, or be the first one to hear his cute attempts at communication, like 'buggabys' for butterflies and 'ong gosh' for orange squash.

It was going to be difficult to manage on Bernard's small grant without my salary. My mother had promised that she would come and support me when I brought my baby home, but when the time came, did not feel well enough to travel to England. My mother-in-law, who lived just round the corner, was very keen and willing to help, but made me feel more nervous and anxious. Bruce was colicky every evening, and cried inconsolably for at least two hours. I felt helpless that I could not comfort him. Bernard was as anxious as I was. We took turns in rocking the baby, and he used to get up in the night and squat over the sleeping baby, to check whether he was still breathing.

After a few weeks, a friend visited with her baby. She diagnosed that Bruce had not taken enough milk to keep it coming, and so my milk had dried up. I boiled and sugared some diluted ordinary milk. Bruce drank it greedily and slept soundly. End of problem. But no, the health visitor came and said it wasn't right to use ordinary milk, and I must use the special baby milk powder. Bruce didn't like the SMA milk. He got violent diarrhoea, and we took him to the doctor. Because he was losing weight, the doctor made me feel like a very bad mother who couldn't keep her baby alive. She made me bring him to the surgery, every day, to weigh him. She changed his brand of milk powder twice, but he still couldn't keep it down.

Fortunately, the friend who had helped me before came round again. She brought me a tin of National Dried Milk and made up a bottle for me. At last, it was something Bruce liked. I stopped going to the doctor, in case she criticised National Dried Milk. After that, Bruce began to thrive.

By the time my mother eventually came to London, Bruce was seven months old and getting plump. My mother couldn't understand why I had been making a fuss, in my letters and phone calls. He was relatively easy to look after. We took him in his carrycot when visiting friends, and left him with Bernard's parents when we went to the cinema.

My first nephew, Markus, was born in February 1962, just five months after Bruce. Our second son, Barry, was born the following year in 1963. When I was pregnant with Barry, it was a hard and cold winter, but I had my little bulge, like a furnace, keeping me warm.

It was snowing when we moved in January from our flat in Finsbury Park to a little house in Twickenham, to be nearer to Bernard's first job as an educational psychologist. Lighting a fire in the cold empty house caused frozen pipes to thaw and burst and we had a bad leak. All told, it was a very stressful move. I had a very lively toddler and was in the later stages of pregnancy. I think Barry understood my need for rest and decided to come a whole month early. Instead of in May, he was born in early April, on 8th April 1963, and he brought the spring with him.

After my horrible experience with Bruce's hospital birth, we arranged for a midwife to come to our home for this one, and she was excellent. She arrived within an hour although it was the middle of the night. She inspired confidence, and had prepared us very well in advance. Because Bernard had been there at Bruce's birth, she made full use of his assistance. Barry took half the time that Bruce had taken to be born. He was much smaller than Bruce, and weighed six pounds, whereas Bruce had been nearly nine pounds. This time the little cleaned-up bundle had a big mop of golden hair.

Nothing woke him, until he was ready to wake up, not even the noise Bruce made with his toys. Later, we had plenty of sleepless nights. Such is life with young children! We were just happy to have two healthy, happy boys.

My second nephew, Martin Bernd, was born the year after Barry, in September 1964, and our daughter, Tania, in February 1965. And that made a new generation of six cousins, who have remained in contact across the English Channel. Tania was another winter pregnancy, although, mercifully, this time, it was a mild winter. Like Barry, she arrived a whole month early, on February 17th, in the early hours of the morning. The midwife only got to us just in time. Bernard and I nearly had to manage it all ourselves. Tania was another plump, little six-pounder, perfect in every way, with a mop of hair that was neither golden nor dark, but somewhere in between. Next morning, she was wide awake when she was introduced to her two brothers. She stuck her tongue out, which made them laugh. We called her Tania Louise Rose, after her two grandmothers.

We now had three children under four years old. It was hard work. We lived at the bottom of a cul-de-sac. I walked up the same road every day, to the local shops or to the little local park, with Tania in the pram and two toddlers sitting back-to-back on a tea tray over the pram. I had no automatic washing machine, only a twin-tub. That meant a lot of heaving and carrying. There were no disposable nappies. The terry-towel and muslin nappies had to be boiled in the twin-tub before washing. Every second day was washing day. When one of the children was ill, Bernard had to come home for his lunch hour, so that I could go shopping. When I had to go to the doctor, Bernard would drop us all there by car. I had to take enough food, drink and toys in case I had to wait a long time and then come back by bus with the three children and a pram.

When Bruce was four, a specialist diagnosed that his tonsils had to come out. I remembered my own unhappy experience in hospital when I had my tonsils out at the age of 10 and asked if I could go into hospital with him. The specialist looked at me and said, 'With two little ones I should think you would be pleased to get rid of him for a week!' Bruce looked panic-stricken. Bernard was furious and told the specialist that he was out of order to say that. Bruce was an anxious child and we simply couldn't leave him in a hospital for a week.

I found out that the Elizabeth Garrett Anderson Hospital in London allowed mothers to sleep in with their children. We booked to go there. Bernard's mother came to stay to help Bernard look after Barry and Tania. It was an interesting, and very valuable experience, in the hospital with Bruce. I was able to explain everything to him in words he could understand.

When Bruce was back home, I joined The National Association for the Welfare of Children in Hospital (NAWCH). For many years, I talked with parent groups about the benefits of a small child having their mother with them, in hospital, or at least, visiting every day. I also visited hospitals, to talk with sisters of children's wards and hospital managers. Several years later, Barry had his tonsils out, and I went into hospital with him, too.

The biggest problem was that Tania wanted her turn at going into hospital with Mummy, but she did not need to have her tonsils out. Bruce and Barry were very proud of having been to hospital and they made it harder for Tania by telling her what a wonderful time they'd had!

Our house was small and I felt claustrophobic. There was a tiny patio at the back, which was not even big enough for the children to play. I took them out every day, when the weather was good enough. Bernard imagined that I could put my feet up with a coffee, any time I liked, and I imagined he could chat over tea with adult colleagues, whenever he liked. But it wasn't like that, for either of us. Bernard was working long hours, and I was lonely and starved for adult company. I tried to make friends with other mothers in the close, but didn't manage it. There was always one or other child crying or needing something and never time for myself. I even gave up reading the papers.

Sometimes I got so frustrated I felt like exploding. I felt I was losing my sanity. Nobody can work seven days a week and be on duty all night, too. I needed an evening off. Bernard agreed. I signed up for a dressmaking class on Wednesday evenings. That was like entering another world: ten women and a teacher, very civilised and sedate, all talking quietly, no-one howling or screaming! I learnt useful dressmaking skills, but that was not the point. I had adult company. I got on particularly well with another mother, whose daughter was the same age as Tania, and the two girls later became long-term friends. I extended the two-hour class, by meeting my friend for a cuppa and a chat, beforehand, and sometimes we went out somewhere afterwards too. My sanity returned. When things got on top of me, I could count the days until the next Wednesday evening, when I would get relief again.

When Tania was just over a year, Barry two, and Bruce four, we moved to a bigger house in Wembley, which was on a corner, and there were five different directions you could go in, instead of one way out of the cul-de-sac. There was room to play indoors when it was wet, and a generous garden for fine days. Local children came into our garden to play.

On the first day in our new house, we bumped into a friend from Reading University. She had two children and introduced me to Housewives' Register – an organisation of mothers who met, with their children, for coffee mornings, and arranged baby-sitting rotas, so that everyone could go out some evenings. Life was good and getting better.

At Tania's batmitzvah – Bruce, Bernard, Tania, myself and Barry (left to right).

CHAPTER 32

Teaching and Psychotherapy

From just before our first son, Bruce, was born and until our third child, Tania, started school, I did not go out to work. It was hard to make ends meet with only one salary, especially when we moved to the bigger house in Wembley, and had a huge mortgage. There were things I could do to save money. I had a sewing machine and a knitting machine. I made sweaters, pyjamas and duffle coats for the whole family, and matching dresses, of the same material, for Tania and me. Children's clothes were expensive, so it was a big saving. Most of our friends' children had clothes handed down or passed on, from children who had outgrown them. But our children had new clothes – made by me.

I painted the whole of our Wembley house, inside and out, over the four years we were there, before I went back to teaching, and that saved money too. Sometimes, the children helped. I painted inside the house, room by room, when the children were asleep in bed, so that it would be dry by the morning.

I managed to earn a bit of money too by marking GCE exam papers at home twice a year, sometimes while rocking a baby to sleep in my lap. I also turned to studying at home, to get a teaching certificate. I managed an hour before the family woke in the morning, and an hour after the children were in bed. I went back to teaching a year before I had intended, to boost our income.

I took a full-time job locally, teaching science, at Wembley Junior High School, a mixed school for boys and girls, aged eleven to thirteen. It was Tania's first year at school, and it was important to me that I took her home for lunch every day. I had done the same for the two boys. It meant hurrying the half-mile between my school, hers and home, and then back again. After a month, I had lost several pounds in weight, and was exhausted.

Bernard was worried about me. He bought an old, green Triumph

Herald car very cheaply. It was just right for going backwards and for-wards between the schools. We called it the Green Tee and we kept it for years. Later we would buy a Volkswagen Camper and go around Europe in it.

The very first day I drove Green Tee to school, I slammed the door and it locked with the keys inside. I was in a panic until the PE teacher managed to pick the lock and retrieve my keys. So Tania was able to have her year of home lunches. After that, all three had school lunches and we employed a plump, motherly lady, who came for an hour every weekday, to make the children their tea, so that I could stay a bit longer at my school.

Going to Wembley Junior High was to be the start of a long un-interrupted career. I can only give you a flavour here, of what I expe-rienced and what was important to me.

Wembley was very different to the girls' grammar school I had taught in before. The comprehensive re-organisation of schools had just begun when I went to teach there in 1969. Local grammar schools and secondary modern schools were combined and re-labelled as comprehensive schools. The views of teachers and children had been ignored by the government. There was little explanation, training, or money, for the changeover, and there were serious problems.

I had to work while the school building was being renovated and extended. It was chaotic, and rather like a continuous obstacle race, getting groups of children to their classrooms, through where the builders and decorators were working. With the students having only two years at the school, you didn't get a chance to get to know them well. Then they were off to the senior high school. It felt like a tem-porary transit camp; there were ten classes in each of the two years.

My science classes were streamed according to ability. The clever-est pupils being in A, and the weakest in E. The head of science took the two A stream classes. Being the most recent recruit, I was given the two E stream classes, a D, two Cs and a B. The behaviour of the children was reasonable in the B class, but got progressively worse in the lower streams. The two E classes were a nightmare. I couldn't teach them anything, because they were determined not to let me. I also taught two mixed–ability geography classes and, in each of them, was one of the two worst behaved students from my E class. Yet, in geography lessons, they were all reasonably well behaved and prepared to learn.

I confronted each of these four children, on their own, and challenged them about the difference between their behaviour in the two classes. They each said, more or less, the same thing: geography was interesting and science was boring. I told them they didn't give science a chance to be interesting, because they never tuned in.

It was clear to me that they felt shamed at being labelled 'E' stream and I told them so. I said I thought they were not stupid, but being labelled had made them angry, and it made me angry too, as mixed classes were a much better idea. They agreed with me, and I said I would ask the head of science about it. He was adamant that science classes had to be streamed, but at least he agreed that the E classes did not have to follow the syllabus. I got interesting science films for them, and sometimes managed to get them to question and discuss the topics. This caused problems for the other science classes, who were envious of my two E classes getting to see interesting films. It also gave a boost to the E class children to know that they had something that other children desired. When I got to know these children, it made me sad that many of them had very little in their lives compared to most children. They carried a lot of anger and resentment around, which stopped them from being interested in, or enjoying, what they were doing.

During this first year at Wembley Junior High, I had to be assessed in the classroom, for my teaching certificate. I arranged for the assessor to come into my B science class, as I felt confident they would behave well enough. I had told the children they would be having a visitor coming to their next lesson, and I prepared carefully. I introduced the visitor and made sure he had a comfortable seat. Not long into the lesson, some sort of distraction rippled through the class. A boy called out to me, 'Miss! Kevin's mouse has escaped!' A mouse scampered along one of the benches, skirting round the Bunsen burners and other apparatus, and jumped to the next bench, to the accompaniment of squeals from the class.

I shouted to the class to turn off all Bunsen burners and freeze.

Then I told Kevin to catch his mouse and bring it to me. When every-one was still, the mouse was no longer frightened and came to Kevin easily. I knew there was a cardboard box of stationery in the prep room. I fetched it and tipped out the stationery, to put the mouse in. I made some holes for air in the lid, and put some paper scraps as a bed, and a piece of my break-time sandwich, in with the mouse, while explaining to the class what I was doing. We then had a discussion, for twenty minutes or so, on keeping pets, before the class came round to the idea that school was a terrifying place for them, and that it was cruel to bring them to school. Kevin even volunteered to take his mouse home at break, and never bring him to school again.

I had completely forgotten the assessor by then. I was hastily adapting the lesson I had prepared because we had lost half an hour. By the end of the lesson, they were all busily writing, while I kept an eye on Mr Mouse to make sure he stayed in his box. I sent Kevin off with Mr Mouse a few minutes early, with a note permitting him to take the mouse home. After I had dismissed the class, I told the as-sessor that the mouse saga had made my lesson plan impossible, and asked to have another chance. He said that would not be necessary, as it had been a real lesson and I had demonstrated my ability to adapt to situations. He awarded me a distinction. I didn't do quite so well in the theory exams, but I got my teaching certificate.

The following year, the local authority decided junior high schools didn't work and that our children should stay up to age 18 or19. The headmaster decided to split the school into four houses, and I was ap-pointed head of one of the houses. I was responsible for all the chil-dren who were in difficulties in my quarter of the school.

Whenever I could, I got the parents to come and see me after school. Behind their child's difficulties, there were often problems between the parents. I found myself being used as a marriage coun-sellor, and would refer those parents with difficult relationships to the local marriage guidance clinic (now Relate). That got me interested in counselling. I was accepted onto a course in school counselling, but my headmaster would not support my application for a secondment for a year. He said he didn't want a school counsellor; he wanted me as head of house, which I was good at.

After he turned down my secondment application for a second time, the following year, I left to take a senior teacher job in Harrow, at Mountview High School. I had been seven years at Wembley Junior High.

At Mountview High, my role was to organise all the internal and public exams for the school. I worked there for two years. While I was there, I decided to train as a marriage counsellor, which led, eventually, to me getting a deputy headship at Reynolds High School in Acton, where I was in charge of staff and pupil welfare. It was a far more interesting job than that of preparing examinations.

I worked with the parents of children in trouble and with teachers who had personal problems. My marriage guidance training was extremely useful. I was able to help trainee teachers allocated to Reynolds for their practical placements, and new teachers on probation. Remembering my own struggle with E classes at Wembley High, I made sure they had reasonable classes and got help with the more difficult students. To my surprise, most of the teachers, particularly the older men who were strict disciplinarians, didn't like me helping the new teachers. They called it 'soft-soaping' and believed that new teachers should be thrown in at the deep end, like they had been. If they couldn't survive without molly-coddling, they shouldn't be in teaching, according to their view. I didn't agree.

I didn't agree with my colleagues about many things. For example, the head of maths complained about children being taken out of his classes for music lessons. He said it made them undisciplined and badly behaved. The school had a very fine brass band that played every morning for assembly, and an orchestra that gave concerts at ends of terms. I argued that there was no finer way of learning self-discipline than working together to make music.

I frequently challenged sexism. I refused to accept the idea of girls' subjects and boys' subjects. As far as I was concerned, all subjects should be equally available to boys and girls. My favourite subject was child development. I had no problem convincing the boys that it would be good for them. I would tell them that they would probably become fathers within the next ten or fifteen years and they soon became interested in the issues. I didn't agree, when other teachers or parents, would tell boys that child development was only for girls, and that 'real exams' were for boys. Children might be a lot better off if their parents had learnt about child development at school.

I also didn't agree with punishment. I had enough punishment in my own childhood to know that it doesn't work. The beatings I had for wetting my bed, as a little girl, didn't help and only made it worse. Being given lines by teachers only made me angry and frustrated, and extra homework put me off both the teacher and the subject! Never in my teaching career did I give lines as a punishment.

I don't believe in punishment, because it is mostly meaningless or vengeful. It is much better to have clear rules and clear, meaningful consequences when they are broken. Teachers used to send misbehaving children to me, and expected me to punish them. I didn't. I talked with them, instead, about taking responsibility. Sometimes a child would plead with me, 'Why can't you just punish me, Miss?' I would reply that they wanted me to wipe out their misbehaviour with a punishment, so that they need not take responsibility, and could go off and do it again. Some children understood what I meant, but not all.

My aim was to get the miscreants to do something towards repairing whatever their behaviour had damaged. For example, apologies can repair damaged relationships or graffiti can be cleaned up. I didn't always succeed, but it was worth trying for the sake of those that were able to grow in responsibility. One of my worst failures concerned a probation officer who brought in a boy who had stolen ten pairs of shoes for his mates, while doing a Saturday job in a shoe shop. He wanted the boy caned. I didn't agree with caning and told him so. The probation officer didn't see the point of making the boy gradually pay for the stolen shoes from his pocket money, because he said the shop had allowed for theft in its budget!

Teachers often had their own problems. Staff depression and absence through illness were big problems, which had knock-on effects on the students. They resented their usual teachers being replaced by other teachers, who were equally resentful at losing their marking and preparation time. Teachers could talk their problems through with me, in confidence. This helped them to find their own solutions.

The most difficult issues to resolve were those of hostility between students, or between a student and a teacher. It seemed to me
to be enormously hard for some people to reach a state where they
could agree to differ. Some had so little self-esteem that backing down
felt, to them, like being annihilated. They had never learnt to back
down or apologise, as this was considered showing weakness. So I included in the students' lessons some sort of experience of how to
manage disagreement. I arranged for the head of careers to show
films, after which he and I would have very heated discussions, drawing the students in whenever we could. At the end of the lesson, we
would agree to differ and left on good terms. Mostly, the students
would watch with rapt attention. For some of them, it was the first
time they'd seen warring adults resolve their difficulties without re-
sorting to violence.

One of the main sources of stress in Reynolds high School was
the conflict between the head teacher, who wanted to phase out caning from the school, and those who disagreed with him. It seemed to
me, that when these teachers caned students, they were in fact vent-
ing their anger at the head-teacher onto the students. Of course, this
did not improve behaviour, but increased the suppressed anger that
frequently broke out in fights in the playground.

It saddened me to see the toll on both teachers and students. I
helped several teachers get jobs elsewhere, and realised that I needed
to protect my own health and sanity too. I could not see myself bear-
ing the stress for another twenty years. It was at this point that I began
the long and expensive training to become a psychotherapist.

Not long after I had begun this training, Reynolds High School
was amalgamated with two other local schools and re-named Acton
High School. Many teachers had to find jobs elsewhere. I was glad to
be offered a deputy headship at Greenford High School. I could have
left teaching at this point. However, although I had graduated in my
psychotherapy training, we had debts and expenses that meant I could
not yet give up my full-time teaching salary.

The deputy headship at Greenford High had been vacant for some
time. Morale was at the lowest ebb I have ever met in a school. Antisocial student behaviour was the worst in the borough. The students

came from three largely separate communities: Asian, Afro-Caribbean and right-wing white nationalists.

All three communities were at loggerheads. The parents' fights in the pubs, at night, were simply carried on by their children in school, the next day. The teachers, many of whom were dedicated and competent, were worn out by the friction and hostility. The rate of absence, of staff and students, was high. Several students who had been excluded from other schools in the borough ended up at Greenford High.

The quarrel between the teachers' unions and the government spilled over into the school. Teachers refused to cover for absent colleagues. It became part of my job to bring in supply teachers. When there were not enough supply teachers, the students had to be sent home. Most of them didn't go home, but wandered the streets creating mayhem, and there were many complaints about their behaviour.

I missed Reynolds High School, where I felt I had been able to do some good work, even though it had been tough going. I was determined not to relapse into ill health, and only the knowledge that I would be leaving soon, kept me going. Those last two years of my teaching career were pretty much of a nightmare.

CHAPTER 33

Psychotherapy and the Reunion of Kindertransport

Although I valued teaching highly, I knew I would not be able to bear the fast pace and enormous stress for much longer. I realised I needed to prepare to do something else. In all the schools where I worked, I saw teachers surviving, by going off sick. Many of them would be absent more often than they were at school, while others would sink into depression from the sheer strain. I started my four years of basic psychotherapy training while I was still teaching.

The training was intensive but stimulating. For three times a week, in personal psychotherapy, I could let go of the everyday stress of school, relax, and learn new ways of thinking and feeling. There were long training sessions – two evenings a week at the London Centre for Psychotherapy in Swiss Cottage – but it was worth it to be with a group of like-minded colleagues.

After two years of training, I began to see therapy clients. I'd see them in a church vestry in Ealing, before school, and later write up notes, which I took to supervision sessions. I continued seeing clients for another five years after I had finished training, before I could afford to give up my deputy head's salary.

I left Greenford High School at an opportune time. The decrease in numbers of school age children in the area meant the school roll had shrunk, and some teachers had to be made redundant. I volunteered for this, in 1986, and got a good pension deal, which made up a bit for my drop in income. For the next two years, I began to build up a practice, with my own consulting room at home. Our three children had grown up, and were either at university, or away elsewhere. I also earned a bit of money from home tuition, teaching children excluded from school.

I had four such pupils. One was a 15-year-old girl, Annie, who had just had a baby. She could not get herself together enough to go to school. She suffered from agoraphobia that made her unbearably anxious to go outside her home. Annie was tense being at home with her baby. She was supposed to be studying for her GCE exams, but was in no state to study. I visited her at her home twice a week. I enjoyed my visits, and she did too. I chatted with her and showed her how to play with her baby. We enjoyed him together. I told her what a good mum she was, and how important she was to her baby. All this built up her confidence, so that she could do some studying between visits. By the end of that year, she was taking the baby out in the buggy, not just with me, but also, by herself. She was able to go out to take her exams and passed them all. It was very gratifying to see her progress.

My other three pupils were not such success stories. They were primary school boys under eleven, who had been excluded from more than one school because their behaviour was dangerous to other children. A place was found at a boarding school for the first, Mickey, so he only came to my house for four months. The second one, Johnny, came to me for over a year. He was often in trouble, yet seemed to admire the police. Perhaps, as he had no father at home, he was searching for one. He enjoyed his trips to the police station and told me all about them. We had some fun reading stories together, and Johnny made enough progress to get the chance to go to an ordinary secondary school when he was eleven. I was anxious that he might not be able to cope without getting into more trouble. I contacted the school, ahead of his starting, and emphasised that he would need help to settle. I met him in the street some years later – he had just done a term in a secure unit for antisocial boys. Once someone is in deep trouble, it is often very difficult to help him, or her, get out of it.

The third boy, Ganwan, was only nine, and very small and thin. His family of eight adults had recently arrived, as asylum seekers, from Africa. All the local schools had refused him a place, as he was violent with other children. I knew something of what Ganwan might be feeling, as I could relate to being a child refugee, too. When I was sent to Germany against my will, I had absolutely refused to go to school.

When I visited him at his home, none of his family could speak English. Ganwan knew a little, so he had to translate for me. They had a tiny flat, it was impossible to find a quiet corner. So I took him to my house. After that, he came to me twice a week. I was surprised that he came regularly, because he would not allow any lessons. He liked to sit on the floor and read stories with me. I never found out how he had learnt English or anything about his background. He was clearly unable to trust anyone. I wondered about what terrible things he had seen, and experienced, in his home country. Often he would fall fast asleep; I would cover him with a blanket and only wake him up when it was time for him to go home.

Out of desperation, I contacted the educational psychologist, who had been one of my husband's colleagues. He told me as much as he knew about Ganwan. He thought the boy was in a state of mind that made him unteachable. He was tired, because he spent nights out on the streets stealing bicycles, and he had begun taking cars. Through the educational psychologist, I was invited to an inter-disciplinary conference on Ganwan's future. Both the psychologist and I argued the case for sending Ganwan to a therapeutic residential school. The local authority representative said it would cost too much. I pointed out that eight years in a therapeutic boarding school would cost far less than a lifetime in prison. I was told, however, that the Home Office, not the local authority, would have to pay for prison! Sadly, I did not hear anything more about what happened to Ganwan.

By 1989, three years after I had left Greenford High School, I had built up a full private psychotherapy practice. In June that year, a determined and enterprising lady, Bertha Leverton, herself a Kinder-transportee, organised a reunion for the children who came to England with her on the Kindertransport. A friend had heard her speak on the radio on *Woman's Hour* and told me about it. I was not even aware of the word 'Kindertransport', but I rang Bertha out of curiosity. She told me the reunion was for all those who came to England as child refugees from the Nazis and who had been without their parents during the war. She said I had to come and Bertha was not a person to whom you could say, 'No'!

For two days, some 1,000 Kinder met in a big sports hall in Harrow. There were speeches and performances on the platform, but mostly we sat at tables, sharing our personal stories with each other, while eating and drinking. I was amazed to hear about so many experiences, some similar to mine and some very different. Every story was unique, and every story made me realise how little I really knew about my own story. Up until that conference, it had not occurred to me that any children, other than my brother and I, had come to England as refugees. Suddenly, there were a thousand of us together, and it was only then I learnt there had been 10,000 children rescued by the British Government. I finally saw my place in history. I had been part of a wonderful rescue mission.

But even this knowledge of the Kindertransport was tinged with regret and shared sorrow. 'If only our parents had been allowed to come too!', we sighed. 'Many of them would have been saved from the Nazi slaughter and they could have supported Britain's war effort.'

Many Kinder regarded me as lucky because I saw my parents again after the war, which they didn't. Of course, I was lucky to see both my parents again. However, I didn't feel lucky; I felt very confused. I was shocked and saddened by the tragic stories of other Kinder but, in a way, I felt I had lost my parents too. The parents I met after ten years were total strangers, who were completely different to the parents I had known before. My inner world was peopled by two sets of parents and three sets of foster parents. How could I not be confused?

That conference was an epiphany for me. It was the moment that I let Ruthchen back into my life. It was as if a mask had suddenly vanished from my eyes and ears; a mask that had shut out a part of the world that I couldn't bear to see, hear and know about. Suddenly I saw everything differently. I realised just how much I didn't know because I had not allowed myself to know. By the time of this reunion, I had become ready to know, and hearing the stories of others, made me want to know. After the conference, I started reading books on our bookshelves at home that I had previously ignored, following up references and asking questions, wherever I could.

From the time of the conference, clients affected by the Holocaust began opening up to me in their psychotherapy. And other clients with bad experiences, started telling me about them. I was ready to hear what these clients had dared not voice before. They seemed to sense my new openness.

When I told colleagues about this, they referred clients to me who had family histories affected by the Holocaust. Gradually, my practice contained more and more clients who had been traumatised. I did some further psychotherapy training with a focus on this, and I used my personal therapy to piece together, and to understand, my own life story.

I tried to get Martin to talk about the past. He was very reluctant to discuss it. He did not want to be reminded of the disturbing things that had happened. He felt it was better to save his energy for the present and future. He had been living in Germany since 1957, and was still anxious about being identified as Jewish. He did not deny his Jewish origins, but he feared that, somehow, it would be to his disadvantage, if his neighbours and friends knew.

It proved easier for him to talk to a stranger about his past, than with me. A few years ago, a German researcher came to England to interview former Kindertransportees for her PhD on what happened to the children in their lives after the war. She was interested in my psychotherapy work and ideas about trauma, and invited me to give a talk about it at Sussex University. Back in Germany, she got my brother to talk with her, and he told her about his experience of being out in the streets of Berlin on Kristallnacht. He had never discussed this with anyone before. It had been such a shocking experience for him that he had pushed it to the back of his mind, and kept it locked away there for decades.

There was a second reunion of the Kindertransport in 1999 and, this time, many children of former Kindertransportees came with their parents. Group discussions were part of the programme, and I was one of the group leaders. The parents and children shared their experiences with each other in a way they had not been able to do in their families. Once they had started, they didn't want to stop talking. As they wanted more discussion, I ran some groups for them with a colleague, enabling them to continue the dialogue between the generations.

In my therapy practice, I had become interested in what Holocaust survivors passed on to children by not being able to talk about their trauma. This was helpful in the dialogue between the generations. The parents had been determined to protect their children from the awful things they had suffered, so they kept them secret from their children. But children always sense when something is being kept hidden and not talked about. In the groups, they described knowing there was something so awful it mustn't be talked about. It felt to them like a dark, foreboding black hole of nothingness. Sometimes they filled the hole with terrible fantasies. They didn't ask questions, in order to protect their parents from having to relive the horror by talking about the past.

Parents and children were also protecting themselves from a catastrophe they imagined would happen, if they talked about the traumatic experiences. I could feel this from my own experience of shutting off my past for 50 years, until I was ready. You have to feel strong enough, and believe that you won't fall to pieces, before you can talk about something deeply disturbing. But, above all, there has to be someone that you feel really wants to listen, and can bear to listen without 'falling apart'.

In 1992, the UK government decided to include teaching about the Holocaust in the national curriculum for all secondary schools students. I knew just how difficult this would be for teachers who had no training to do this. How could they teach what they had not learnt about, or experienced, themselves? Teachers need guidance to help them understand what the Holocaust tells us about human behaviour. I believe it takes courage to accept that the Nazi perpetrators were ordinary people, and that we too, could have been perpetrators, or victims, if we had been there at that time. It is easier to whip up violence and hatred in people, against a different group, than it is to get them to accept each other.

I joined a group of Holocaust survivors who were prepared to go into schools to tell their personal stories to groups of students and help teachers with any problems with Holocaust teaching. It is something I still do, through various organisations – the London Jewish Cultural Centre, the Holocaust Education Trust, Beth Shalom in Nottinghamshire and the Anne Frank Trust. I enjoy going into schools again. It gives me a chance to combine my two main areas of professional experience – teaching and psychotherapy. Teachers who feel undervalued welcome my support and I can also help engage the students in the subject.

I tell students that by learning about the Holocaust, they can understand why my generation failed to stop it happening, and how it might be possible to prevent such atrocities in future. I ask them how they might feel being sent away to a strange country at age four, as I was, and then how they would feel, if at fourteen they were taken against their will to a country where atrocities had been committed.

I invariably get questions about why Hitler appealed to the German people. To most students he seems a repellent figure. He was nothing like the perfect, blond, blue-eyed, Aryan supermen he wanted to create. I explain that his attraction is to do with power, and that powerful people who do bad things can exert an intoxicating pull on our imagination.

Not long after I started going into schools, I realised that it was dangerous to focus exclusively on the Holocaust, because it made the issues seem remote. So when students ask if I think the Holocaust could happen again, I say that anything that has happened once could happen again unless we prevent it. When they argue it couldn't happen in England, I discuss the part that every country in Europe played in allowing it to happen. I tell them about other genocides. How bullying, prejudice and racism can lead eventually to genocide unless it is stopped.

I am passionate about this. Just as students who witness bullying don't have to be passive bystanders, we all need to learn about genocide and each of us can do something about the bad things we know about; whether it be by joining protest movements, marching or sending letters to MPs. We can become active 'upstanders'.

I also believe that if we ignore genocides that have been denied by the perpetrators, such as Turkey still does, for what happened when the Ottoman Turks slaughtered over a million Christian Armenians, Greeks and Assyrians, between 1915 and 1923, we create impunity for later genocides. Hitler is recorded as saying to his generals, 'Who now remembers the Armenian genocide?'

Many Turks have never heard about the Armenian genocide because it is banned from discussion in Turkey. This ignorance means that the genocide continues. The offspring of the survivors feel as though their ancestors are being murdered a second time, as if they never existed. To raise awareness of the Armenian Genocide of 1915, I went with a group to Armenia in August 2007 and planted a tree in the name of Britain's Liberal Jews, in the memorial garden in Yerevan.

There are other examples. Some years earlier, in 1984, I went to spend Christmas with Joan Goodricke in Tasmania. I especially wanted to see Mr and Mrs Goodricke again, before they got too old, to thank them for giving me a home during the war. They all made me so welcome, but then they were the sort of people who would make anyone welcome. We had a picnic in the garden on Christmas Day. A week later, on New Year's Eve, we went to a firework display at the harbour in Hobart, and joined 2,000 people in lighting sparklers at midnight. But it was a visit to Port Arthur Prison Museum that made the deepest impression on me. In the 19th century, convicted criminals were transported there from London. The prison regime was brutal. Many prisoners died from starvation, beatings or hard labour. Those who survived to complete their sentence, together with ex-guards and a few adventure seekers, became the first settlers. In a very short time, they had wiped out the native Aborigines. This was a genocide inflicted by British people. It is another reason why we cannot shrug off shocking deeds by saying they only happen elsewhere.

A simple memorial can help us reflect on, and learn about, things that have happened in history that should be known about and never forgotten. So it was very moving for me to see the Kindertransport memorial at Liverpool Street Station, the terminus where I had first arrived in Britain, along with thousands of other children. A bronze sculpture depicts a group of children with their suitcases, and a little girl is clutching her teddy bear. It was erected in 2006, as an expression of our gratitude to Britain for taking us in and giving us a chance to live. There is a quotation from the Talmud, an ancient collection of Jewish sacred writings, which reads, 'Whosoever rescues a single soul is credited as though they had saved the whole world.'

Scultpure commemorating the Kindertransport at Liverpool Street station in London.

Talking in a school while holding a doll given to me by a friend from Berlin. It's just like my old one.

On one of my school visits, talking about the Holocaust.

207

CHAPTER 34

Grandchildren

There is a biological clock that starts ticking in parents as soon as their children have all left home. It is the desire for grandchildren, which can be as strong as the desire to become a parent. We did not want to put pressure on our children to have babies. When our children left home, Bernard and I got ourselves a puppy and a kitten to keep us busy.

Then, in December 1992, our daughter, Tania, produced our first grandchild, Adèle. I could just gaze at her and play with her tiny fingers and toes for hours. My daughter was very generous. She didn't keep her baby anxiously to herself but welcomed us all to hold her as much as we liked, between her feeds and sleeping.

Tania was a much more relaxed mother than I had been. As my mother hadn't been there when my first baby was born, I never really learned to relax as I might have done if she'd been around. I was glad that I could help Tania and that she was not resentful.

But first, I had to come to terms with the transition from mother to grandmother. I felt Tania had robbed me of my role. I was a little envious and longed to be a young mother again, and to put right all the things I had failed at, as a mother. Then I realised I needed to give up motherhood to Tania and make 'the grandmother' my role.

I remembered how confused and criticised I had felt when my mother eventually turned up. I gave my daughter all the encouragement I would have liked. I offered help and accepted it when she didn't want it. I kept quiet when I didn't agree. My daughter blossomed into a confident, competent mother, and all the family enjoyed Adèle.

As I sat looking in wonder at my newborn granddaughter, I realised for the first time something important about life. She made sense of life for me, because she was worth both living for and dying for. She was the reason why I could begin to face my own death. If I lived forever and didn't eventually die, there would be no room for her

Ruth and Bernard with grandchildren Raphi and Adele

and her children and her children's children. In the meantime, I had the important job of grandparenting to do.

Adèle and her brother Raphael, born three years later, grew up to be very sociable, with three uncles, two aunts, seven first cousins and four grandparents. They have lots of friends too because they learnt to make relationships very early in their lives.

Most children of Kindertransportees have grown up without grandparents because their grandparents were murdered by the Nazis. Children of Kinder often have no family stories about them, either because their parents were too young to remember them or because the parents did not want to talk about the horrors of the Holocaust.

The children of traumatised refugees, or asylum seekers, grow up like trees that have had their roots chopped off. If their parents can't talk about the family roots in their original country, these children have an unspeakable empty void where their grandparents should have been.

Fortunately, with the passing generations, a greater openness becomes possible. Quite often, when these children grow up to have children themselves, things change in the family. The survivors sometimes find it possible to tell their grandchildren things they were not able to tell their own children. Nowadays, grandchildren will encourage family members to go and visit the towns or villages where the refugees came from. Severed roots that had been rejected for decades can then be reclaimed, and wounds can begin to heal.

PART TWO

Living with Animals

CHAPTER 35

Workhorses

A nimals were, in may ways, as important as people, on the Halt-ings' Farm. We all had to learn to live together in harmony.

In the 1940s, horses did most of the heavy work on the farm and in the fields. Most farmers couldn't afford tractors. I remember a wagon that was carrying dung; it became bunged up in mud in a swampy part of a field, after heavy rain. The wagon was a bit over-loaded, too. Poor old Damsel, a placid, rather elderly mare, flatly re-fused to try to pull it out. I was sent to harness up Dawn, a younger mare. We hitched her in front of Damsel, to take the strain. The two of them together couldn't manage it, even when we unloaded most of the dung. The wheels of the wagon simply sank deeper and deeper.

A traction engine was sent for – a big, heavy brute of a tractor – but it promptly got stuck in the gateway into the field. Dawn should-n't have been able to see the machine but I had put on a bridle with-out blinkers. When the driver gave full throttle, she saw the tractor out of the corner of her eye, reared up, ripped the reins out of my hands and then she bolted. The wagon came up out of the soggy mud with an almighty squelch, and the two horses raced off across the field, until the far hedge stopped them. So you can see why tractors were not very highly thought of on the farm, in those days! Later the Halt-ings got their own little yellow tractor we called Alice, as it was an Allis-Chalmers model.

All the workhorses on the Haltings' farm were pedigree Suffolk Punches. There are many breeds of workhorse. Shires and Clydes-dales were the most common, at that time. These were bigger than Suffolk Punches and had bushy-feathered fetlocks (ankles). The Suf-folk Punches were slightly smaller, with very little feather on their fetlocks, and much more elegant and agile, and were a beautiful, golden chestnut colour. I fell in love with them at first sight when I came to the farm.

I used to look over the hedges when I got off the bus from school. If I saw Ron, the stableman, working with horses in the fields, I would dash over to him. He would hoist me up on one of the horses, to ride home. That was very special! But I often got into trouble if Mrs Halting found horsehair on my school uniform.

In the summertime, some of the Suffolk punches would compete for prizes at the royal county shows. I loved helping get them ready. Several weeks before the shows, the horses were given extra corn rations, and had only light work in the fields, so that they wouldn't spoil their coats with sweat. I would groom them, every day, until their coats shone like copper warming pans! They had exercise sessions, where they wore special tackle, to make them arch their necks and pick their feet up extra high. Then, on the day of the show, I would help Ron and Mr Halting plait their manes and tails, and tie them with ribbons.

A high-stepping Suffolk Punch prancing with her neck arched and coat gleaming is a wonderful sight. Sometimes a mare would be shown with her foal and then I was allowed to lead the foal in the show ring. I would wear a white coat with an armband showing our entry number. I felt very proud leading my foal. I was amazed at how difficult some of the other foals in the class were to lead. They pulled back or jumped forward and lashed out. My little Daisy was as good as gold. She and I adored each other from the day she was born. However, she did manage to nibble off all the buttons of my white coat while we were parading round. She and her mum both won second prize at that show, and someone bought them for a big price. I was heartbroken to say goodbye to Daisy. But that is farm life. Although there are many enjoyable times, it is not a game, but a way of living, and there is no place for sentimental attachments.

Whenever I felt low or upset, and could no longer hold it in, I used to slip out to the stables and tell it all to the horses, often in the night as well as daytime. You can safely say absolutely anything to a horse. They will never contradict you, or laugh at you or look down on you. I mostly sought out Viking when he was in the stable. He was big and strong and made me feel protected. I would sob into his neck and he would turn his head and nuzzle me, comfortingly. One day Mr Halting discovered me asleep in Viking's stall. He was very angry and said I could have been trampled to death by the stallion. I simply couldn't imagine my friend, Viking, doing that to me.

One Sunday at lunchtime, we were sitting at the kitchen table with some of the farm hands and there was a discussion about Viking making an awful noise all morning. He had not had any exercise for three days as Ron, the only horseman who could handle him, had been off sick. As soon as dinner was over, I slipped out to the stable and comforted Viking. I asked him if he wanted to go out for a walk, and he nodded his head. So I untied his rope and led him out into the yard and onto the road, away from the ducks and chickens. He was very pleased, arched his neck and wanted to trot. So I ran and he trotted beside me.

Meanwhile Mr Halting had discovered his stallion had gone from his stall and all pandemonium was let loose in frantic efforts to find him. I went about a mile with Viking and when I turned back, there was Mr Halting, on horseback, with three farm hands on bicycles. I couldn't see what all the fuss was about. Mr Halting explained that any commotion could have alarmed Viking, and he might have reared up and trampled on me, or bolted and done a lot of damage to himself and others, and it would have been my fault!

When I was about thirteen or fourteen, I was allowed to work with some of the horses. Sometimes, there were accidents with them, and these could be memorable. One day, I was working two horses, Dawn and Darling. They were harnessed, side by side, to a chain harrow, a metal chain with spikes sticking down that was used to break up the clods of newly ploughed earth into fine soil.

It was a fine sunny day and I was enjoying the smell of the warm, damp earth and the autumn breeze. Suddenly, as we were near the roadside hedge, a group of motorbikes roared by, making not only a roar, but intermittent bangs. Dawn and Darling reared up and bolted away from the hedge. This time I let go of the rope reins at once and watched as the pair flew off up the field. I was not too bothered, as I thought they would stop at the far hedge. To my amazement, the pair of them jumped in unison and cleared the hedge, with the chain harrow flying up behind them. They cleared it like steeplechasers, and continued up the next field, until they came to an exhausted halt. By the time I reached them, they were quietly munching grass together, as if nothing happened. The horses were unhurt and their harnesses intact. I unhitched them and led them home. no-one believed my story, until they saw the chain harrow on the pasture field, instead of the ploughed field!

EXCERCISING VIKING

CHAPTER 36

Ponies

I was a lucky child to live on a farm with several ponies. My first ponies were Rufus and Senorita. I was the first to ride each of them, but Rufus's mother, Queenie, was very suspicious of me, and would keep me away from Rufus, by coming between us and snorting at me.

I was frightened of Queenie, who was Luvvy's pony. Luvvy wouldn't let anyone else ride her, except her father, Mr Halting. Although she was only a medium-sized pony, she could carry an adult and was very difficult to manage. She would swish her tail round and round in a full circle, and dance sideways with the whites of her eyes showing. Quite scary!

Gradually, Rufus's curiosity got the better of his mother. First, he would peep round from behind her, and then he would trot out towards me, because he wanted to have what I was holding out in my hand. Queenie was getting fed up with heading him off, when she was sent away for a few weeks to mate with a stallion. Rufus broke out of his loosebox looking for her, but when Queenie came back, she was very distant and rejected him.

That is the natural way for ponies to prepare for the next foal. Rufus had to grow up and become independent of his mother. When he was 18 months, he was gelded. That means his testicles were removed, making him easier to control. As a gelding, Rufus became much more placid and content to be without his mother. When he was two, he was old enough to ride.

First, I put a canvas girth round his middle in the loosebox. He bucked and kicked and turned round, and tried to bite it off. Gradually he got used to it. Then I tied a bag on each side of the canvas girth, with a brick in each bag. Rufus didn't mind this. I led him round the yard, and then down the road, and rewarded him with corn cake and apples. Little by little, I put more bricks in the bags, until he

Ruth on Queenie

was used to carrying the equivalent of my weight, and I replaced the canvas girth with a leather saddle. He didn't mind this much because I let him sniff and lick it for as long as he wanted, before I put it on him. He expressed his distaste for having the saddle on his back, by giving me a playful nip as I was doing up the saddle girth.

Then I decided it was time for the big step. With the yard gate closed and Mr Halting watching to see everything went OK, I saddled and then mounted Rufus. He stood stock still, as if he was shocked that I had suddenly disappeared. I braced myself for him to start bucking and rearing. He simply turned his head to see me and nuzzled my knee as if to say, 'Now I know where you have got to!' I walked him round the yard and we trotted up the road as if we had ridden together for years. It isn't necessary to break in a pony like they do so cruelly in cowboy films.

Like many geldings, Rufus tended to get fat and lazy. He was adorable because he was so friendly, but he was not as exciting to ride as Senorita. She and I made friends before she was even a day old. Her mother, Eve, and Queenie were always together. Queenie was a good hand, maybe two hands, smaller than Eve but she was boss. Some days, she would be nice to Eve and they would stand head to tail, swishing the flies off each other with their tails. Or they would nibble each other's withers, the top curve of their shoulders, to get salt. Other days, when Queenie was in a bad mood, she would kick Eve and drive her away. Eve didn't seem to mind. She simply waited till Queenie was in a good mood again and didn't pester her.

Queenie and Eve were sent together to the thoroughbred stallion. Both got pregnant. Eve gave birth to Senorita, but Queenie had huge problems. She became quite ill, went off her food and got very weak about two months before her foal was due. The vet had to be called. He examined her carefully and then said, 'I can save either the foal or the mare, but not both. Which one do you want?'

Luvvy went into hysterics at the idea of her beloved Queenie being put down to save the foal. Nor could she bear the idea of the vet killing the unborn foal to save Queenie. So the vet gave Queenie an injection of something, and gave us some medicine for her. She revived enough to keep going for another month before she went into an early labour. It was very difficult for Queenie, as her foal, Prince, was tiny and very weak. Usually, foals can stand up on their legs immediately after they are born, and begin to walk and run within hours.

We put Prince in a big basket on the Aga cooker, to keep him warm. Queenie wouldn't let us express her milk for him, so we fed him cow's milk with a bottle. He could only suck a very little, and then he had terrible diarrhoea. He only lived a few days. We were all very sad and upset; Luvvy most of all. On a farm, you have to get used to animals dying. Queenie never had another foal. Luvvy wouldn't risk it. And, because Queenie didn't go back to the stallion, neither did Eve.

For a time we had another pony, Copper-Knob, that was owned by a family that had to go away for a year. She was called Copper-Knob because she was an Exmoor pony, and Exmoor ponies all have light brown, copper-coloured noses. She was a good hand smaller than Queenie, and Queenie couldn't stand her. Copper was not placid like Eve. When Queenie was in a nasty mood, Copper would kick her and Queenie did not like that!

Copper was mischievous. When the fancy took her, and you were too relaxed and not controlling her properly, she would suddenly go down on her knees and roll over. It could be nasty if she rolled on top of you. She only did that once with me. I learnt the signs as she would go a bit wobbly and I would have to give her a thump in the ribs with my heels. Yet, whenever there were tiny children on her back, she was as gentle as a lamb.

I had two accidents riding Copper. Once, I was making for home after rounding up sheep on the Downs, when a group of motorbikes suddenly emerged over the crest of the hill. Copper reared up and charged down the side of the hill. She had the bit between her teeth, which meant there was no controlling her by the reins. I clung on as best I could. She headed straight for a chalk pit where there was a vertical drop of about twenty feet, which might have been fatal. I dropped one rein and, with both hands, hauled on the other rein with all my might, until I pulled Copper's head round and threw her to the ground. She rolled on my leg, and I couldn't get up. It was a bad sprain with huge bruises, and I couldn't move.

I had to get a message out, somehow, about what had happened. I fished a pencil out of my jodhpurs' pocket and a tiny sketchbook, which I always kept on me, because I liked sketching animals and landscapes. I made a sketch on the paper of precisely where I was and fixed it to Copper's reins, and then I told her to go home! She ambled off down the rest of the slope, skirted round the chalk pit and trotted off on the road leading home. I didn't have to wait too long before Mr Halting came in the car and picked me up. Fortunately, it all cleared up in a few days.

The other accident happened one summer evening after school, when I was setting out to find the sheep. Copper liked to gallop through the long grass off the beaten track. It tickled her and made her frisky, which we both enjoyed. I wasn't paying too much attention, when Copper suddenly shied in mid-gallop and deposited me at the feet of two people lying in the long grass. Of course, they were shocked and apologetic, though it wasn't their fault. Copper thought it was rather funny too, and she made friends with the couple, before I re-mounted and rode her off to find the sheep.

One Saturday morning, I was peeling potatoes in the farmhouse kitchen when Mr Halting came in and said excitedly that the Cowdray Hunt was coming over the hill. I dashed out with him and, sure enough, there were riders on the Downs, and even in our fields. Hounds were searching for scent all around. I said I would love to go up there. Mr Halting encouraged me to do so. I said, 'What about the spuds?' He said he would sort that with Mrs Halting. So I quickly saddled up Eve and rode up onto the Downs. The hunt was gathered just over the crest of the hill, with hounds and riders milling around.

Suddenly, the horn sounded, just as we reached the crowd. Dogs and horses turned and galloped off across the level grassland, and up the next hill. It was exhilarating! The horses snorted and the hounds bayed. I had never seen Eve arch her neck so high. She loved it, but as she was not hunting fit, we fell behind. The hunt disappeared into a copse of bushes and small trees.

When we caught up with them, they were all together again, waiting. The hounds had lost the scent and were weaving back and forth trying to find it. A very smart huntsman in a pink jacket, immaculate white breeches and black cap rode up to Eve and me, and asked me where I was from. I told him. He said I should become a member and I could join, if I wished, but I had to be dressed properly. As I was wearing dungarees, a pullover, and no cap, he said I must go home and leave the hunt. I had not even noticed that every other rider was dressed in a black jacket, smart tie and hunting cap. I felt belittled and humiliated.

I arrived home very downhearted. Mr Halting said they were snobs. He wrote a letter to the master of the hunt saying that I should have been allowed to join them as he had given permission for the hunt to ride over his land. The master of the hunt wrote back that I would be allowed to take part in future, but I had to wear a hard hat for safety and, if possible, riding breeches and jacket.

Later on, I joined the hunt several times and loved the excitement of it all, though most of the riders took it far too seriously and hardly smiled. They frowned at me when I whooped with joy as we galloped. Curiously, I never saw a fox. From the noise the dogs and horses made, I should think every fox in the area (and they are intelligent creatures) would have made sure they were not seen. I didn't think catching foxes was important. What mattered to me was the sheer pleasure. I don't think the townies who object to hunting would feel the same way if they'd ever been out with the Cowdray Hunt!

CHAPTER 37

Sheep

Mr Halting's pride and joy was his flock of Romney Marsh sheep. They spent most of their time on the hills above the farm. The first time I walked up there with Mr Halting, he told me about the escapades of individual sheep. I was rather sceptical when he assured me that every sheep looks different, but I soon discovered he was right.

Because there were no fences up on the Downs, the sheep had to be rounded up and brought back, if they strayed too far. Mr Halting had grazing rights only on the unploughed grasslands nearest the farm. Beyond that, a flatter, gentler dip slope facing southwards towards the sea was ploughed for growing corn, where the sheep were not allowed to go. During the winter, the grass became frostbitten, brownish, tough and stringy. The young shoots of oats, wheat and barley came up from the earth, long before the greening of the pasture, and they were a lot tastier than what the sheep got from their own pasture. So, of course, they tried to get into the cornfields for a feast. One or two sheep, like Jez (short for Jezebel), were so clever at getting through any fence that they had to be brought down into the farmyard, at that crucial time every spring, until the corn shoots were taller and less sweet.

After about a year on the farm, when I had learnt to ride, Mr Halting trusted me to ride up alone with Julie to check the sheep. Julie was an Old English sheepdog, a big, shaggy dog. She was young and not properly trained to work sheep. But Patrick, the smooth-haired Border collie, was so well-trained that he would work with nobody but Mr Halting himself. Julie was happy to go with me, and she was good company. On the long path up there, if I sang, she would join in with eager yaps and mournful howls. I would ride up, all the year round, to check the sheep. Sometimes, in winter, there would be frost or snow and a howling wind up there, and the pony just would not go the way I wanted, if it meant heading into the wind. I remember times when I had to go backwards, until we were back in the lee of the wind.

One early spring day when we were up on the hills, some youths came roaring by on motorbikes. My pony, Rufus, ignored them, but Julie was hardly more than a puppy and took fright. She took a running leap onto the back of my pony. Now Rufus was a very placid, rather lazy pony, but he took offence at being ridden by a dog! He reared up and, when Julie dug her claws in to cling on, he bolted like a bullet from a gun. He was a fat pony and he did not have much stamina. I pulled his head round to the slope up to Beacon Hill, and he soon came to a halt. Amazingly, Julie and I were still on his back! I had to dismount and comfort both of them, as Julie was shivering with fright, and Rufus was sweating and had a coughing fit from all the exertion.

Later that day we couldn't find a sheep called Patsy. I counted and double-counted. I sent Julie into the patches of bush several times. Patsy was nowhere. But I had learnt not to give up easily. Eventually, after we trekked round the ploughed parts, we found her. Poor Patsy! She had managed to get into a field of wheat shoots. There had been heavy rain so that the shoots were particularly juicy, and Patsy had pigged herself. Not only was she damaging the owner's crops, but she had made herself seriously ill. As they digest in a sheep's tummy, juicy wheat shoots produce a tremendous amount of gas.

Patsy's tummy was so swollen that she had toppled over and was lying on her back with all four hooves in the air. She was very much still alive and protested when I yanked her over onto her feet. She tried to run away, but immediately toppled over again, and was on her back with her legs akimbo. As she was near enough to the edge of the wheat field, I dragged her to the fence and pulled her under it, onto the grass. She was no longer trespassing. If the wheat farmer had happened to come long, he would have had no right to take her away. I galloped over the flat grassland, Julie racing beside me, and we scrambled downhill to the farm.

Mr Halting saddled up Queenie and whistled for Patrick, who appeared from behind the barn. In no time, we were back up there with Patsy. I stood there watching, enthralled and horrified, as Mr Halting pulled out a jack-knife from his breeches' pocket, gently held Patsy's head down and away from him, and plunged the tip of the knife into her tummy. It was just like a balloon being popped, only the hiss was much louder and longer. Patsy immediately struggled to get up. Mr Halting held her down and massaged her tummy, both to get all the air out and to encourage the skin to tighten back and allow the wound to heal quickly. He then got a little bottle of ointment out of another pocket and rubbed it in the place where he had punctured the sheep's tummy. When he tried to show me, neither of us could find the wound beneath Patsy's thick, woolly coat. It was hardly more than a pinprick, anyway. But it had to be at exactly the right spot, or else Patsy might have aborted her lamb or carried it dead. As soon as Mr Halting released her, Patsy struggled to her feet and ran off. Mr Halting whistled to Patrick, who had been lying prone nearby, waiting for his master's command. Patrick knew just what to do and very quickly had Patsy back with the flock, even before we had remounted and reached them. Mr Halting said, 'Well done, little maid! That sheep would not have lasted more than a few hours more.' It sounds old-fashioned now, but he always called me 'little maid'. Nowadays, we would say 'sweetheart' or something like that. Anyway, you can imagine how proud I felt. It's not every day that you save a sheep's life, when you are only 13 years old.

In the late summer, Mr Halting would either buy or hire a ram to serve the ewes. Rams are difficult creatures, with uncertain tempers. One year, we had great difficulty with the 'man of the flock', Old Rambo. He was adept at making holes in fences and taking the flock on safari over the cornfields. Most of the ploughed land belonged to Lord FeatherstoneHaugh, whose grand mansion and estate were near the top of Harting Hill, on the Downs. The FeatherstoneHaughs were usually very friendly, but they were fed up with Rambo taking his flock rambling across their fields. One day, when I rode up on the Downs as per usual, there were no sheep anywhere. On my return, Mr Halting told me they had been impounded at the mansion at Uppark. The FeatherstoneHaughs demanded a huge fine. Mr Halting did not have very much money and refused to pay. Things got worse. They complained that Rambo had gored one of their servants and they doubled the money they were demanding.

That night, I saddled up Senorita. She was the most reliable of the ponies, and a hand taller than the other ones. Senorita and I went up Harting Hill in the moonlight, trying to keep in the shadows so as not to be seen. Moonlight is beautiful, but it makes eerie shadows, and the night creatures make scary sounds that you don't hear in the daytime. Every owl hoot made me jump and shiver with anxiety. When I reached the big double doors of the Uppark yard where the sheep were impounded, I positioned Senorita alongside the doors, and stood up on her saddle. I had to jump three times to gather enough momentum to vault over the doors. Once inside, I unbolted them, and Rambo immediately led his harem out, onto the Uppark home pasture. I did not dare to stay and drive them further away, in case I was caught. I left them and made my way home on Senorita as quick as I could.

I told Mr Halting what I had done as soon as I woke up next morning, and he rode off with Patrick to get the flock to their own pasture, as I had to go to school. Nobody ever found out who had let the sheep out of the pound, not even Mrs Halting! Rambo had done his job by then and it was time to return him to his owner in Yorkshire. After that, the flock settled down again.

Lambing was always a difficult business. English weather is so erratic. It was difficult to house the whole flock in the home farm without overcrowding the buildings and ruining the little fields around them. The lambing season was spread out from late January to April, or even May. If the weather was reasonable, the ewes were left to birth their lambs on the Downs. If they needed more attention, someone would go up once a day or even more often. Sometimes, a ewe would get stuck giving birth, and need assistance. If the weather got bad, those ewes that looked about to lamb would be driven down to the farm. One or two ewes that had had difficulty the previous year would be brought down early. So, from January to May, there were always sheep around the farm. I loved the newborn lambs. They were so cuddly and frisky. As soon as they were strong enough, they would be driven back up to join the rest of the flock. But there were always a few who stayed. I was allowed to keep one or two as mine. These were usually lambs that had no mother. Although many of the Romney

Marsh ewes had twins, very few could manage to raise them, as they could not produce enough milk early enough. Quite a few lambs would die. I found that very difficult at first, but that is nature's way of keeping the flock strong. The weakest died during birth or soon afterwards.

Ewes are usually good mothers, and they become distraught if their lamb dies. Mr Halting used to take the dead lamb away quickly and skin it. Then a twin from another ewe would have the dead lamb's skin tied over its back. The mother of the dead lamb would be overjoyed, because it smelt like her own lamb. She imagined her lost lamb had been found and she would happily suckle it. After a day or two, the skin could be taken off. It was a bit more difficult if a ewe lost her lamb up on the Downs. You would be unlikely to find it. Sooner or later, a fox would get it. The distraught ewe would then be given another lamb, but there was no skin to make it smell like her own. The new lamb would instead be sprayed with molasses. All animals find molasses delicious. By the time the ewe had licked off all the molasses, the lamb would smell of her own saliva, and she would adopt it.

At least one lamb left over, each year, would be nursed in a basket on the back of the Aga stove in the farmhouse kitchen. We children would compete for the privilege of bottle-feeding them. After a few days, they would revive enough to live out in the farm buildings, but they still needed bottle-feeding and then milk from a bucket for several weeks. These lambs would follow you around as soon as you went out of the house, and suck your clothes, or anything they could get hold of, and they loved being picked up and cuddled. Sadly, there were usually a few dead lambs, and even a dead sheep or two, every season. There was no sentimental burial in the garden, as you would for a pet dog or cat. The skins were sold for curing as leather. Every bit of the carcass was used – for stews and pies, or for feeding the dogs.

CHAPTER 38

Poultry on the Farm

Of all farm animals, chickens are the most stupid and least love-able. Newly-hatched baby chicks are cute, especially while their coats are glossy and fluffy. However, they grow very fast. Their fluff soon loses its shine, and they develop straggly, little feathers. Their legs grow faster than their bodies and they look very ungainly. Even the adult hens seem to be moulting all the time. Any noise startles them, and they squawk and flutter, sending up clouds of loose feath-ers. Very stupidly, they tell you just when they are going to lay an egg, by a sort of urgent soft clucking and then, even more stupidly, they shout out triumphantly when they have just laid an egg. I used to know, from their clucking, exactly when, and where, to find their eggs. There is nothing quite like following a hen after she has given the sig-nal and then, when she settles down into the nest she has made, put-ting your hand under her fluffy petticoats and feeling a warm, damp egg drop into it. Of course, you can't just do that; you have to get to know the hens first and then, when one gives the signal that she has an egg coming, you have to cluck soothingly to her, so that she does-n't take fright and run off.

When they begin to get broody, hens get a bit craftier and they go further afield, and make a nest somewhere in a hedge or in the skirts of a haystack. I used to be very good at finding these nests and getting the eggs, because the hen would always give her secret away by boast-ing out loud. Sometimes, a hen would manage to hide her nest really well and fill it with about a dozen eggs. If she had already started sit-ting on the eggs, it would be no use taking them, as there would be half-grown chicks inside them. I could tell by the look of the eggs, dull and sort of glassy, instead of fresh-looking. The farmer would get into trouble, if he sold stale eggs or if they had embryos in them. The egg collection depot would check the eggs carefully for size and quality.

Some hens would get away with hatching a brood. They would

suddenly appear in the farmyard with a clutch of ten, or a dozen, tiny, fluffy, yellow chicks surrounding them. Most hens are not very good mothers and seldom rear more than half their chicks. Rats steal them from under the hen at night, and, in the daytime, they get lost or stuck somewhere. As I said before, hens are stupid. I can't think why a bride-to-be's party is called a 'hen night'. It must have been a man who thought that one up, and a rather stupid townie at that. Stags and hens just don't go together. Deer are elegant and intelligent creatures. 'Stag' and 'hind' would be better, or 'buck' and 'doe'. Anyway, bride parties were not invented until some time after I married, so I never had a problem.

The hens on the farm were mainly various shades of brown mixed with white Leghorns, but, from time to time, Mr Halting would get some Plymouth Rock chicks. These became black and white striped hens. There was always only one adult cock. The young cockerel chicks were weeded out for selling or eating before they became fully-grown, otherwise they would have challenged the reigning cock. Cocks naturally fight to the death, and both are likely to be badly hurt, before they can be parted. Every few years a cockerel was selected to replace the ageing 'king'. The new cockerel had to be kept safely away from the old king. You couldn't sell the old cock. He would be too old for breeding and too tough to roast. So he would be made into a delicious stew with herbs and vegetables.

Of all the breeds of chickens we had on the farm, the most intelligent, and interesting, were the Chinese bantams. They were only about half the size of the ordinary chickens but much more lively, in fact downright cheeky. They would fly up and perch on my hand or shoulder, especially if I had some grains of corn in my hand. Each bantam was a different mixture of bright colours, in stripes and speckles, and they all had feathers on their heels. The bantam chicks were very tiny, brown and yellow, and quite gorgeous. The bantam cock was magnificent and he knew it. He was truly very vain.

Every now and then, the farmyard king cock would get angry at the bantam cock showing off and go for him. The bantam would neatly step aside, or flutter up and jump over the other cock, and give a sharp peck from behind. It usually only lasted a few minutes before the farmyard contender slunk away humiliated. We couldn't sell the bantam eggs, because they were a lot smaller than the ordinary eggs, so they were used for cooking.

Ducks' eggs are a wee bit larger than hens' eggs. They are a rather pretty, pale blue and as delicious as the boiled eggs from hens, and richer. Ducks are also a lot more interesting than chickens. They go off for walks, all waddling in a line, like soldiers. If you make a noise, they stop and all heads turn towards you, just as if you had given an order, 'eyes left turn!'

I used to love the Beatrix Potter books, and *Jemima Puddleduck* was one of my favourites. Once, I made little bonnets and aprons for the farmyard ducks. It was very difficult to catch the ducks to put them on, but they looked very cute. They went in the duck pond and put their heads in the water to fish for insects and the bonnets and pinnies soon came off. Ducks are quite elegant in the water. The duck pond was about a hundred yards down the road from the farmyards, and the ducks would waddle down there and back, several times a day. Some of them got quite tame, and would eat corn from my hand, tickling me with their beaks, like little paddles.

Country people liked to have a nice, fat goose for Christmas. Townies were said to have turkey, because they couldn't digest goose fat. Some town friends of Luvvy once sent us a turkey as a present. It was very dry and we all preferred goose, but the turkey wasn't wasted. With lots of herbs from the garden, it made a delicious stew.

Every year, all the geese would be fattened and sold for Christmas dinners, except for the gander, Old Toosie, and one or two young females, who were kept as his brides-to-be for the following spring. He was called Toosie because he was a pure breed, an aristocratic gander from Toulouse. Each goose would lay about twenty eggs, which were about four times the size of a hen's eggs, before she got broody. We would sell these goose eggs, or, occasionally, eat them. I didn't like the taste of goose eggs. Each goose was allowed to sit on six to eight eggs. She would be much more likely to break them, if there were more than eight.

While his wives were brooding on their eggs, Toosie would get very bad-tempered. He imagined that everybody within twenty yards was a threat to his babies. When the eggs hatched, and the geese started strutting round the farm with their little lines of fluffy goslings, Toosie would be a real menace. He would stick out his neck and charge with his wings outstretched. If he caught you, he would not only peck you hard with his powerful beak, but his immensely strong wings could knock you over!

The villagers learnt to avoid using the road that ran between the farmhouse and the front yard. One young man sped down this road on a bicycle. Toosie got to him before he could get past, stuck his whole head between the spokes of the wheel, stopping it dead, and toppled the man. Mr Halting came running out and grabbed Toosie before he could get his head out of the wheel and bite the man. Toosie was shut in the duck house in disgrace while the man was taken into the farmhouse for a cup of tea, and given first aid for his grazes and bruises. The bike too needed a bit of first aid!

One day, Toosie met his match. He made the sad mistake of charging the Old English sheepdog, Rough. Rough was no longer a working dog; he was very old and spent most of his time sleeping in any patch of sunlight he could find. He was really a good-natured dog but he had got a bit grumpy in his old age. As he was almost blind and nearly deaf, he scared easily and, when he was scared, he turned aggressive. The first time I saw him he looked so cuddly with his shaggy, woolly coat that I went to stroke him. That scared him, and he turned round and bit my arm – chonk! I had to have three stitches and a tetanus jab. Toosie fared even worse. Rough sunk his teeth into Toosie's crop, where his neck joined his body, and wouldn't let go. Toosie squawked and beat Rough with his wings, but Rough clung on. Toosie's squawking brought everyone running to the front yard, to see what was going on. Now, the only way to make a dog as determined as Rough let go is to pinch his nose so that he can't breathe. Then he has to open his mouth to breathe and let his victim go. Nobody would go near Rough, except Mr Halting, who had been his working master.

Mr Halting got Rough to let go. Poor Toosie lay there with his breast torn almost right off, and his crop hanging out. He had no more squawk left in him but he hissed menacingly. Mr Halting scooped him up and carried him under one arm, into the farmhouse. Toosie's wings had to be tied close to his body, to stop him beating them.

Up on a soft blanket spread on the kitchen table, he was given alcohol, through a funnel and down his throat, to calm him. Mrs Halting then got out her mending box, dowsed Toosie's breast with white spirit to numb it, and proceeded to sew his breast flap back into place with a darning needle and waxed thread. She sterilised the needle, first, in a flame.

After he was patched up, Toosie's wound was covered with gentian violet. We didn't have antiseptic creams then. Gentian violet worked well for most wounds. The trouble was it took a long time for the purple colour to disappear. I made a straightjacket for Toosie out of scraps from the mending basket, and we kept him doped up with alcohol for a couple of days, to give his wound time to begin healing. Very soon, he was back in the yard checking on his wives and threatening everyone - except Rough.

CHAPTER 39

Plenty Of Pigs

Pigs are one of the most maligned of creatures. You wouldn't call someone a 'dirty, stupid pig', if you knew any pigs. Pigs can be as intelligent as dogs, and it can be very rewarding looking after them, but they do need a lot of care. They can be dirty, of course, but that's usually due to their keeper's neglect. With enough space, and plenty of clean straw, pigs are very house-proud, and do not foul their nests. Their strong smell is nowhere near as unpleasant as bird droppings or human sewage. I never minded cleaning out pigsties.

As soon as piglets are two to three weeks old, they have to be dosed with various things to protect them from pernicious diarrhoea and worms. I used to like holding the little piglets while Mr Halting opened their mouths and popped in a spoonful of ferrous sulphate, or some other liquid. Soon after that, the male piglets have to be castrated. That is not such a nice job, but if you don't do it, they will not fatten for market and they will get very troublesome fighting each other.

Have you ever seen a litter of newborn piglets? They are beautiful! After their mother has licked them clean, they have a strange and lovely shine that lasts only a few days. In this first week, they are fascinating, and it is no wonder their mother falls in love with them, and will attack if she thinks they are going to be harmed. But take the trouble to get to know a sow, before she gives birth; she will trust you and share the joy of her family of piglets with you, and let you fondle and handle them after they are born. Pigs, like humans, want company during labour. Ponies, however, are usually different, and prefer to be on their own, when foaling.

I remember spending the night in a bed of straw, next to Ruby, when she was farrowing. Ruby was a headstrong, rather flighty, young sow and needed a lot of reassurance. Her labour was painful. She thrashed and rolled around a lot. I quietened her, by rubbing her tummy and back, and she would gradually calm down and lie still, grunting blissfully, until the next attack of pain. It was a long, weary night for both of us, but in the early hours, she gave birth to six lovely, red piglets with black spots. You can imagine how cute they were.

The piglets were not all born at once. There was half an hour, approximately, between each. In her thrashing around, Ruby probably would have rolled onto the ones already born, and they might have suffocated. I knew this, and that is why I spent the night with her, although I had to go to school the next day. Ruby trusted me, and following each birth, after she had cleaned up, she let me take hold of the new piglet. I put them in a corner of the sty with a wooden gate across to keep them apart from Ruby, and I made a little nest there, with a hot water bottle to keep them warm.

When, finally, the afterbirth comes out, that is a dangerous time. Quite often, the last piglet is wrapped inside the afterbirth, and the mother sow may be too interested in her other piglets to notice. In the natural state, the other piglets would all be feeding by then. The afterbirth has a strong smell, not so much for humans but for other animals. There are nearly always rats on a farm. You don't often see them, because the farmyard cats are there to catch them. If you get too soft and feed the farmyard cats too much, they become lazy, and don't catch so many rats; some rats grow too big for the cats, which may then back off from chasing them.

A big, full-grown rat can jump from the rafters in the barn roof onto a newborn piglet and climb up again with the piglet in-between its teeth before the sow notices. Rats stay mainly outside, but in the winter, they come into the barn. I remember, on cold winter nights, the cows had to stay in the cowshed, and did not go out in the fields. I used to help Mr Halting give the cows their last feed of hay. When we turned the light on in the barn, we would see, high up in the rafters, a row of beady eyes glistening in the half-light. Then, as my eyes got used to the light, I would see the rats scamper along the beams and disappear.

The mother sow knows instinctively that her piglets would be in danger if a rat were to smell the afterbirth, so she quickly eats it. If she doesn't realise there is a piglet inside, she might eat that too. I was waiting for the afterbirth, and, sure enough, there was a tiny piglet in it. He was quite difficult to get out, and although Ruby was working with me, I don't think she would have managed on her own. He was only half the size of the others, but he looked just as beautiful, once he was breathing properly and his coat was shining.

We called him Coco, because his head was too big and top-heavy so that he wobbled on his tiny legs like a clown. Coco spent his first couple of days in a little basket at the back of the Aga cooker, in the big farm kitchen. I fed him milk, every hour, from a bottle and, each day, I took him to Ruby in her pen, so that she and his five siblings would not forget his individual smell. I made sure he got a teat to suck on Ruby's belly. That was no problem, because Ruby had six teats. It can cause huge problems, when some sows give birth to eleven or twelve piglets, as they seldom have more than eight teats.

Because of his enriched diet, Coco's body caught up with his head very quickly. When he jumped out of his basket, I made him a little pen out of three cardboard boxes, in the corner of the kitchen. It had to have a cardboard roof, because Rookie, the pet rook, and Squeak, the Siamese cat, did not take kindly to the new lodger. The dogs took no notice – it was beneath their dignity! It was not very long before Coco caught up with his siblings in size, and could re-join his family permanently.

Ruby and Amber were different in every way. I went with Mr Halting to collect two gilts (young female pigs) – red Tamworths. Two red and pink snouts poked out be- tween the slats of a little wooden crate at Peters- field station, and grunted a high-pitched greeting to us. They enchanted me. The moment I opened the car door, back at the farm, they managed to break one of the slats, and scamper

Amber and her piglets

out of the crate. I knew we were in for trouble. With their unusually long, pointed Tamworth snouts and slim bodies, they could go through any hedge. And, sure enough, they did, whenever they smelled vegetables or flowers in a garden! They could jump over the wall of any normal pigsty, which made containing them quite a problem. They were litter-twins, and stuck together for both protection and fun. The other pigs, when let out in the farmyard, gave this formidable pair a wide berth.

Ruby was the leader and Amber always followed her into mischief. Ruby had a mind of her own, and liked chasing anything that would run, especially squawking chickens, and sometimes it was a problem finding the pair! I had read in *Farmers' Weekly* that when you mate Tamworth and Berkshire pigs together, you get red piglets with black spots. So, I saved up my pocket money from breeding and selling rabbits, and I sent away for a black Berkshire boar to mate with Ruby and Amber.

The Berk turned out to be rather fat and lazy. So we gave him ginger – to increase his testosterone. He managed to get Ruby pregnant, and her piglets had similar patterns of black spots on red coats. But he failed to impregnate Amber. Black Billy, a Large Black boar, had got their first. So Amber gave birth to five pure black piglets. Some of her piglets had pricked ears like hers, and some had floppy ears, like Billy's, but they were all pure black.

PLENTY OF PIGS

CHAPTER 40

A Pig Story

One cold, grey winter's morning, Maurice Faxton, a farmer from the other side of Petersfield, came with his son, Michael, to fetch Black Billy to have him serve his two sows. He didn't keep a boar himself because, he said, 'They be ornery critters and do more mischief than they be worth.'

The place was quiet. Mr and Mrs Halting were at Petersfield market. I heard him say to Basher, 'Now where be that 'ere boar I come to git, like the guv'ner said?' A few moments later, Billy trotted out, with Basher shooing him from behind. Black Billy was a kind and gentle creature normally, but there was something he didn't like about what was going on, and he was sizing up the situation.

Mr Faxton opened the back of his van and lowered the ramp to the ground. 'C'mon me boy! Git b'hind 'im', he ordered Michael, who was about fifteen years old. Mr Faxton shouted to him, 'Put a bit o' oompf into it!'. Michael jumped up and down, and shouted, 'Raa! Shoo!' Billy was as still as a statue. Then Michael picked up a broom and slapped Billy on his rump with it. Billy charged the ramp, swerved between Basher's legs and ran round behind Michael. All three men were chasing him in a circle. I was watching all this from an open window, and I couldn't help laughing.

Michael looked up and then the other two did too. 'What's so funny?', demanded Michael. 'Bet yer couldn't git 'im in the van!', he added. 'Betcha I can!', I yelled down at him. I ran out into the yard. 'Hi Billy', I called, and he trotted up to me. I stroked him, but as soon as Michael came up to us, Billy scampered off. So I picked up a milk bucket from the dairy door and went over to the barrel in the corner. I dripped a little molasses into it. Then I rattled the bucket and called, 'Billy, Billy, Billeee!' He trotted up to me and stuck his head into the bucket. He was so absorbed in the scrumptious taste that I was able to push him backwards up the ramp and into the van. As I turned round, I saw Mr and Mrs Halting had come home. Mr Halting was opening the yard gate for the van to go out. 'Well done, little maid!' he said. I leant into the van and tickled Billy's snout, which was poking through the grid between the front seats and the back. 'Bye, Billy. Have yourself some more fun!' I said to him. Michael scowled at me as his father drove off.

'I hope they are kind to our Black Billy,' I said to Mr Halting as we went into the house together. 'Don't 'ee worrit, little maid,' he replied, 'That there pig can take care o' hisself well enough.'

CHAPTER 41

Ginger

Of all the pigs I came to know on the farm, Ginger was the most intelligent and fabulous of all – the perfect English Gentleman and a real Beatrix Potter pig. He was the first red Tamworth pig I had ever seen, and I fell in love with him at first sight. I will tell you how that came about.

Squire Hawthorn and his two sons were in some sort of big business, to do with government in London, and they had a big mansion in East Harting, which was their second home. Hettie Hawthorn was much younger than her brothers, and was away at a posh boarding school. But she came to Harting with her mother and auntie for the whole summer and some weekends. The Hawthorns laid on a wonderful fireworks display every year, on Bonfire Night, starting in 1945. (You weren't allowed to make any light after dark during the war.) A whole pig was roasted on a spit. There were roasted chestnuts, hot baked potatoes, mugs of soup, chunks of homemade bread and jars of ale. There was a big bonfire at the bottom of their garden and a pyrotechnic specialist from London let off the fireworks.

I used to help Hettie gather the chestnuts for roasting. We rode our ponies up over the Downs to a wood where there were sweet chestnut trees, which are very different to horse chestnut trees. Villagers brought wood for the bonfire. Hettie and I begged to be allowed to make the guy, but, no, – the guy had to come down from London and had to look like a Member of Parliament, whichever one was out of favour with the Squire! Every year, the Hawthorns used to fatten two pigs, one of which was for Bonfire Night. Why two pigs? Because one pig would be lonely, and would not thrive, like two would together. People were thoughtful and humane in Harting. What happened to the second pig after Bonfire Night? I don't know. Then, every spring, a new pair of pigs would arrive. Sometimes they were Large Whites or Wessex Saddlebacks, or even Gloucester Old Spots.

One year, the Squire rang Mr Halting and said he had been sent three Tamworth pigs and they wouldn't take one back. He said Hettie thought I might like the odd pig. Of course, I ran up the hill to the Hawthorn's mansion to see the new pigs, as I always did.

The Hawthorn's gardener, who looked after the pigs in their pen at the bottom of the garden, said I could choose one of the three. I chose Ginger because he looked at me as though he wanted to be the one for me. He was about the size of a large cat. He didn't struggle when I picked him up. I carried him, proudly, all the way back to the farm with Hettie. I gave him one of the sties in the piggery where I kept rabbits. He was quite comfortable, until a nosy rabbit jumped the divide and startled him. After that, I often found one or two bunnies snuggled up with him in his pen. He never hurt any of them; in fact, he never hurt anyone or anything at all. I made a collar for Ginger and led him out like a dog for exercise. He always trotted at my side, keeping pace with me just like a sheepdog. Then, as his neck got fatter and his collar became too tight, I didn't bother with a new one. He still trotted at my side, always answering me with a few suggestive grunts, whenever I spoke to him. Everyone was amazed. Sometimes, I took a short cut to the farmhouse through the orchard and the kitchen garden. Ginger would look longingly at the fallen apples and juicy flowers, but when I said, 'No! Ginger', he just looked at me and grunted, without touching anything. Of course, I gave him lots of apples and other juicy treats, at other times.

I taught him to sit on his haunches and beg for apples, with his front feet in the air. News of Ginger's feats went round the grapevine in the village, and I got lots of requests to show people how he could sit up and beg. So Ginger got fatter and fatter! As a hog (a castrated pig), he should have gone for bacon at five or six months. But I couldn't bear to think of that, and pleaded with Mr Halting to keep him.

Now, it is not good farming practice to keep an animal eating its head off, long after its sell-by date. After six months, the value of a hog pig starts to go down rapidly. So just before Ginger was a year old, Mr Halting said his time was up and promised me a Tamworth gilt who would have lots of baby piglets. Nevertheless, I was inconsolable. I loved Ginger like a pet.

To have slaughtered Ginger ourselves would have been unbearable. How could we eat meat, knowing it was Ginger!? All the family loved Ginger, and everyone agreed that was out of the question. So he had to go to market. Although I was offered the day off school to go to market with Ginger, I couldn't bear to see him being sold and carted off to the slaughterhouse. So, I went to school, but cried most of the day. I couldn't even bear to go out at lunchtime and see him in his market pen. I had said my last goodbye earlier, at home.

Ginger had his picture taken for the local paper, as he sat up and begged for apples in the market. I wished that a circus owner could have bought him and given him a place in the circus. Sadly, there were only farmers there and no circus people. So, that was the end of Ginger. But he has lived on in my memory. We had a good time together, Ginger and I. He had a good life, if short, and he was well-treated, and that is what matters. He is one of the few celebrities I know who did not let fame spoil him!

CHAPTER 42

A Cat Called Squeak

Rats and mice are cute, little, furry animals, but they are very destructive. They like to chew holes in sacks of corn and animal feed, to get at what's inside and eat it. They make a horrible mess, and a lot of the feed is wasted. They are dirty creatures, and leave droppings wherever they happen to be. They visit dustbins and refuse heaps, and then go into feed sacks, or cow mangers or pig troughs, without cleaning their messy feet. This spreads diseases. So farms need lots of cats to keep their rodent population down.

There were more than a dozen moggies, non-pedigree cats, on the Haltings' farm and every one had at least a little bit of ginger and tabby in their coats – because the dominant tom-cat in the area, Tom Sawyer, was a big, ginger cat. Moggies were chosen, as they were tougher, and hardier, than the pedigree cats.

The farmyard moggies were never fed, except for a little milk at milking times. After the machines had finished gathering milk from the cows, a little of what was left would be milked by hand, and poured into two tiny dishes. The moggies would crowd round and lap up these strippings. A big, burly, but gentle Danish farm hand, called Niels, would squirt a stream of milk at the waiting moggies, straight into their open mouths. That was a sight to see! If the moggy and Niels didn't quite get their act together, the poor cat would get an eyeful, and let out a painful meeeouch! If Mr Halting happened to see this performance, he would be angry. Wasted milk on the floor meant less milk to sell, and it encouraged germs. But worst of all, if you fill a moggy's tummy with rich milk, she won't bother to go out and stalk mice.

One day, Luvvy came home with a Siamese kitten in a cat-basket, though Mr Halting had warned her that a pedigree would not survive on the farm. You could hear it coming, before you saw either Luvvy or the basket! The kitten had a high-pitched, squeaky voice, not like any of the farmyard moggies. Luvvy told us the kitten's name was Susannah, but Kevin said she should be called 'Squeak'. After a few days, Luvvy gave up trying to get us to call her Susannah, and Squeak became her permanent name.

Jack said that the farmyard moggies would eat 'that scrawny, squeaky, little, half-pint critter in two mouthfuls'. So Squeak stayed in the farmhouse. But she soon got bored and sneaked out into the back garden. She was a beautiful sight, walking daintily with mincing steps across the lawn, and holding her tail up high behind her like a flag on VE Day! Luvvy and I were forever rescuing her.

Then Squeak found a milk dish in the cowshed. She didn't notice the farmyard moggies coming in for their regular tot of milk. When she looked up from the dish, there were six of them sitting in a row, eyeing her. Suddenly Squeak's hackles rose. Her hair stood on end and it made her look twice the size she usually was. Her elegant tail had become three times its normal thickness. It looked comical, like a loo brush! The moggies' coats were scrawny compared to Squeak's, and all they could do was to crane their necks forward, with jaws open menacingly. Then Squeak let off a long hiss, ending in a blood-curdling screech. All the Moggies turned tail and vanished. Squeak placed herself, proudly, beside the empty milk dish as if to say, 'It's all mine now!'

Two fox terriers, Willie and Patch, thought the farmhouse was their special territory. They were twice the size of Squeak, but they were heavy and clumsy. Patch tried attacking Squeak in the flank and bit hard. Quick as lightening, Squeak turned and fastened her claws into Patch's nose. Patch let go of Squeak's flank with a howl of pain. Squeak didn't let go. Patch leapt into the air, shaking her head, in a futile attempt to dislodge Squeak. Squeak clung on and they dropped to the floor together, and rolled over and over, snapping and snarling, until Squeak eventually let go. Patch was quickly up and out of the room. Willie, the younger dog, who had been watching, ran after Patch. She was not going to wait for *her* turn.

The territory was Squeak's by right of battle, or so she thought. What she had not bargained for was Rookie, the crow. Rookie was an unusual pet. He had been rescued as a chick, when he fell out of his nest. He had been lucky to survive the fall with only a broken wing, and a cat would certainly have eaten him, if Kevin had not rescued him. Kevin fed him milk with a fountain pen's filler when he was a chick, and we all grubbed up little worms for him from the garden. His damaged wing was bandaged in a splint and healed quite quickly, but he was never able to fly. When he became an adult, he was able to use his wings to flutter up onto the backs of chairs, and his favourite perch was on the top of the big kitchen cupboard.

Before Squeak took over the kitchen territory from the terriers, Rookie kept out of the way, up on his cupboard. He only came down for food and drink when the coast was clear. Rookie had never challenged the terriers, or they him. They had somehow agreed to live in peace together until, that is, Squeak came along.

One day, when Rookie had come down on the floor of the kitchen for a snack, in walked Squeak. She immediately swelled her fur to maximum size and hissed her usual insults. Rookie fluttered with shock, and battered Squeak with his wings. Squeak went for Rookie, but she could not get either her teeth, or her claws, into his feathers. Rookie nipped round behind her, and gave her tail an almighty tweak. Squeak let out a howl that would have awakened the dead! No matter what she did with her claws, Rookie was deftly in behind her for another tweak of her tail. And another and another! Poor Squeak eventually turned tail and ran. I think it was the first time in her life she had been defeated in battle. So a pecking order had been established, literally. Visitors to the farm never failed to be amused by the cabaret act that was usually laid on for them by Squeak. She would amble into the kitchen, and wake the sleeping terriers with a hissing insult and chase them out. This was a signal for Rookie to flutter down to give Squeak's tail a friendly peck, and then chase her round the kitchen table a few times.

We suspected, one day, that Squeak had given birth, because she disappeared for a long time, and when she reappeared she was ravenously hungry and looked a lot thinner. We hunted for her babies but couldn't find them. She curled herself up by the Aga cooker and fell asleep. One of the farm hands heard a mewling sound, up on the cowshed roof. So Jack got a ladder, and eventually found three newborn kittens in the nook where the cowshed and milking bail roofs joined.

Squeak had not even bothered to make a nest for them, and one had died from exposure. She had rejected them. The other two kittens revived after a few hours in the bottom drawer of the Aga cooker, in a basket lined with a soft fur glove. We tried to feed them milk with a dropper, but they didn't get the hang of swallowing, and got covered in milk.

A few days earlier, one of the moggies had given birth to five kittens, in the hayloft, and had made a lovely, warm nest for them. So I brought Squeak's little 'orphans' to her. Because they were covered in milk, the mother licked them tenderly, and let them suckle on her teats, while her own well-fed babies were asleep. That little moggy-mother reared all seven kittens. Her own five had ginger and tabby stripes, but Squeak's two were pure black with little, white paws. The kitten that died would have looked like Squeak, but its Siamese characteristics had made it too delicate to survive the cold, up on the roof. I felt very sad about that, as Siamese kittens are very beautiful. Squeak just was not cut out to be a mum. Not everybody is.

SQUEAK GETS A SQUIRT

CHAPTER 43

Cows and Calves

Cows
Do nothing but browse,
And drowse
And now and then moo.
That's all they do.

From Richard Armour's poem Comment on Cows

A cow doesn't just browse and occasionally moo to her friends. She is a grass-digesting machine. The nutrients in the grass she mows up with her tongue, and chews to a pulp, are absorbed into her intestines and transported through her bloodstream to her mammary glands where they are used to make milk, which collects in her udder. So she is also a milk-making machine.

I learnt to understand cows by the tone of their mooing, and by what they do with their ears. When a cow is not feeling well, her ears droop, her head sinks down, and she stops grazing and looks forlorn.

In wintertime, the grass doesn't grow very fast, so the cows needed to have extra food. I used to put the food rations into the mangers and help the farm hands bring in the cows. Each cow had her own stall in the cowshed. One or two naughty ones would try to snatch a mouthful from someone else's manger, on the way to their own. You had to watch and scold them.

In spring and summer, when grass was plentiful in the pastures, the cows would receive just a panful of corn in their mangers. It would be a mixture of rolled oats, linseed cake and cow cake. Oats were grown on the farm, and the farm granary had a machine for rolling them, to crack open the grains and make them easier to digest. We had to order cow cake from farm stores, and it would be delivered in big sacks. Cows think cow cake is delicious, and even some of the farm hands would chew it. I tried it once and found it better than the everlasting porridge we used to have for breakfast, or the pre-cooked oats you find in today's supermarkets.

In autumn and winter, the grass was less nutritious, and the cows would get a basketful of chaff and mangolds, with their corn ration on top. Golden oat straw and hay went together through the chaffing machine. Mangolds have big fat roots, up to the size of a football. They had to be fed into a slicing machine that was rather like an oversized cheese grater. You had to wind a handle to work the chaffing machine and the mangold slicer. It was quite hard work, and usually, one person would wind the handle, while another person fed the stuff in. Once, I was slicing mangolds on my own. It was winter and very cold. My hands were freezing. As I pushed the mangolds down into the slicer, I did not notice a small piece of my thumb had been sliced off, until I saw blood all over my hands and wondered where it came from. I hadn't felt a thing, because my hands were too cold to feel. I tied a hanky round it and carried on till I finished the job. Later, when I soaked my thumb in warm water, it began to ache agonisingly, and it throbbed for a very long time. I had to have a tetanus jab.

Milking was the high point of the farm day. Cows need to be milked in their stalls for two hours, twice a day, at the same times, 12 hours apart. There were always two milkers. The first one would come with a bucket of warm, soapy water and wash the mud off the cows' udders, to prevent muck getting into the milk. The second milker would then put a milking machine on the first two cows, and watch carefully to see that the milk was passing through the transparent tube into the bucket. The milk was poured into two clean buckets and weighed, and charts kept for each cow. The buckets were taken into the dairy and poured into a steel tank at the top of the cooler. The milk would run slowly down, over both sides of a corrugated steel plate, and into a milk churn at the bottom.

The milkers would continue until all the cows had been machine milked and washed. Then they would squeeze the remaining bits by hand, from each cow, into a new clean bucket. If the machine was left on too long, it could hurt the cow. It was important to milk these last strippings by hand. If the strippings weren't taken, the cow would make less milk next time. The strippings were worth taking for they had the highest butterfat content, and so raised the value of the milk. The Guernseys averaged 4.5% butterfat.

After the cows were milked, they would go out to the fields. There was still a lot of work to do. The dung had to be cleaned out and taken to the dunghill in the yard, and fresh straw put down. Food rations had to be put in the mangers, ready for the next milking. Then there was washing up. All the stainless steel milking machines, buckets and cooler, had to be thoroughly washed in boiling water, and then rinsed with steriliser in rinsing water. Germs love milk. If you have ever spilt milk and not cleaned it up very well you will know the nasty smell of milk germs. If germs got into the milk, whole churns would be wasted.

Every day, a milk lorry came to collect the churns, and at the dairy depot, each churn would be tested for germs, butterfat and general quality. The farmer was paid according to the quality of the milk, and he got animal feed coupons according to the quantity. So milking was a very serious business.

Cows quite frequently got infections in their udders and would need a special ointment squirted into their teats. They still had to be milked, and this could be painful for them. Without milking, the swelling would be even more painful, and they would give less and less milk until they became 'dry'. While a cow had an infection, her milk could not go into the churn with the other cows' milk. It would spoil all the milk. So the milk from an infected cow was given to the farmyard cats, or the pigs, after it had been boiled to kill the germs.

The loss of this milk meant less money and fewer coupons to buy cow cake. So it was important to get a sick milking cow well again, quickly. Most farmers would shoot a cow if she didn't recover quickly, and she would then go for dog meat, as her carcass would not be fit for human food. This was a terrible loss, but after a week or two of sickness, she would not give much milk any more, and she was no longer economical to keep and feed.

Mr Halting and I were fond of a cow called Bumblebee, who was kept much longer than usual. She was a crossbred golden brown South Devon Guernsey without any white markings of a pure-bred

Guernsey, and somewhat larger. She had been a very good, high-yield milker in her prime, but was getting a bit past it. She had recently had twin bull calves, Glorybee and Letmebee. As they were bull calves, they were sold when they were ten days old to be fattened for beef. Bumblebee missed them terribly. Mr Halting felt sorry for her, and let her nurse the baby female heifer calves. There were always a dozen or so heifer calves, which were kept to replace the milk cows, when they grew up. Bumblebee was very placid and sensible and a good influence on the calves, which would become skittish and break through fences, when they were big enough to go out in the fields.

One day, Bumblebee was clearly not well. She was put in a loose-box by herself with lots of straw, as she couldn't stand up. The vet said she had a high fever and there was no point keeping her. But I couldn't bear her to be shot. The vet said she would get bedsores if she didn't get up. We couldn't get her up; she was too weak. So I designed a sling out of a sheet of thick rubber to go underneath her. By attaching ropes to the sling and throwing the ropes over the beam that held the roof, we were able to turn her onto her other side. We did this twice a day for several days, until she sat up of her own accord. She let me give her water, but she could not be tempted to eat. The vet came again and was amazed she was still alive. He told me that if she were to start eating again she wouldn't be able to digest anything, as she would have already lost the bacteria in her stomach.

Then I had an idea. When the cows had been milked, they often lay down and chewed their cud. This means they were chewing on a regurgitated bolus, a partially digested lump of grass teeming with healthy micro-organisms that aid a cow's digestive process; so I went into the cowshed at milking time, sat beside Angel as she was chewing her cud and told her about poor Bumblebee.

I waited till she swallowed and then, as she brought up a new bolus to chew, I put my hand in the side of her mouth and caught the bolus. I ran round to Bumblebee's loosebox and tucked the bolus in her mouth. She looked surprised, but she automatically began chewing, and at last swallowed. Now the bacteria from Angel's bolus would grow in her tummy. And, sure enough, it was not long before Bumblebee started to eat a little warm corn mash. She recovered fully and went back to her calves. She had another pair of twins the following year, and these were both heifers that would grow up to be milk cows.

Everyone thought it was crazy and didn't believe it, but Mr Halting had a method of telling if it was going to be a heifer or a bull calf. Somehow, he knew how to get cows pregnant with heifers, not bull calves. It was something to do with the timing of mating the cows with the bull, Bullyboy. Our herd gave birth to a much higher proportion of heifers than any other farm in the district. This was important, because heifer calves were needed when cows got too old to milk, and they sold in the market for nearly twice as much as a bull calf.

To sell milk all the year round, calves have to be born throughout the year. Cows give a lot of milk just after calving, then a steady yield for several months and then tail off before they have their next calf. In the summertime, cows usually calved out in the field. The calves would be up on wobbly legs within an hour. By the time they came in for milking, they would be trotting along beside their mothers.

After a few days, the calves would be fed milk from a bucket and given some corn mash. That was often my job, and I loved it. Newborn calves are very cute. You have to let them suck your finger, which they think is their mother's teat, and then lower your finger, with the calf sucking it, into the bucket, so they get the hang of drinking milk from there.

Another job I liked doing was drawing the newborn calves on their registration forms. To register a pedigree calf in the *Guernsey Year-book*, Mr Halting had to fill in a complicated form. Then, I would just draw the calf's unique white markings on the form in the outlines of a calf, left side, right side and head front.

In winter, the calves would be born in the cowshed. This was more difficult than in the field, where they could move around much more. The best way for human babies to be born is head first. Calves are different. They present with their two front legs straight out in front. Their head should be down, between their front knees, but sometimes it gets pushed to the side or back. Then it is very difficult for the cow to give birth, and she will need help. Calves are just like human babies, sometimes they have to be turned round inside the womb, before they can be born. I watched many calves come into the world. The cows liked someone to be there, to talk to them and make them feel safe. When the two little front hooves appeared, we would loop a rope around them, and then pull when the cow pushed, being very careful not to pull when she was not pushing.

Calves are born in the slippery, transparent bag that grows inside their mother. Sometimes the calf needs help to wriggle out of its bag, and its nose needs to be kept free to breathe. Once the calf is born, the cow gets up to lick the calf clean of all the gooey stuff that was in the slippery bag. Then she will eat the slippery bag and the afterbirth, unless you take it away.

Agnes was a heifer that had a difficult birth. She was shivering so much that Mr Halting took his coat off and wrapped it round her. He carried her into the house, and put her in a basket on the back of the warm Aga cooker. By the time Mr Halting and I came down to the kitchen, at 6 am next morning, Agnes was trotting around. It must have been a big jump for her off the Aga, but she had not hurt herself. And she joined the other baby calves out in the yard.

She was small, but was the ringleader when it came to mischief. Agnes always tried to get more than her share of food. She quickly learnt to open the gate of the calf byre, by putting her head over it and wiggling the catch, till it opened. Then she would lead all the calves out for a game of tag!

Agnes was, soon, permanently out in a field. She had a sweet tooth for dahlias. When the gate was padlocked, I watched her systematically trotting along the fence, looking for weak spots. She always found some way of getting out of any field. In despair, Mr Halting tied her up in the cowshed, and only let her out for exercise in the back yard with the pigs. The pigs would scuttle back into their pens when Agnes came rushing out and pranced round the yard. Even the bull, Bullyboy, didn't fancy her at first. Agnes flirted with him until she won him over. Soon after, Agnes, who was nearly two, became pregnant. She was tied up in the cowshed, next to the baby calves' byre. When the calves were let out, to drink the strippings, they would suck Agnes' teats too, so she began giving milk before she had even given birth to a calf. She had also become much quieter, and so she was allowed out with the milking herd. She was now a milk cow. Agnes went on to be one of the best milkers in the herd. But, at certain times, particularly when there was a full moon, she would get restless and skittish.

CHAPTER 44

The Big Bad Bull

When people don't like a girl, or they are angry with her, why do they say, 'She is a right cow'? Cows are very nice animals. They give us milk, out of which we can make yoghurt, butter and cheese. So why is calling someone a 'cow' such an insult? Now bulls are different. They don't really give us anything but a load of trouble. They don't produce milk. Their meat is tough and stringy, their skin is not best quality for leather, and they can be awful bullies and quite dangerous when they get angry. Why then don't we call a person who annoys us 'a right bull'?

Nowadays, bulls are kept at purpose-built centres just made for them. Cows are impregnated with these bulls' semen, by vets who visit the farms. When I lived with the Haltings, there were no spare vets to do the bulls' work. You couldn't keep a herd of cows without a bull on the farm to make all the cows pregnant. That was Bullyboy's job, or Colebrook Centurion, to give him his official name.

He was a magnificent animal, a pedigree Guernsey bull, and a lovely light golden-brown colour with white patches and shiny, beautiful, little horns. He had to be kept very fit, because it was a big job keeping some 20 pedigree Guernsey cows happily in calf. He was well fed, groomed and exercised. He was a good-natured bull mostly, unlike the Jersey or Ayrshire bulls, which tended to be bad-tempered and dangerous.

Bullyboy spent much of the time out in the fields with the cows. When they came in to be milked, he would go into his own special loosebox, where he got his regular corn ration, while the cows had theirs in the cowshed. It was a very good life for a bull. When too many cows came 'on heat' at the same time, he got a bit tired and jaded. Then he became reluctant to leave his loosebox. But when there were no cows on heat, he got frisky and mischievous.

One of these times, he got very frustrated. It was February, and cold and wet for days on end. None of the cows had been on heat for some time, and he hadn't been out in the fields for ages. The cows used up their energy making lots of good milk, but Bullyboy got increasingly fractious from lack of exercise. Mr Halting let Bullyboy out in the yard for a bit of a run. It was fun to see him kick up his heels and race round the yard, scattering the squawking chickens, until he ran out of energy and went meekly back in his box. Next day, he pounded the side of his loosebox and made an awful noise, bellowing until he was allowed another run in the yard.

Then, one day, he charged the manure heap in the yard, which had grown higher than usual. For some reason, this annoyed Bullyboy. It got in his way, so he charged it, but the dung-heap stayed put. This annoyed Bullyboy even more. With his head down and his horns forward, he charged again. His whole head got stuck in the heap. His feet thrashed about but got no grip and he fell onto his knees. What an indignity! He pulled his head out, bellowed with rage, made for the yard gate, and then turned towards the water trough.

With a huge leap, he jumped right into it, and with another huge leap, he was out the other side into the road, between the yard and the farmhouse. A cattle lorry came down the road and screeched to a halt. Bullyboy stopped and snorted at it, but then decided it was too big to challenge. He turned and made to bolt up the road. One of the cow-hands caught up with him and talked calmly to him. But Bullyboy was not going to go meekly back in his box. He had other ideas! He turned again, halfway round, and charged the wooden gate to the nearest field. With head down and tail standing high, he went clean through it, scattering splinters of wood, and bolted off again, up the field, snorting and bellowing.

The cow-hand went out after him – not an easy job with a frisky bull in a field. He would have to catch Bullboy by the ring on his nose, using a pole, as the only sensitive part of a bull is his nose. Bullyboy, however, was determined not to be caught, and ran circles round the poor cow-hand, who had to give up.

I had an idea, and Mr Halting liked it. I knew that Bullyboy spent most of his time with two particular cows when he was in a good mood out in the fields. So we brought these two cows and coaxed them into the field. They were none too pleased to be shooed out of their warm stalls into the wet, slippery field, especially as it was getting dark by that time. But Bullyboy came trotting up to them. The two cows nuzzled him, as you might hug a friend you hadn't seen for some time. When we opened the gate again, the cows led Bullyboy into the yard, and he was quite happy to go in his box for a feed.

That still was not the end of the story. A few days later, he was bellowing and banging on the walls of his loosebox, where he had been confined after his escapade, when I saw him leap at the tiny window and get stuck halfway! He pounded the air with his front feet. His massive shoulders wouldn't come through. His bellows turned into frightened screeches.

Mr Halting and two farm hands rushed to the rescue and tried to push his head back in. It didn't work. Bullyboy was firmly stuck. The three men went into the loosebox and tried pushing Bullyboy from behind. They were piling the straw and dung of the loosebox under Bullyboy's hind legs, and begun wheel-barrowing in more dung from the dunghill in the yard, so his legs could be nearer to the level of the window. This went on for some time. Then, suddenly, Bullyboy shot out of the window.

He stood in the yard, snorting and looking around, not quite realising where he was or what had happened. Then he charged clean through the yard gate and the patched-up gate that he'd wrecked earlier, and thundered up the field. Then he heard one of his favourite wives calling from the cowshed. Like a good husband, Bullyboy came whenever one of the cows mooed to him. He was never allowed into the cowshed, but I could see he was making up his mind to charge in. Mr Halting saw that too. He got two hands to stand with pitchforks at the two doors into the cowshed, while he went in and untied Dolly.

Dolly stepped daintily out of the cowshed door and gave Bullyboy a coy look. Bullyboy bellowed an amorous greeting. But Dolly was not going to be won over too easily. She led him a dance, round and round the yard. She teased him by heading straight for the dunghill, and then stepping aside at the last minute. Poor Bullyboy was not as nimble on his hooves as Dolly, and he smashed into the dunghill!

Just at that moment, Mrs Halting appeared and ticked me off for watching the proceedings. She told me that what was going on in the yard was not good for little girls to see. She had not realised that Bullyboy usually served his cows in the back yard or the fields, and I already knew all about it. Country children learn to understand sex, and making babies, very early. It is a natural, important part of farm life.

The weather got better, and Bullyboy went out in the fields with the herd. I don't recall any more mayhem involving him after that. But I did tell you that bulls don't give milk like cows, and, instead, casue a lot of trouble. Besides leading us all a dance, Bullyboy had smashed two gates and they had to be replaced with new ones.

CHAPTER 45

Rabbits

At the Haltings' farm, there was a farm hand called Joe Hibbitt, who kept twelve hutches, full of rabbits, against a sheltering wall. His rabbits didn't struggle in his hands, like the Goodrickes' rabbits, but would look at me inquisitively. Joe let me stroke them and hold them, and I enjoyed their nuzzling and tickling.

Popsy, one of his doe rabbits, had just had babies. Joe took me to see them in their nest box. They were three days old. You could just see five pairs of wriggly hind legs sticking out from under her. Their eyes were closed, and they hardly had any fur at all. They looked more like mice than rabbits. I was disappointed. So he opened another nest box. Inside were four beautiful, slightly older, fluffy babies. They all woke up and one sat up on its haunches, with both front paws in the air, and looked at us with its little nose and whiskers twitching.

She was gorgeous – flecked brown, with a snow-white stripe down the front of her head, and little white paws. 'What's her name?', I asked. 'Lor' bless'ee!', he replied, 'She baint no more'n two weeks ol'. I baint nam'd 'un yet.'

He told me I could have her, 'if t' guv'nor ses 'ee may.' I decided to call her Alice. She became my first ever rabbit.

Joe sold most of his rabbits when they were big and plump enough to fetch a good price in the market, and make a good rabbit pie. So one or two hutches became empty, and Alice moved into one of them, when she was ten weeks old, and old enough to leave her mother. It became one of my first chores to feed Alice and help Joe to feed all his many rabbits.

Every day, after school, and sometimes before school, I went along the roadside hedges with a big hessian sack, and filled it with grass from the verges. I very quickly learnt which plants the rabbits liked. Just like humans, they don't like to eat the same thing all the time. Alice's favourite food was dandelions – leaves, roots and, most of all, their flowers. I can see her now in my mind, sitting chewing a dande-lion stalk, with the yellow flower bouncing on the end. The stalk got shorter and shorter, until the flower disappeared into her mouth. Then I would offer her another ... and another ... She liked cow parsley, clover and hogweed very much, too.

I adored Joe. He showed me a wasps' nest in the bank under a hedge, and all sorts of things around the farm, like a thrush's nest in the apple tree. He allowed me to watch, when he mated Major, his biggest buck rabbit, with the doe rabbits. He was gentle and patient with his rabbits, and with everyone else. He never found me a nui-sance, as other people did sometimes. Then suddenly he was gone. All his rabbits and hutches were gone too, except for Alice and her hutch. I don't remember why Joe left the farm. I don't recall him say-ing goodbye. Perhaps he did, and perhaps he didn't. I had got used to people coming into my life, and then disappearing again.

The ground by the wall where the hutches had stood was turned into a raspberry patch, with a little stone wall round it. It was a good place for raspberries, which grew plump and sweet, but there was no room there, any more, for Alice. Mr Halting let me use the disused piggery, which housed a giant saw for cutting wood, at one end. There were four pigpens, and Mr Halting cleared two of them for me.

Alice could not believe her luck to be in a straw-laid, open pen. She was, by now, heavily pregnant and she danced and pranced about with joy at her unexpected freedom. One day, she made a nest in a corner, by rolling straw into a circular band. She had filled the mid-dle with soft down that she had scratched off her own chest. I knew that doe rabbits liked to keep their babies in the dark, so I made a lit-tle shelter over her nest, out of an old, wooden crate and some thick cloth, to make her feel safe.

She had six babies that first time. They had no hair and looked like scrawny rats, with their eyes closed. But I knew they would soon be fluffy and cute. And, of course, they were. In due course, Alice's babies filled up the second pen. When they were big enough, I bor-rowed a school friend's buck rabbit, to mate with the does.

Then I ran into problems. The rabbits started fighting, because there were too many of them. They began jumping right over the sides of the pens, into one another's territory, and fought even more. They managed to get out when someone left open the door at the sawmill end. When the little gate in the wall was left open, you would meet them hopping around the yard, eating the raspberry plants. They jumped right over that wall too. Mr Halting said it couldn't go on. Some of my rabbits would have to be sold. I selected six rabbits and he took them to market. I couldn't go, because I was at school. In the evening, he gave me 15 shillings. That was what my rabbits had fetched. For me, that was a lot of money – way more than my six-pence a week pocket money.

I reckoned I was onto a good thing. I kept my favourite doe rabbits; Alice, of course, Snowy, a lovely white rabbit, Jemima, a pale orange-brown and very beautiful one, and a couple of grey ones, with white markings, like Alice's. They were Alicia and Angelina. They were all Alice's babies. The others I gradually sold in the market. I used to go on the bus on Wednesdays, which was market day in Petersfield, with a rabbit, or two, tucked under my school blazer. I would get off one stop further than the school bus stop, at the town square, register the rabbits, and put them in one of the little wire cages for rabbits. Then I would walk back to school. After lessons, I would go back to the market and collect my money.

One Wednesday, I arrived at the market with two rabbits, only to find the rabbit section closed. Oh dear! If I took my rabbits back home to the farm, I would be dreadfully late for school. I decided to go to school with the rabbits under my blazer. I sat in the cloakroom with the rabbits, until everyone had gone to their form rooms, so that I could shut the door, to keep in the rabbits. But someone was late, and left the cloakroom door open. There was a panic all round the school when one silly girl, who had gone to the loo, met a rabbit hopping along the corridor. It just had to be a flighty, town girl who probably didn't even know what a rabbit was! She shrieked and fled.

Teachers came out of classrooms to see what was up. Soon there were people milling around everywhere. The biology teacher caught the two rabbits, and I had to own up that they were mine. I was sent to the headmistress. She was very understanding, and banished me to the science laboratory prep. room, so that I could look after them and

do my lessons there, until home time. She even made sure that someone brought me some lunch. After that, Mr Halting used to ring up,
to find out when the rabbit market would be closed, as it quite often was.

In wintertime, the hedgerow plants are not nearly as nourishing as
they are in the summer. To keep their coats sleek and healthy, rabbits
need a bit of corn to supplement the plant food. So, at the end of the
summer harvest, when the corn sheaves had all been collected in, I
would go gleaning. That's what my namesake, the Ruth in the Bible,
did. I would go out with a big sack, just before the stubble fields were
spread with dung and ploughed in. There would always be lots of single straws that had escaped the binding machine. I would take my full
sack home, and tie it to the beam in the roof of the piggery with wire.
It had to be high up, otherwise the rabbits would gobble it up, and it
had to be tied with wire, otherwise rats would come down from the
beam, and eat it. (Rats' feet can't get a grip on wire, though they can
with string.)

The next bit of trouble came when I acquired Ginger, the pig. He
had one of the three pigpens, and that meant putting more rabbits together in the other two pens. That was no problem. The difficulty
arose, when the rabbits started jumping over, and paying Ginger a
visit. At first, Ginger was terrified. He was only a baby, not long separated from his mum. He had obviously never met a rabbit before.
He didn't know how to cope with half a dozen of them pouncing on
him. I heard him squealing from the kitchen garden, where I was
picking vegetables. I ran into the piggery, to calm him. Ginger was a
very gentle-natured pig, and the rabbits were only being curious. He
soon made friends with them. It is amazing how different animals,
with a little bit of help and encouragement, can learn to live together,
and even enjoy each other's company. It always makes me wonder why
humans often can't get on with people who are a little bit different to
themselves. If a pig and a rabbit can be friends, why can't we do the
same?

As he grew bigger, Ginger would stand up with his front paws on
the pen wall, and watch the rabbits. He even talked to them in little
grunts. The rabbits would sit up on their hind legs, and twitch their
noses at him.

One night, I was with Mr Halting in his little old Austin Seven car, BXR (she was called by her number plate), when we saw a baby rabbit hop out of a hedge into the road, in front of us. It stopped dead when it became caught in BXR's headlights. Mr Halting stopped the car, and I sprang out and picked it up. It didn't try to run away, or even wriggle, when I lifted it up. It was trembling with fright. I got back in the car, nestling it against my chest under my coat. Mr Halting warned me that you couldn't make a pet out of a wild rabbit.

When we got home, I put the baby bunny in a soft wrap in a little basket on the Aga cooker, for the night. It was still trembling, the next morning, when I opened the wrap. I tried to feed it milk, from a little dropper we kept for feeding baby animals. It wouldn't take it. So I put it in Alice's pen. Alice had a new family, about the same age as the little wild bunny. She was always a very good mother, and immediately sniffed and then licked the baby. But it was no use. The baby bunny would neither suckle Alice, nor eat grass with the other babies. Mr Halting said it would die slowly and painfully of starvation. I felt helpless and very sad. I didn't want the baby bunny to suffer, so I let Mr Halting take it away and put it out of its misery.

Sometimes, when the wild rabbits were seriously damaging the cornfields, the men would go out and shoot a few, for rabbit pie. I would help Jack and Kevin to catch rabbits in a trap we made of wire netting. There would be a small hole for the rabbit to enter through a tunnel, to get at an aniseed ball inside, and then it couldn't get out again. We often caught wild rabbits that got stuck in wire fencing, too. But I never again tried to tame a wild bunny.

CHAPTER 46

Farm Life Today

The countryside of my childhood made a very deep imprint on my mind and feelings. Though I adjusted to town living, I would later take every opportunity for a weekend, or even a day out, in the countryside. Even today, I never cease to feel sad that we are all born on a beautiful planet, a Garden of Eden, but instead of enjoying its lovely landscapes, fascinating living creatures, and rich colours, sounds and scents, we mess it up, terrorising and killing each other, through greed and intolerance!

Farm life is not what it used to be. It has become just another industry. Farms are now big firms, managed by directors and supervisors, with workers clocking in and out, and everything is controlled by computers. When I lived with the Halting family, farming was still a way of life. It was possible for farmers with smallholdings to earn enough money for the necessities of life. It was hard, but a good and healthy way to live. It was magical for children, filled with camaraderie and adventure. Children were active rather than passive, as there were no electronic gadgets to distract them.

That world has gone. After the war, young people were attracted to the higher wages and opportunities available in the towns, and did not want to struggle on the land in all weathers. With the scarcity of young workers after the war, farmers either became businessmen or left farming. Entrepreneur farmers bought up small farms to create huge units. More machines came, and fewer people were needed to work them. Animals were then crowded into fattening pens, so that mechanised conveyor belts could feed them. Computerised milking bails began to cater for all milk cows, needing only one milkman in charge.

Working the land had also changed. It's all tractors now, and no more lovely, big, proud workhorses. I was never lonely working with horses. They are such good companions. But you can hardly talk to a

tractor, or make a friend of it. It must be very lonely, sitting on a tractor, or a big combine harvester, all day.

Sophisticated machines now do virtually everything, on a huge
scale. Farmers don't even have to work out seasonal winds or the sun's
movements. There are computers for everything. Invoicing, ordering,
and efficiency are now all done at a desk, somewhere.

Motoring through the countryside, as we often do now, I notice
many changes. The hedges are all cut by machine and are getting less
and less effective as windbreaks, or at keeping animals in the fields. It
was one of the winter jobs to go round all the hedges and to 'cut and
lay' them. They were pruned, and the tallest branches were carefully
bent and laid crossways. That way, you kept the hedges trim, but nice
and thick, so that they would keep the stock in and the wind out.
Nowadays, you hardly ever see cattle or horses sheltering by a hedge
in the lee of the wind, because the wind blows straight through them.
Machine-cut hedges are not thick enough, or private enough, for
birds' nests, and that is partly why we have many fewer birds than
there used to be. Where there were rows of very tall, spindly trees,
there used to be at least six or more rooks' nests, right at the top, in
springtime. Now you seldom see any.

The fun and *joie de vivre* are no longer there. With so much po-
tentially dangerous, heavy equipment, children are no longer part of
the farm scene. In my childhood, there was always a group of children
around, wherever the action was, in the farmyard or out in the fields,
watching and learning, and always eager to be allowed to help. Parents were less worried about them roaming far from home. There
were dangers, of course, and Robin's death was a tragedy, but, most
of the time, you could rely on the adults and older children to keep an
eye on the younger ones.

There are very few small farms left and most children have no
chance of visiting a farm that is like the Haltings' farm, which is no
more. Its fields, and those of other small neighbouring farms, have all
been merged into a huge farm of 2000 acres. The beautiful, old farmhouse, a typically solid, flint house with picturesque redbrick window
surrounds, is still there, more or less as it was from the outside, but
modernised inside. The farm buildings, the cowsheds and stables, and

the huge two-storey barn, have been converted into an estate of sep-arate maisonettes and flats.

The yard, always full of animals and dung heaps waiting to be carted to the fields, is now an immaculate lawn, with tidy paths to the dwellings. The granary, where the corn was milled for animal feed, and the bull's loosebox below it, have been converted into a little house, where my eldest foster brother lives. The bustling life of the farm, as I knew it, is gone. An empty silence now greets you, as you drive up. No more can one hear the fluttering, squawking hens or gag-gling geese. Doors were never locked, as the dogs would be barking in the yard to announce any approaching visitor. But there is no longer the same concern for others, or for other people's property.

I still hear about the problems of farmers today, such as all the government forms and quotas, because I have kept in touch with my schoolmate, Joyce, who married a farmer, Edward. He used to go to the boys' grammar school in Petersfield, Churcher's College. His sis-ter, Mary, was in my class at Pefe High, and we used to go riding to-gether. I often went to tea at Mary's, and got to know her family very well. I keep in touch with Joyce and Edward; we meet two or three times a year – especially to go to Goodwood races – for old times' sake.

Martin's Story

Martin's Story

My brother, Martin Michaelis, was seven years old when we arrived in England, whereas I was only four. So he understood why things were happening to us, better than I did. Before he died, earlier this year, he wrote about many things that, until now, I only partly understood, or misunderstood, or didn't know at all.

My understanding of how badly adults can behave came suddenly, and prematurely, as a young boy on *Kristallnacht*, the Night of Broken Glass, in November 1938. I was walking along the streets of Berlin with my father, when we saw grown-ups, on lorries, throwing bricks at the glass windows of shops and offices. It was an organised event, with nobody stopping them.

At the age of not quite seven, I did not understand what was going on, or why, but I knew that it was naughty. This naughty action was not being done by children but by adults. And it was a surprise, as I had assumed all adults were well-behaved, because they were always telling mischievous children to behave properly. Yet I had no reason to doubt the decency of my parents, and many other adults.

So that night, I learnt that growing up is not concerned with changing from being a 'naughty' child to becoming a 'well-behaved' adult. I realised that growing up meant learning to avoid sweeping conclusions. I began to listen and to observe what people of any age were saying, or doing, and select what made sense.

I would still be a child for many years to come, but that night prepared me for a purpose, though I did not know it then, which was to be an anchor for Ruth. Just three months after Kristallnacht, Ruth and I came to England, on our own, leaving everyone we knew, behind.

I vividly remember the day we travelled by train from Berlin to the Dutch coast, to board the night ferry to Harwich in England. It was a sunny day, in February 1939. Ruth and I sat on a bed in the nursery, for hours, with our toys all spread out. We chose a few to take with us in our trunks, and waited to go to the station to board the train.

I cannot recollect being harassed by anybody, neither on the way to the station, nor when boarding the train, nor at any time on the whole journey. It was an ordinary passenger train, not one specifically for children on the Kindertransport. There were no tearful goodbyes on the station platform in Berlin, as there were for many families. Our mother and a nurse travelled with us, all the way to London. Mother came as far as the first foster parents, the Steads in Kent, but returned to Germany almost immediately.

Ruth felt this as a personal desertion, but Mother had no alternative. England did not allow parents bringing children to stay and she had to finish organising Father's departure to Shanghai. Father had presumed that Mother would come back to England to collect us, and that we would all join him in Shanghai, but the outbreak of war put an end to all plans to reunite us, and the family was split in three places.

The experience of coming to our first foster parents in England was hard for both of us, as Ruth has described. Reverend Stead was a very kindly man. He would take us for long walks, and he took us everywhere, before his health deteriorated. I loved the magnificent sitting room, where I could look out onto the lawn through large big windows, while he gave me lessons.

But Mrs Stead and Miss Wright, our governess, did not treat us well. I think the Steads were worried that we would have a difficult time as foreigners, and, later on, they wanted to send us to an English boarding school. So we were refused food, unless we asked for it politely in English. As a result, we both learned English very fast and forgot our German. But there was no logic to their cruelty; we could just as easily be punished for not eating enough!

They did many other things that were strange and alarming. They refused food to Ruth, because she did not go to the toilet when she should have done. I attribute this to ignorance of how to handle young children, rather than deliberate cruelty. It was certainly a distorted attitude towards the punishment of young children.

Miss Wright could be very harsh at bath time, scrubbing our

backs, fingernails and toenails with a very spiky brush. One day, I snapped the brush out of her hand and threw it out of the window, saying, 'The next time you do that, I'll throw it at you, so you had better not.' She was frightened, and that made for a certain amount of respect. 'You will also get the brush too, if you don't treat Ruth more gently in the bath,' I added. After that encounter, she was even in a good chatting mood when she bathed us.

It must have been a difficult time for the adults, with aeroplanes fighting above, day and night, and dropping bombs all around. Sometimes Mrs Stead would come to me – out of the blue – almost in tears and with a mild apology. She would say she wanted the best for us, instead of quarrels, but we were so naughty.

After the war, I visited her and she was very nice, and she apologised profusely. She said it had been a hard time for her in the war, when Ruth and I were young and her husband was ill. She had wanted children of her own, but she was never able to have any.

But taking out her problems on us left its mark. Ruth was too young to understand why bad things were happening to her. She thought she was to blame for everything. She would deflect the unintelligible behaviour of adults onto herself, and intensify efforts to please them. This was a very natural reaction for a young child, and would have been healthy in relation to loving parents, and other trusted relatives and friends.

The behaviour of the Steads, and our unpredictable situation, also had an affect on me. Kristallnacht had taught me to understand that adults behave in different ways. I felt the need to take on responsibility in a sudden emergency, and I felt strongly protective of Ruth. That's why I stood up to Miss Wright and Mrs Stead. I found ways that Ruth and I could survive, without being punished. I am sure that other children in a similar position would have done likewise, just as the oldest child of a bereaved family with several children to look after, in a poor country, must feel responsible for their welfare.

I adjusted more easily to being in England during the war with our various foster parents than most people around me thought. The view of the Steads, and the Goodrickes, was that I was not adjusted and that I was unhappy. Indeed, the Goodrickes were so concerned about me that they took me to see a psychiatrist. In retrospect, their reaction was understandable. My behaviour was different to most children's, because of what I had been through. I was sometimes stubborn and argumentative, or fearful and withdrawn, for good reasons to my mind, but it may not have been intelligible to others, as I didn't make any effort to fit in, nor did I want to please anyone. I just made myself busy, finding out as much as possible about as many things as possible. That was my way of dealing with the trauma of the situation.

I was absorbed by science, and I can still remember discussions and experiments at school, like they happened yesterday. For instance, in the first term at the Friends' School, we learnt phlogiston theory, about what happens when substances that can burn in air are burnt. In the second term, we learnt that fires are known about which don't involve air at all. I was fascinated to learn that magnesium will burn under water, producing the same ash as when it burns in air. I loved doing the experiments at school that proved, or disproved, theories.

Mr Goodricke allowed me to carry out experiments with chemicals at home, in a kind of scullery side room of the house, or, better said, he tolerated it with increasing (justified!) apprehension after the first frightening incidents. In one case, a cloud of dirty, black smoke penetrated the whole house, and required a lot of cleaning up. I must credit it in his favour, he did not forbid my experiments after that, but insisted that anything with the remotest likelihood of becoming dramatic, had to be carried out at the remote end of the lawn, instead of in the house.

Of course, I obeyed, and true enough, there was a loud explosion, which would have done serious damage in the house. I had tried to dissolve the metal fragments of a doodlebug in water mixed with citric acid, meant for making lemonade, in a gallon glass flask that I had wrapped in a towel. Fifteen minutes later, it exploded; the glass flask had disappeared completely into fine powder, the metal had gone and the towel was just wet with solution.

My science experiments, my fear of the doodlebug bombs and my withdrawn behaviour had no doubt contributed to the feeling of the Goodrickes that I was unhappy there. I did feel I was unfairly treated at times. But I simply wanted fair play, to be seen as part of the family, with the same close relationship as between the Goodrickes and their children, but without feeling that I could be pushed around. I yearned to have a family of my own, like theirs.

I liked Mr Goodricke. We had many good talks together and I learnt a lot from him. He taught me to read music and to play simple accompaniments to songs. But there were a lot of misunderstandings which overshadowed our relationship. For instance, Mr Goodricke didn't understand, that when I built my crystal set, I was tuning in to the BBC's continental service – not German radio stations. He called the police, who laughed at the idea I might be a spy.

On other occasions, I was wrongly accused of stealing. I had saved up so much lunch money, by buying lunch cheaply from a baker's near the school in Tunbridge Wells, that I often was able to buy small electrical items, bulbs, wires, chemicals and other things. Mr Goodricke thought I had stolen the money to buy them, though he later accepted my explanation.

Mr Goodricke also misinterpreted my friendship with his daughter, Ursula, when I was twelve and she was sixteen. He had to be told by the psychiatrist that it was all perfectly normal, and the various other things that worried him about me were also normal. Later, he was able to accept a more serious, close friendship that developed between me and Ursula's younger sister, Joan, which continued by letter for three years, till my second year as an undergraduate at Cambridge University.

Ursula was different from the other Goodricke children, in many ways more like an adult. She liked reading, and spent much time in her room, the only attic room in the house, with its own stairs to get there. We shared an enjoyment of reading and learning about the world and the universe, so it was natural that we talked about such things.

When I read, in a big astronomy book, that the sun was an ordinary star, it fascinated me, and, in retrospect, was probably the start of a lifetime's interest in cosmology and astronomy. I told everyone that the sun was just an ordinary star, which set off a huge storm of laughter and teasing on the part of all the children, and even the parents. Mr Goodricke thought it was a subject for the psychiatrist: 'The boy is not in his right mind – it is obvious that the sun shines in the daytime, and that the stars come out at night, and they are quite different.' The psychiatrist said, 'Why do you come to me, instead of asking a school teacher, who would have told you that the boy is right?'

My fear of the doodlebugs was the one aspect where it was felt that some action was required. The psychiatrist thought it a normal and appropriate response, for a boy of my age, to be frightened of bombs and aware of the dangers, but I was relieved when it was suggested that I would be happier in a more peaceful environment, and this led to our moving to our third foster family, the Haltings. Though I also felt that the Goodrickes wanted me to leave.

There was a period when the doodlebugs were falling over Westenhanger, every ten or twenty minutes. They made a tremendous noise. They flew too low for anti-aircraft guns to be much use, and were faster than piloted aircraft, and hard to shoot down.

Ruth remembers the bombing of Britain as being like an exciting fireworks display in the sky. She was too young to realise the real peril we were in. I also knew that Germany was on the brink of having the atomic bomb, which was intended for London. So the war might have ended with the destruction of London, instead of Hiroshima. We are fortunate that most of the German physicists who decided to stay in Germany, and work on the German atomic bomb, actually did the best they could to delay it, while those who had escaped to America contributed to the atomic bombs used by the Allies; some, like Einstein, did this very reluctantly.

I was grateful to escape from all this and go to the Haltings. I was glad that Mrs Halting had insisted that there be no separation, and that Ruth should follow me as soon as possible. I feel similarly to Ruth, that though we were made to work hard by the Haltings in the house and on the farm, and it wasn't always easy for me, I learned a lesson for life – to cherish honest endeavour, in preference to scrounging and laziness.

Mrs Halting was a slave driver, sometimes overestimating what we could do; but I learned a lot from her. She practised what she preached, by working hard herself, and would listen, if I disagreed with her on

Martin in Royal Air Force uniform

how things should be done, or on the time a task might take.

Mr Halting paid generously for work on the farm, which I did in the summer months, as I was keen to earn some money, whilst I was a boarder at Midhurst Grammar School. I was not supposed to leave the school in the evenings, to do chores outside, and I had to persuade the teachers to give me permission. They did not like the idea at first. I said, that by letting me go, they were allowing me to learn the value of honest work. They accepted my argument.

I got on very well with one of my teachers, Mr Stuck, who taught chemistry and swimming, my two favourite activities. As I was a prefect, I was allowed to look after the laboratories and supervise swimming lessons. Much later, Mr Stuck came and visited me, and my wife, Maria, in our home in Germany.

While I was still a boarder, at Midhurst Gammar School, I made my first journey back to Germany. Ruth has described the traumatic experience of her forced repatriation, and I certainly felt the friction of her unhappy return, and the tensions between our parents due to their wartime suffering.

The first time that I went from England to Germany, and back again, was a moving experience. I did not know what to make of it, or how to react. I did not feel that I had been forced to come back to Germany, to be where I did not want to be, nor did I think that anybody was going to try to prevent me from returning to England. I never had any such fear of restriction on the many subsequent visits to my parents in Mainz. I vividly remember, once, on a walk with my father in Mainz, saying to him, 'Things in Germany are not as green as England, and I cannot imagine ever being repatriated to Germany.' And I recall him replying, 'Never mind. Nobody is going to force you to repatriate. You will settle it, of your own free will, in due course.'

Neither of us knew, then, that my future destiny was to return to Germany. After I left school, I went to Cambridge University, where I met Maria, who was to become my wife. She was learning English in Cambridge at the time. She is the second oldest of five daughters of a farmer in South Germany. Ruth has described being at our wedding.

At first, Maria and I did not want to settle in Germany at all. After two years of National Service in the Royal Air Force, I wanted to emigrate to Australia, where there had never been a war. First, though, we needed to marry in Germany, to fulfil the eligibility requirements. My parents didn't object to the marriage, but were strongly opposed to the move, as they felt this would be separation forever, after successfully being reunited. After much argument, Maria and I gave up on the idea, and we came to settle in Germany, where we have stayed ever since.

Now I think of England and Germany as if they were one country, and all the others as being 'other countries'. I am completely bilingual, so that it is hard for anybody to notice that I have anything to do with the other country when I am in either one of them. And, amazingly, I live in a house in the exact spot in Mainz where I told my father I would make up my own mind about where I would live. It had not yet been built when we had the conversation. Maria and I have lived in this house for fifty years, and we brought up our three children here. I feel I have fulfilled the dream I had, when at the Goodrickes, to have a family of my own, where everyone feels close, and the children are respected for who they are.

Maria, Ruth and Martin

271

Note for Teachers

I hope this book will become a useful resource for students, teachers and parents. I hope it will inspire people to take a stand against injustice, and provide ideas about how to help people recover from loss and trauma. Every year, I go up and down the country, discussing the Holocaust with groups of students, and other organisations, and, though I am in my 70's, I hope to continue for at least a few more years – but much more needs to be done, to develop such dialogue within schools.

The foundations need to be laid in the formative childhood years. There are young people with difficult past experiences. They need to learn to understand what has happened to them, and to learn to accept themselves. Teachers and parents need to think about their own struggles of childhood and adolescence, so that they may be better equipped to help their young charges understand their turbulent feelings. It is not easy to be in touch with, and own, the potential in oneself to be a killer. But this is part of being human and, if we deny it, we are less likely to realise our potential to be helpful, compassionate people.

This process of communication and understanding can start with circle time for pre-school groups, and then continue for all school-children. Reflection, wholesome curiosity, empathy, and compassion, are valuable traits that don't come through testing and exams. These qualities have to be developed through dialogue.

The Nazis deprived all Jews of German citizenship with the Nuremberg Laws of 1935, and I had no nationality until I was 18, when I became eligible for British nationality. Although I will never be fully English, as I was not born in England, I am very proud to be a British citizen. The value and importance of citizenship is a key theme, and a useful base for discussion. Citizenship can, perhaps, best be understood through its absence.

The Holocaust has been acknowledged worldwide, and mourned and memorialised by the whole of humanity. This means that the survivors can achieve a measure of resolution, because their murdered ancestors have a place in collective memory, and their story is passed down to subsequent generations. Students could discuss the value of recalling such events, and consider something they might do as an act of remembrance.

There have been more than 50 further acts of genocide worldwide, since 1945. These have been systematic killings of people from different national, ethnic and religious groups all over the world. So, as the Holocaust fades into history, as survivors pass away, there is no shortage of shocking alternatives to uncover. Students can learn how ignorance, prejudice, racism, and petty violence, can escalate to wholesale killing and genocide.

There are many Rwandans, Cambodians, Chagossians, Dafurians, and others, who could be invited to come into schools, and elsewhere, to tell their stories. First, they have to believe that they will be welcomed and their stories heard. That is not easy for people who have been viciously persecuted and ill-treated. Once students have heard these stories, they often feel moved to become active 'upstanders', and will not want to be passive bystanders to injustice.

I hope, too, that students can develop confidence and feel inspired to tell their own family stories. Every life is a story in the making, and to describe one's own story, addressing people who want to hear, is a way of developing understanding of one's own identity, and finding a meaning to life. The absence of someone who can give meaning to a young person's experiences can have long-term consequences. My brother made meaning for me, about the absence of our parents and the upheavals in our lives, by responding to my questions and trying to give me answers. As a result, I was able to overcome my distress and hold onto my sense of self.

I found refuge with animals. They were the companions I could trust. They had a calming effect on me and helped stop me from becoming fixated on the past and on negative events. Just being in the stables was enough to change my mood, and make me feel less lonely. My self-confidence increased in leaps and bounds, when I was leading animals around the farm, feeding them and keeping them under control. It is well known that animals have a therapeutic effect on human beings. So I hope these stories inspire children to want to spend time with animals. Parents and teachers can do something about that too, and look around for interactive, hands-on experiences; they can discuss the way we treat and respond to animals, and even consider how they could be introduced into the school environment. Children benefit greatly from growing up with animals, learning their ways, and such an experience can develop understanding and respect for all life.

Through working hard with household chores, and on the farm, during my adolescence, I made a valuable contribution to the family economy. Urban teenagers today often neither want, nor are required, to contribute. So, finally, I would ask, how can young people today participate in society, distracted as they are by computer games, gadgets and TVs? And there is the age-old question: Is it the town, or the countryside, that offers the better quality of life?

Some Key Dates

1933   Hitler becomes chancellor. Jews are barred from entering professions.

1935   Ruthchen Emma Clara Louise Michaelis born in Charlottenburg, Berlin. January 23.

Nuremberg Laws deny citizenship to Jews, September 15.

1938   *Kristallnacht*, the Night of Broken Glass: some 200 synagogues destroyed, 7,500 Jewish shops looted, at least 91 Jewish men murdered and 30,000 sent to concentration camps, on 9 and 10 November. A few days later, all Jewish pupils were expelled from German schools.

1939   Martin and Ruth arrive in England and go to the Steads, their first foster parents, February 22.

Ruth's father is one of 20,000 Jews who flee to Shanghai in China, where no visa is required for entry.

Germany invades Poland on September 1. Britain declares war on Germany. WWII begins.

1941   Ruth and Martin go to the Friends' School, a boarding school run by Quakers.

1943   Ruth's mother goes into hiding in Germany because she takes part in the Rosenstrasse protest. She is one of 6,000 non-Jewish women married to Jews calling for the release of Jewish husbands in prison or concentration camps.

Ruth and Martin go to live in a hostel in Richmond, in July, before moving, in October, to the Goodrickes, their second foster parents.

1945   The war ends. The Germans surrender in May, the Japanese in September.

Another move of home, this time to the Haltings, their third foster parents.

1947   Ruth's father returns to Germany from Shanghai.

1949   Ruth's father takes out a subpoena to force her repatriation to Germany.

1950   Her parents allow her to return to the Haltings' farm during holidays.

1953   On 23 January, her 18th birthday, Ruth becomes a British citizen. Elizabeth II is crowned Queen on June 2nd. Ruth becomes a student, at Reading University, in October.

1956   Graduates from Reading and goes to Mainz University, Germany.

1957   Returns to England and starts working for a biscuit firm.

1958   Converts to Judaism and marries Bernard.

1959   Starts her teaching career.

1961-5 Motherhood. Bruce, Barry and Tania are born.

1969   Returns to teaching.

1986   Retires from teaching to build up psychotherapy practice.

1989   Goes to 50th reunion of Kindertransport refugees.

1991   Holocaust education required in National Curriculum.

1995   Starts going into schools as a live witness to the effects of the Holocaust.

2008   Ruth celebrates her golden wedding, 50 years of marriage.

2009   Ruth winds down her psychotheraphy practice and retires (almost completely) from clinical work, but increases school visits. In October, she makes her first journey to China and visits her father's wartime flat in Shanghai.